THE WORKS OF SRI CHINMOY

QUESTIONS & ANSWERS

VOLUME III

THE WORKS OF SRI CHINMOY

QUESTIONS & ANSWERS

VOLUME III

★

SRI CHINMOY SPEAKS

LYON · OXFORD

GANAPATI PRESS

LXXXVII

ISBN 978-1-911319-10-8

See appendix for notice regarding this edition.

FIRST EDITION WENT TO PRESS ON 27 AUGUST 2015.
2ND PRINTING, WITH REVISIONS, 27 DECEMBER 2017.

QUESTIONS & ANSWERS

VOLUME III

SRI CHINMOY SPEAKS

SRI CHINMOY SPEAKS

BOOK 1

scs 1. *My Puerto Rico*[§]

My geography tells me that you are the land of unmatched charm and beauty. My history tells me that you have significantly learned the meaning of suffering. My literature tells me that your culture is flooded with the soul's spontaneous sincerity.

My body tells me that your body is the perfect expression of nature's simplicity and candour. My mind tells me that your mind is looking pointedly into the golden vision of the future. My heart tells me that your heart is full of loving warmth and snow-white affection; and that your heart's tearing efforts to transcend the ill-fated barriers of poverty will, before long, be crowned with success.

Yesterday they came. Yesterday they conquered. Perhaps they helped. But they could have made better use of their paternal concern. Today they have come. Today they are helping. Momentous is their contribution. Yet you need more of their attention, sympathy and opportunity.

Let them come and let them go, if so is the Will of God. But you try to live dauntless, deep within. You try to listen to the dictates of your inner soul.

Yours is the mounting cry. Yours is the Golden Shore. Yours is the Promised Land. May God shower His choicest Blessings upon you, my Puerto Rico!

SCS 2. *O my Puerto Rico* [§]

O my Puerto Rico!
Your soul is Beauty's flow,
Your heart is Duty's glow.

O my Puerto Rico!
Your simple life of Truth
Is God's Perfection-Ruth.

To you I bow, to you I bow,
In our Lord's Eternity-Now.
To you I bow, to you I bow,
O my Puerto Rico!

SCS 3. *Mother Earth* [§]

Mother Earth, Mother, we bow to you. We see you with our searching eyes. You see us, your children, with your glowing soul and flowing heart.

We love you with our heart's feeble capacity. You love us with your life's all-embracing reality.

Mother Earth, you are God's Sacrifice-tree. You are God's Realisation-flower. You are God's Perfection-fruit.

You are beauty's inspiration and duty's aspiration. You are inspiring God's entire creation to be beautiful, soulful and fruitful. You are aspiring in and through God's universe for God-satisfaction in God's own Way.

God blesses you constantly with His universal Delight and His transcendental Pride because you teach your children that transformation of human nature and not extinction of human nature is God's supreme choice.

God loves you most. Why? Because you love Him only. Because you suffer for Him only. Because you prosper for Him only. Because you have taught yourself that His choice is your choice, His voice is your voice. You have no choice of your own; you have no voice of your own. Your eternally and unconditionally surrendered oneness is your perfection-cry and God's Satisfaction-Smile.

You are at once God's Silence-creation and His Sound-creation. With your Sound-might you tell us, your children, how divinely great God is. With your Silence-height you tell us, your children, how supremely good God is. You also tell us that God's universal Greatness we eventually will become and that God's transcendental Goodness we sempiternally are.

Mother Earth, powerfully you concentrate, soulfully you meditate, fruitfully you contemplate. In your concentration we see God the infinitesimal atom. In your meditation we see God the ever-expanding Infinity. In your contemplation we see God the Beloved Supreme. In the inner world you are God's confidence in Himself. In the outer world you are God's assurance to Himself. God is your teacher. God is our teacher. He has taught you how to give to us unconditionally. He has taught us how to receive from you soulfully. The teacher says that you have done extremely well in the examination, while we have sadly failed. Therefore, Mother Earth, we congratulate you, we admire you, we adore you. Mother Earth, Mother, to you we bow and bow.

SCS 4. *Patience* [8]

There is not a single human being on earth who does not need patience. And we who are seekers of infinite Light and Truth need patience more than others, for we are consciously, soulfully and devotedly aiming at the highest Goal. We want to climb up Mount Everest in the spiritual life. So naturally we need conscious, constant and unending patience. It is not like climbing up an ant-hill or even an ordinary hill; it cannot be done in the twinkling of an eye. The higher the goal, the more patience we need.

In our ordinary human life we have problems with our superiors, inferiors and equals. We have need of patience with our superiors when they exploit us and misuse our capacity and humility. We need to have patience with our inferiors when they mistrust our sincere appreciation and goodwill, or anything that we want to do for them. We have need of patience with our equals because there comes a time when they do not want to stay with us or live in and for us any more; but, at the same time, they want us to live only for them. They feel that they have to surpass us; that becomes their inner joy, that becomes their duty, while they feel that our duty is to remain where we are and please them in their own way. They want to surpass us and lord it over us just like our superiors.

We have need of patience with our human mothers, who tell us, "Don't go out, children. Stay inside. The outer world is dangerous; it is a devouring tiger. We don't want our children to be devoured by the world's cruelty, temptation and destruction. We want our children to stay at home cheerfully and peacefully with our constant affection, love and blessing."

We have need of patience with our human fathers who tell us, "Children, it is high time for you to go out of the house and walk around to see the world at large. It is time for you to receive from the outer world what it has to offer and to offer to the world what you have. The outer world needs your aspiration to fulfil itself, and you need the outer world's dedication to fulfil yourself. So don't stay inside any more. You are no longer a tiny plant but a strong tree. Go out and offer yourself to those who are in need of your guidance and protection."

We have need of patience with Heaven. Although Heaven will eventually grant us its infinite Peace, Light, Bliss and Power, unfortunately it delays at times in spite of our having the necessary receptivity. The only explanation we can find for this is that we are beggars. Heaven tells us that beggars cannot be choosers. Heaven will give according to its willingness. Therefore, we accept our deplorable fate.

A beggar cannot demand. But we know well that we shall not always remain beggars. We know well that when our full awakening takes place, we will see that we are none other than God's chosen instruments to fulfil Him here on earth. As spiritual seekers, we discover that our aspiration grows and glows; we realise that God wants only to please Himself and fulfil Himself in and through us. We feel that the best thing is to please God according to our awareness. Sooner or later we come to realise that it is not we who fulfil God but God who fulfils, satisfies and manifests in and through us.

We have need of patience with earth. Earth is constantly crying. It wants us to elevate its height to Heaven. We try to help earth in its upward movement since earth has a legitimate reason to ask us for a favour. Earth has blessed us with concern, oneness and sacrifice; naturally earth can make a request. But in spite of our best efforts we fail to elevate the earth-consciousness even an inch from where it is now. But this sad experience cannot last for good. One day our incapacity and inconscience will see that we are simply trying to please God, and there will come a time when all our inner failures will be transformed into success. On that day our name will be gratitude.

We have need of patience with God. At God's choice Hour, God will greet us and give us illumination-salvation, illumination-liberation. We try to expedite that choice Hour of God's, but God says, "Children, My decision has been made and will not change. I am not going to change the Hour." We cry and God tells us, "In your lamentation is sincerity. Cry more soulfully. Let Me see what I can do for you." But we feel the necessity of crying not only soulfully but also unconditionally. We wanted God to expedite His Hour, but we are now ready to wait for God's Hour. God says, "You have made considerable inner progress. I see you are ready. I have changed your Hour." When we are ready to wait for God's choice Hour unconditionally, God offers us His soulful Smile and sooner than at once He greets us with what He has and what He is. What He has is infinite Concern and Love for us and what He is is immortal Consciousness.

scs 5. *Desire-life and aspiration-life*

Before the seeker entered into the spiritual life, he had a friend. His friend's name was desire. His friend said to him, "Life is pressure, life needs leisure. Creation is torture, creation needs pleasure. God is self-assertion, God needs Compassion."

The seeker is now in the spiritual life and he has a new friend. The name of his new friend is aspiration. This aspiration says to him, "Life is temptation, life needs illumination. Creation is imperfection, creation needs perfection. God is Eternity's salvation, God needs satisfaction here on earth, there in Heaven."

Before the seeker entered into the spiritual life, he used his love-power for world-possession, he used his devotion-power for world-recognition, he used his surrender-power for world-admiration. Now the seeker is in the spiritual life and he uses his love-power for self-expression, he uses his devotion-power for self-illumination, he uses his surrender-power for self-perfection.

Before the seeker entered into the spiritual life he thought that there was nothing in God's creation that he could not do, if he cared to. Anything he wanted to do or achieve, he felt that he could accomplish and achieve without fail. This was the dream-experience that he treasured and cherished in his everyday life. But reality had a different story to tell him. When he had to face reality, he saw, felt and learned that nothing — nothing at all — was within his easy reach. For every little thing he had to make a personal effort. He had to try and cry and cry and try; yet satisfaction always remained a far cry. In his dream-world he felt that he was the possessor of everything. In his reality-world he felt that he was the possessor of nothing. His dream-world made him feel that he was a prince. His reality-world made him see and feel that he was nothing short of a veritable beggar.

Now he is in the spiritual life and he feels that he can do nothing, for he himself is nothing. But to his wide surprise, when he dives deep within he sees that everything has already been done for him by his Inner Pilot, his Beloved Supreme. On the one hand, if he is asked to do something for himself or for the world at large, he feels he will fail. But when he realises his inseparable oneness with his Inner Pilot, he sees that everything is done for him by his Beloved Supreme, the infinite Absolute, and not only for him, but for everybody, for the entire creation. When the Creator created the creation with His Silence-Light, He Himself came into His creation as revealing and manifesting capacity.

Before he entered into the spiritual life, the seeker quite often, if not always, felt that he was an object of pity. The world pitied him because he was not contributing something substantial to the world. Humiliation was his lot. Now the seeker is in the spiritual life and he sees that, unfortunately, he has two more names which have been thrust upon him by the world-community: doubt and suspicion. His aspiration is doubted, his aspiration is suspected. Until the Goal is won by him, the world is bound to doubt him and suspect him. And even when he has reached the Goal, world-ignorance may not recognise him, not to speak of acclaiming him. His God-realisation is no guarantee of world-acceptance. His God-revelation is no guarantee for world-acceptance. But his God-manifestation is undoubtedly a guarantee of world-acceptance. For when he manifests God in and through himself, or when he manifests God in the world-body, or when he manifests God in the universal life, then the atheists, the agnostics and the lovers of God all see and feel that some illumination has taken place in their own lives. This illumination they observe according to the power of their own receptivity. Here at this point, the seeker is not an object of doubt and suspicion; he becomes the world friend, world comrade, world leader, world guide, world dreamer and world saviour. At that time the seeker is known as humanity's most precious cry and Divinity's most gracious Smile.

SCS 6. *How can I maintain my inner strength during my meditation?*[5]

Sri Chinmoy: Here the strength is aspiration. During meditation, how can you develop more aspiration in order to go deeper. When you meditate, please do not think of diving deeper. If the mind operates, then you will not be able to go deeper at all. When you feel that you are in a sublime meditation, you will see that the meditation itself has its own power. So you only have to try to surrender to the meditative power within you. At that time do not use your mind. If you are having a profound meditation, then there cannot be any intervention of the mind. The meditation that you are having is the result of the meditative power within you. Just allow this meditative power to play its role. This meditative power will always have a free access to the deeper reality within you. Let it dive deep within if such is the Will of God. But sometimes the meditative power does not enter into the inner or deeper reality because it feels that the entire being is not fully ready. If it enters into the inner reality, there may be a revolt from the outer being. So when you enter into deep meditation, let the force that has already created this sublime meditation flow or grow inside you according to the Will of the Supreme. At that time do not bring your mind forward in order to go deeper or higher. The force that has already shown you its capacity can easily carry you into the deeper parts of your being, but it waits for God's Command or the Command of the Inner Pilot.

When you start meditation, the only thing you do is to make your mind calm and quiet, and then let the meditation do anything it wants to do. You do not act like a doer any more; your responsibility is over. When you have made your mind calm and quiet, your responsibility is totally over. Then you have to let the force, the divine force that is giving you the experience of a good meditation, do whatever else it wants to do in you and for you.

SCS 7. *Consciousness*[8]

Consciousness is the connection between human aspiration and divine Compassion. Consciousness is at once man the preparation and God the ever-transcending Perfection. Man is the eternal preparation. God is the eternal Perfection.

Let us be conscious. To be conscious is not to become great in the desire-world. To be conscious is to be good in the aspiration-world. A conscious individual is he who inspires the world. A divinely conscious individual is he who aspires for the world, for the world's success and the world's progress. An eternally conscious individual is he who loves, serves, saves and liberates the world. A loving consciousness knows no forgetfulness, no procrastination, no destruction. An aspiring consciousness is a perfect stranger to tardiness, illusion, delusion and ingratitude.

In the spiritual world, to be conscious means you are striving, searching and longing for something. You are consciously crying to accept the Command of the Inner Pilot and become His chosen instrument to please and fulfil Him in His own Way. You are not escaping from the world but you are accepting the world with all its teeming ignorance with a view towards ultimately transforming it.

When you are conscious, blinding doubt surrenders to the aspiring heart in you. It also means that fear surrenders to you, the fear which has prevented you from giving up your little "I". When you are conscious, you realise that you need total oneness in both the inner world and the outer world. You feel that satisfaction comes not from the ego's supremacy and autocracy but from your loving and serving oneness with man.

Consciousness is the seed in our life's multifarious activities. We are all the silence-seed and the sound-fruit. The silence-seed was God, is God and shall be God in His Vision-Life. The sound-fruit was, is and shall remain God in His Reality-Life.

Consciousness energises the eternal traveller in us and expedites our divine journey. Human consciousness is the boat. Divine consciousness is the passenger. Supreme Consciousness is the Boatman, the Consciousness of the ever-transcending Beyond.

scs 8. *Could you say a few words on your purpose in coming to the West?*

Sri Chinmoy: In 1964 I came to the West to be of service to the Supreme in the aspiring mankind. To be absolutely true and honest, the Supreme in me, who is my Inner Pilot, commanded me to come to the West and serve Him in the West.

scs 9. *Thank you very much. There seems to be a growing number of young people in the West who are interested in spirituality. Could you comment on that — if you see any reason for that or any future to it?*

Sri Chinmoy: In the West people are very interested in the spiritual life and yoga. Especially the young generation is deeply interested in yoga. As we all know, yoga is conscious oneness with God. In order to establish this conscious oneness with God, we need to love from within, love from without. Young people today are crying for love. The love that binds is not the love that they are seeking. The love that expands, the love that emancipates, the love that makes them feel that they are of one and, at the same time, of many — this is the love that young people are seeking. Young men and young women have taken to the spiritual life precisely because they have felt an inner hunger for the divine love. I beg to be excused, but perhaps this love they did not get from their families or from their individual churches. If they had discovered or found this love in their parents, in their religious leaders, in their churches, then they would not have had to look for it in the Eastern approach.

The spiritual life is not the sole monopoly of India. Spirituality is for everyone. But there are different approaches. A Westerner is bound to have one approach to Reality; an Easterner will have another approach to Reality. But the Goal is the same. The Western approach is the approach of prayer, mostly of prayer. The Eastern approach, or Indian approach, let us say, is the approach of meditation. In yoga we try to synthesise the two approaches: prayer and meditation. We feel that one *can* realise God only through meditation, but again, if we know how to synthesise prayer and meditation, then we can expedite our spiritual journey. When we pray with folded hands, we feel that we are speaking to our Almighty Father and that He is listening to us. And when we meditate, we feel that He is talking to us and we are listening to Him. It is like the conversation we are having right now. You are asking me something and I am listening. Then it goes the other way. When we pray, we reach high, higher, highest. And when we meditate, we bring down into our system Peace, Light and Bliss from above. Seekers in the young generation want to speak to God and also they want to hear God's Voice. Only if we pray can we go up, up, up and tell God what we have to say. And when we meditate we also hear what our Lord has to tell *us*. So the seekers feel the need of both approaches; that is why they are inclined to follow the path of yoga.

SCS 10. *Why at this period in history is the West, which has been developing materialistically, now beginning to develop spiritually?*

Sri Chinmoy: Now that the West has reached the pinnacle of material prosperity, the West feels in the inner world that it is totally bankrupt. In this world everybody wants satisfaction. A poor man wants satisfaction, a multimillionaire wants satisfaction. But a multimillionaire may come to realise that no matter how much money he has, even if he wallows in the pleasures of wealth, he may not or, let us say, he cannot get even an iota of real satisfaction. That is because satisfaction is an inner awakening, an inner achievement, an inner realisation. The West has been blessed by material wealth, material gifts; but what the West has is not enough to make it happy. So now the West wants to be blessed by inner wealth, which is satisfaction. The West feels that if it dives deep within and listens to the dictates of its inner being, the Inner Pilot, then inner satisfaction is bound to loom large. The message of matter the West has always listened to and fulfilled. But now it wants to listen to and fulfil the message of spirit. Not only is material perfection needed, but the perfection of the spirit is also needed.

It is like having two friends. I have listened to one friend all the time and now I feel I have to pay some attention to the other friend. Matter is not to be neglected; it is also God's creation. But if we listen to the dictates of the spirit, then only can material wealth be used for the right cause, for a divine purpose. Let us say matter is the body and spirit is our inner existence. If there is no body, how can we manifest? The soul is within us, but in order to manifest its divinity, the soul needs the body. And again, the body needs the soul in order to realise the highest, the Absolute. If there is no deity inside the body, then the body is of no use. Again, how can a deity remain in the street? It has to have a home.

What the West is doing now is diving deep within in order to become the life of silence. Once it has become the life of silence, then it can become the life of sound, expression, revelation. At this stage, the West feels that realisation is of paramount importance. And once realisation has taken place, then this truth can easily be offered to mankind. So the West is entering into the inner world in order to bring to the fore the wealth of the inner world.

SCS 11. *Could you say something about your activities at the U.N.?*

Sri Chinmoy: At the United Nations there are many nations united together. The United Nations is like a lotus that has many petals. Each petal is necessary in order to form the lotus. Each nation has something to offer to the world at large. Twice a week we offer our devoted and dedicated service to the soul and the body of the U.N. We go there to invoke the presence of the soul of the U.N. We try to elevate the consciousness of the delegates, representatives and members of the staff. The delegates and representatives are trying to bring to the fore the good qualities of each nation in a political way. They want to bring about Peace, Light and Bliss in infinite measure so that the world will not surrender to war, but to love. Through our prayer and meditation we are trying to do the same thing, so that the world will not surrender to war, but to love. Through our prayer and meditation we are trying to do the same thing, but our approach is the inner approach. We are not saying that our approach is better. Far from it. But we feel that if we sow the seed, then it will eventually become a tiny plant, and finally it will grow into a banyan tree and produce flowers and fruits. This is our way. We feel that the seed has just germinated. They feel that the tree is already there, that the flowers and fruits are there, and that it is up to the world to accept the fruits, to eat the fruits and become energetic and dynamic.

SCS 12. *How do you find the response; do you find it is growing?*

Sri Chinmoy: Yes, it is growing like anything. Previously it was like a hard rock, but now we feel that it is like fertile soil. It is responding. It is not only because we are praying and meditating, but because the U.N. members also have an inner urge to do the right thing, to grow into the divine light. It works in two ways.

We will never say that we are working very hard and that is why we are getting the benefit. No. I have taken one step ahead and you have also taken one step ahead. So we are coming to a meeting point. The inner world is coming forward with its inner wealth and the outer world is then entering into the inner world with its aspiration. So they are meeting together.

SCS 13. *How did you come to begin doing this work at the U.N.?*

Sri Chinmoy: The U.N. authorities were kind enough to give me the opportunity to be of service. That was in 1970. Since then, it has been extremely easy for us to be of real service. Also, the late Secretary-General, U Thant, was extremely nice and kind to us. He showered his goodwill, affection, love and admiration on us for our selfless service. I had the golden opportunity to meet with him on a few occasions. He came to one of our functions and he encouraged our activities right from the beginning. He observed our activities and he was extremely nice, sympathetic, kind and appreciative of our spiritual activities at the U.N. I have dedicated a copy of one of these magazines, *Meditation at the United Nations*, to the late Secretary-General. There are many dignitaries who offered their soulful tributes to him in this magazine. I will send you a copy. Pope Paul has also been very nice to us. He deeply appreciates our activities at the United Nations. I have had the occasion to have a private audience with him twice, so he knows all about our activities at the United Nations.

scs 14. *Do you have any comments on the world food problem — the fact that many people are starving and more will be starving? Some people say that that is due to the fact that it requires much more grain today to feed a cow than a person would eat directly.*

Sri Chinmoy: Speaking from the spiritual point of view, I wish to say there will always be some problem, either a food problem or physical problems, mental problems, vital problems, psychic problems. There will be no end to our problems. What we have to do is go to the root of all these problems. The root is ignorance. If I am making a mistake, then I have to rectify it all at once. If you are making a mistake, then it is your bounden duty to rectify it. If I know that I have done something or I am doing something wrong, then my inner awakening will prevent me from doing that thing. So it is not a matter of too little meat or too little grain. The real problem is ignorance. There are many things we do wrong every day; we can't help ourselves. We have surrendered to ignorance. That is why problems are in our mind, problems are in our body, problems are in our vital. Problems are everywhere. These problems can be solved only when we can surrender to the light, the inner divinity within us.

scs 15. *Can you explain to us your philosophy of love, devotion and surrender?*

Sri Chinmoy: We all know human love. Human love is to possess and be possessed. We feel that today or tomorrow we will possess someone. But to our wide astonishment, we find that before we possess that person we ourselves are mercilessly possessed by that person. Once we have possessed someone, we feel that we are strangling that person in the name of love, or we are already strangled in the name of love. But divine love is not possession. Divine love is only expansion. Real love is total oneness with the object loved and with the Possessor of Love. Who is the Possessor of Love? God. Love is the inner bond that connects man with God. We must always approach God through love. Love is the first step. The second step is devotion. The third step is surrender.

In the human world, devotion is attachment. We feel that if we are attached to someone, then we will get Peace, Light and Bliss from that person in abundant measure. But eventually we come to realise that our attachment is nothing short of our ignorance. We feel that if we are attached to a human being, we will get what he has and what he is. But, unfortunately, what he has is darkness and what he is is ignorance. And when he is attached to us, we do not feel that we are able to give any light to him. So attachment is something that constantly is taking us away from our reality. But if we have real devotion, devotion to a higher cause, to some higher reality, to the light within us, to the truth above us, at that time the highest Truth can operate in and through us. Attachment is to the world around us, the world which is full of ignorance. But when we are devoted, we enter into a higher world to bring down Peace, Light and Bliss from above and bring to the fore our own inner divinity. This is devotion.

Then comes surrender. We can surrender to our boss, who is equally ignorant and who will lord it over us, or a slave can listen to his master out of fear. That is one kind of surrender. But spiritual surrender is different. It does not arise from compulsion; it comes spontaneously from our joy, inner joy. In surrender to God, I become one with Infinity and I feel Infinity as my own reality.

There is a great difference between the surrender of laziness or utter helplessness and dynamic surrender, which is surcharged with aspiration. If out of laziness or helplessness we say, "I have surrendered. Now I don't have to do anything," this is not enough. Our surrender has to be dynamic, constantly aspiring to grow into or merge into the Infinite. Our surrender has to be conscious and spontaneous. When we surrender consciously and spontaneously to the infinite Truth, Peace, Light and Bliss, we become a perfect channel for these qualities to manifest in and through us on earth. In the West, surrender has been badly misunderstood. Here surrender is seen as submission to something or to somebody else. It is seen as a loss of individuality, an extinction of individuality. But this view of spiritual surrender is a mistake. If we really want to be one with the Infinite, the Ultimate, the Boundless, then we have to enter into it. It is like the tiny drop surrendering its individuality and entering into its source, the vast ocean. At that time, it doesn't lose anything. It becomes the ocean itself. When we enter into the Ultimate, we do not lose our so-called little individuality. On the contrary, we become the Infinite itself. On the strength of our total oneness, we and the Infinite become indivisible.

When we surrender to God, we feel that God is our most illumined existence. The difference between man and God is this: man is God yet to realise totally who he is, and God is man yet to be fully manifested. Man is God; he is definitely God, but he has not realised fully who he is. And God is man, but He has not yet fully manifested Himself on earth. When we surrender our earthly existence to the divinity within us, we come to realise that man and God are one and identical.

scs 16. *What is the cause of this separation between man and God?*

Sri Chinmoy: The cause of this separation is ignorance. We feel that "I" and "my" will give us real joy. It is like a child. If he is very energetic, dynamic or aggressive, he feels satisfaction only when he strikes someone or breaks something. That is his satisfaction; that is his peace. But a grown-up gets joy only by remaining calm and quiet and tranquil. Unfortunately, individuals feel that by maintaining their individuality and personality they can be happy. But that is wrong. Only by entering into universality can we be happy. Individuality and personality will derive satisfaction only from universality. A tiny drop, when it enters into the ocean and loses its individuality and personality, becomes what the infinite ocean is. But before that, if it fights for its own individual existence, what can it do as just a tiny drop? So it is the ignorance in the drop that makes the drop feel that it can be satisfied by maintaining a sense of separativity. It is absurd.

SCS 17. *What about the fact that we take physical incarnations? Isn't that separation right there? I mean, just the fact that we all live in individual homes and do different tasks and things like that?*

Sri Chinmoy: Yes, but this is not individuality; It is only the necessity that comes from having respective tasks. With my hand I write, with my mouth I eat, with my eyes I see. But even though I do different things with the different parts of my body, we have to know that all are members of the same family. Each individual also will do what he is supposed to do, but not with a sense of ego. He will do it with a sense of oneness. God has given me the capacity to do a particular thing. He has given you the capacity to do something else. So let us combine our capacity. But I will not say that my capacity is superior to yours and you will not say that your capacity is the only capacity worth having. The difficulty with the world is that everyone feels that he is infinitely more important than everyone else. Here is where the problem starts. You stay with your capacities, I stay with mine, and we don't unite our capacities. That is why problems start.

scs 18. *When people in America began to take an interest in Eastern spirituality, many of them were disillusioned with social action and the consciousness of social problems, and they just wanted to meditate and be quiet. But now people are beginning to form communities to work together and to develop a little bit of that sense you were talking about. What is your view of the relation between spirituality and social consciousness?*

Sri Chinmoy: Spirituality and social consciousness must go together. Spirituality is not for the recluse. It is not only for a limited number of people who go off to the Himalayan caves. If someone feels that by entering into a Himalayan cave he will do the best type of meditation, he is making a deplorable mistake. Again, if someone feels that he will go to Central Park and sing and dance, and that this is spirituality, he is also wrong. We are going from one extreme to another. We have to have a balance. In my own way, I shall pray and invoke the Supreme, who comes first in my life. Then I shall go to the office and share with my colleagues the inner wealth which I have achieved, or I shall throw light on the activities that I am involved in. Meditation and the everyday life have to go together.

But first we have to know the supreme secret. The supreme secret is God comes first. From the One we go to the many. It is like a tree with many branches. How am I going to get to the branches unless I first climb up the trunk? Early in the morning, if I pray and meditate, that means that I am climbing up the tree. Then after two hours, when I enter into the office, that is like going to the different branches of life. This is how we can combine spirituality with society. Society is like the branches and spirituality is the tree trunk.

SCS 19. *What is the purpose of ignorance?*

Sri Chinmoy: In this world there is light, more light, abundant light, boundless light and infinite Light. If we take ignorance as destruction, then we are mistaken. We have to see that what we call ignorance consists of limited light. Even in the darkest night there is some light. Otherwise, we couldn't exist at all. A child, in comparison to his elder brother, naturally is ignorant; but the child also has some light in him. So what we call ignorance is light in a different form. I as an individual, you as an individual and she as an individual have limited light — let us say infinitesimal light — compared to God, who is infinite Light. But through our prayer and meditation, we are growing into God's boundless and infinite Light and becoming all that God is and all that God has.

This life, as you know, is a kind of game that we play; we call it a cosmic Game. What we call ignorance is nothing short of an experience which God is having in and through us. If we become conscious of the fact that we are only His instruments, then we are not bound by ignorance. We see that there is someone, the Inner Pilot, who is playing His cosmic Game in and through us. If we know that we are mere instruments, then there is no ignorance, there is no light; there is only the Supreme, who is everything. He is the Doer, He is the action, He is the result; He is everything, everything. But if we feel or think that we are doing everything, we are making a Himalayan mistake.

scs 20. *Is it necessary to have a Guru, or teacher, to come to this realisation?*

Sri Chinmoy: The person who realised God for the first time didn't have a human Guru; God was his Guru. But, at the same time, we have to be wise. In this world for everything we need a teacher. Knowledge we can get from books, but still we go to a school for years and years and study under the guidance of a teacher. We feel that if there is a teacher, then the teacher can expedite our journey. Otherwise, in the morning I shall study something and in the afternoon I will doubt whether the thing I learned is correct or incorrect. I am confused. But if the teacher says, "Yes, it is correct," then immediately I will believe it. We need a spiritual Master in order to expedite our realisation.

A spiritual teacher is like a private tutor. In the ordinary life, when we go to school, the teacher gives us marks. If we fail the examination, then we have to study again and again. In the spiritual life it is not like that. In the spiritual life the tutor privately, and with much affection, teaches us how to stand bravely in front of ignorance and fight ignorance. A private tutor does not give marks; he only teaches the student how to pass the examination. This is what a spiritual Master does.

When I go to school and advance from primary school to high school to college and university, my teachers give me a diploma. But once I have my diploma, I don't remain in the school. No. My professor has helped me in getting knowledge, wisdom; but once I have it, I don't always remain his student. In the spiritual life also, once I realise the highest Truth, at that time I don't have to be under the guidance of a Master.

If I know there is a way to reach my destination sooner than otherwise, then why should I act like a fool? I can come to Boston from New York by plane or by car. By plane if I come, it is a matter of half an hour, or forty-five minutes, whereas by car it takes me five hours. Now, if I can come here in half an hour, then I can do many things. I can have a most significant interview with you; I can hold a meditation in the evening, I can do many things. So time is a great factor. The sooner we can accomplish something, the better for us. God-realisation is our first goal, God-revelation is our second goal, God-manifestation is our third goal. We have three supreme tasks to fulfil. Our first task is still a far cry. So if we have a little wisdom, naturally we will try to run the fastest.

SCS 21. *The opportunity is not open to everyone. Not everyone finds the right teacher.*

Sri Chinmoy: No sincere effort will end in failure. If I am sincere and if you are meant to be my teacher, God will bring us together. But again, there are many wrong forces operating in the world, and I may be deceived by somebody who is not meant for me. But this cannot go on forever. After some time, my own inner being will tell me that this Master is not meant for me.

There are many ways to know which Master is meant for me. The person who gives me the greatest joy is my Master, even if he is not someone who has millions of disciples. Many people make a Himalayan blunder. When they see that somebody has thousands and millions of disciples, immediately they think that he has something; otherwise, nobody would have gone to him. But this is absolutely wrong. Yes, he may have many disciples, but that doesn't mean that you have to become his disciple. If you feel inner joy in his presence, if you feel from within that he is the right person, this is what matters. Unfortunately, it usually does not happen like that. People have no sense of discrimination; they don't go deep within. To accept a Master is a most important thing, because it is the Master who guides, moulds and shapes the student in his life of aspiration.

If somebody says that there is a set fee, that if you give him thousands of dollars then God-realisation will come, kindly don't believe him. If God-realisation could be achieved by material wealth, then all the rich people on earth would have realised God. But, unfortunately, it is not like that.

We are in a terrible hurry. If we hear that somebody can give us God-realisation overnight, we go. In the ordinary life, it takes us twenty-two years to get a Master's degree, which represents ordinary human knowledge. So how can we expect to get the highest knowledge, inner knowledge, if we don't study for ten or fifteen or twenty years? Our difficulty is that we want to simplify everything. We want to get everything ready-made, like instant coffee. But it is not like that. How can one get a Master's degree in one day? He goes to kindergarten, high school, college and then one day he gets his Master's degree. But if a kindergarten student feels that he can get his Master's degree today just because his elder brother has got it, then he is just fooling himself. His elder brother has studied hard for twenty years. But then again, there are, unfortunately, some false Masters who tempt the seekers and say that they can give it overnight. Unfortunately, I don't have that capacity.

I take my disciples' spiritual life as a serious matter, a most serious matter. What I can give you will take time, and what you have to offer me, your aspiration, will also take time. Aspiration has to increase little by little. My role is to bring down Compassion from above and this also has to increase little by little. It is like this. On your part you will climb up and on my part I will come down and bring down light. There should be a simultaneous effort by the spiritual Master and the disciple. With his inner cry the disciple goes up, and the Master comes down with the Smile of God. This is the role of the spiritual Master. At this moment he identifies with the seeker and he climbs up with his disciple's inner cry. Then the next moment he comes down with God's Smile. The perfection of the seeker is his cry and the perfection of God is His Smile. When a seeker can cry from the inmost recesses of his heart, this is perfection. And when God smiles with his heart's Delight, this is perfection.

scs 22. *Do you believe there is only one teacher for each individual?*

Sri Chinmoy: In the spiritual life there should be only one teacher, because spirituality is one subject. It is not like history, geography and science. In school we study different subjects and we need different teachers. But God-realisation is one subject, so we don't need more than one teacher. But if you have studied under the guidance of a teacher and that teacher is unable to take you any farther, then what will you do? History you studied in primary school and you are also studying it in college. The teacher who taught you in primary school was not in a position to teach you in college. So naturally you had to find a different teacher since your first teacher could not take you to the highest course.

scs 23. *What happens if you disagree with some of your Master's teachings?*

Sri Chinmoy: If the Master is the right one, then the student is bound to feel the truth in the Master's words, because the Master is the disciple's own higher reality. If somebody is my Master, I have to know that my Master is my own illumined reality. He is not a different reality. No! Just because he is my higher, more illumined reality, I have to listen to him. If he is a different person, a different reality, then naturally I won't be able to listen to him all the time and subscribe to his views. This moment he is telling something right, but the next moment he may tell me something totally wrong. But if he is my reality, which is infinitely more illumined, then how can he be different from me? And it won't be difficult for me to listen to my highest reality.

scs 24. *In the East there is more of a tradition of seeking a teacher like this. But in the West we are more into being individual. Could you comment on that please?*

Sri Chinmoy: What you are saying right now does not apply. There was a time when the West did not feel the need of a teacher. But now the West does. Now you see the Indian Masters are coming and many people go to them to get inner instruction. There was a time when the West felt that it was beneath its dignity to listen to Eastern philosophy. But right now Eastern philosophy is not only accepted but embraced by the Western world.

scs 25. *You experienced God-realisation. When did this happen and how did it change your life afterwards?*

Sri Chinmoy: When I was twelve years old, I realised God. Actually this realisation took place in a previous incarnation, but it took me twelve years to revive and assimilate my inner powers in this incarnation. The inner book that I studied I knew well, but in this incarnation I had to revise it. To revise the book it took me about twenty years. I lived in an ashram in south India from the age of twelve to thirty two.

SCS 26. *And then you came to America?*

Sri Chinmoy: Then I came to America. I did not have the vaguest thought of coming to the West, but my Inner Pilot commanded me to come here to be of service. I was brought up in a very small place in India and from there I was thrown into New York, the capital of the world, let us say. From where to where!

So again, it was my obedience that brought me here. I listened to the dictates of the Inner Pilot. Tomorrow if He tells me to go to some other place and be of service to Him there, I will gladly go, because for a God-lover there is no specific home. Wherever he is needed, wherever he is wanted, wherever he is commanded by the Supreme to go, there he has to be.

SCS 27. *How do you go about spreading your teachings? Do you write?*

Sri Chinmoy: I have written considerably, That is to say, the Supreme in me has written about 240 books. Whether they are worth reading or not, God alone knows. But as I said, I am the instrument; He is writing in and through me. I just entered into the art world. Very recently I completed ten thousand paintings in three months' time. But if I say that I did it, then I am telling the worst possible lie. The Supreme in me is doing it. And according to my receptivity, I am offering Him the opportunity to act in and through me.

It is just like sunlight. I can leave my windows and doors open and, again, I can keep all my doors and windows shut. If I allow the sunlight to enter into my room, then my room will be illumined. If I don't allow it, then my room will be all darkness. It is the divine Grace that is operating.

SCS 28. *What is the greatest thing we can do for our children?*

Sri Chinmoy: Here in the West, there is a kind of freedom that I do not endorse. Some parents say that America is the land of freedom and they give their children the freedom to find out for themselves what is best for them. I tell you, this policy has ruined thousands and millions of young children. In the formative years, when children are being brought up, parents should always tell the children what is best for them.

Parents say, "Let them grow up. When they get older they will see for themselves what is best for them." This is what many parents have done in America and they have lost their children. When the child comes into existence I know the child needs milk. I feed the child milk. I do not say, "Let the child drink milk or water, whichever he prefers, and when he gets older he will realise that milk is better for him." By that time he will have left the world. So what I know is best I will give. Let the child drink milk until he is ten or twelve years old and then, if he does not like milk, I shall let him drink something else.

If I know that the best thing for me to do early in the morning is to pray, I will encourage my child to do this. But if I say, "No, I have come to this realisation at the age of forty, so let my son also wait until he is ready," then I am making a deplorable mistake. For forty years I did not accept the spiritual life but wallowed in life's ignorance. How much I suffered and how much suffering I caused for my dear ones! But now I know that the spiritual life is the answer. So when I have the child in front of me, I will inspire him to pray and meditate. The thing that I feel is best I will tell my child. Then, when he grows up, if he feels that what I have said is not the right thing for him, then he can accept something else. But I shall guide him along the road I have discovered to be right until he is old enough to choose his own road.

In the beginning, if the child is not instructed, if the child is not taught, how will the child learn? The child cannot be left to learn in his own way. The lesson has to be given right from the beginning. I know a truth which I will tell my children. Later, if they discover that there is a higher truth or that the truth I have taught them is wrong, then let them reject it. But unfortunately, it is not happening this way in the West. Here I see thousands of children who have been misguided by their parents in the name of freedom.

scs 29. *At what age can you get a child to start meditating?*

Sri Chinmoy: Anytime, at the age of six months, even. Perhaps the child cannot utter a word, but if you are Christian, you can show him a picture of the Christ or something beautiful. God is expressing Himself through beauty. A child can appreciate the beauty of a flower. At that time, the flower itself is God for the child. Then, when the child can speak, let him say, "God" a few times as his prayer. As he advances in years, he can be taught higher meditations. We give our children the only real freedom when we give them the truth, the reality. Real freedom is not just to go and strike someone and move around like a vagabond. No. Real freedom is not to do anything we like. Real freedom is to do everything the way God wants us to do it. That is our freedom. God is all-Light, all-Freedom, and if we listen to Him, only then do we enjoy freedom.

scs 30. *What do you think of marriage? And what do you think the spiritual place of a man and a woman is in this life?*

Sri Chinmoy: It entirely depends on the individual. If an individual feels the need of marriage, I tell him that if he gets married, he can feel that he has four hands, four eyes and so on. He has double strength, double capacity.

Then again, if someone is not meant for marriage, if he doesn't feel the necessity of marriage, then I tell him that he should feel he is running the fastest. There is nothing holding him back from his goal, whereas if he is married and the marriage does not work out, there will be tremendous suffering and life will become unbearable. So the individual has to make the choice.

There is no hard and fast rule that one cannot realise God if he is married or if he is not married. No! It all depends on what God wants from him. If he feels from within that God wants him to get married, that God wants him to have that experience, then he is doing the right thing by getting married. If he feels that God does not want him to marry, then he should not do it.

scs 31. *Can a husband and wife have different teachers?*

Sri Chinmoy: If the husband and wife have different teachers, it is like going to the same goal along two roads. Problems will arise if the husband says that his road is clear, sunlit, whereas the wife's road is full of obstacles. Then trouble will start. But if the husband says, "I like this road and you like that road. So you go your own way, I will go my way, and we will reach the same destination," then it is all right. If the husband does not try to convert the wife and the wife does not try to convert the husband, that is the right thing. But when a feeling of comparison or competition enters, then all is lost.

SCS 32. *But does the union of two people diminish at all when they are following two different paths to the same thing?*

Sri Chinmoy: No. The only thing we have to know is how much understanding and respect they have for each other's path. But it is always safe if they have the same Master, if they are walking along the same road. If the husband and wife follow the same path and the husband becomes tired, exhausted, assailed by doubt, then at that time the wife becomes his helper. And if the wife becomes assailed by doubt or fear, then the husband can be of real help. So if they follow the same path, it is a great advantage.

But if the wife says, "I want to follow the path of the heart," and the husband says, "I want to follow the path of the mind," what can they do? At that time the husband and wife have to be very careful. Each has to know that the other is doing the right thing, according to his or her own capacity and understanding. They should have mutual respect for each other's realisation.

SCS 33. *What about the place of women in the spiritual life at this time of "women's liberation" and all that? What is the woman's real place in a spiritual sense and a man's real place?*

Sri Chinmoy: In God's Eye, there is no man, there is no woman. In God's Eye they are one. Man is the face; woman is the smile. Without the face, how can there be a smile? Again, if there is no smile, what good is the face? So both are equally important.

SCS 34. *We don't want to take much more of your time.*

Sri Chinmoy: I am so grateful. Nothing gives me greater joy than to be of dedicated service to you. Both of you have extremely beautiful souls, devoted, spiritual souls. You are serving God the Supreme, and I am also serving the Supreme. Here I have been doing something and you have been doing something. We are members of the same family. If I kept my capacity only for myself and if you kept your capacity only for yourselves, then we couldn't become one. When we unite our capacities, then only is God pleased with us.

Journalist: Thank you very much.

SCS 1–7. *(p. 5)* This section consists of several lectures delivered by Sri Chinmoy in recent years.

SCS 1. *(p. 5)* Sri Chinmoy gave this short talk to a group of young students on 19 July 1966 while visiting Puerto Rico. It was held under the auspices of the Young Men's Christian Association of Santurce.

SCS 2. *(p. 6)* This poem was written in honour of Puerto Rico's Governor Rafael Hernández Colón on 21 February 1975.

SCS 3. *(p. 6)* The celebration of Earth Day 1975 took place on 21 March — the first day of spring — in Manhattan's Battery Park. The Earth Day Committee invited Sri Chinmoy to commence this year's activities with a silent meditation and a short spiritual talk about our planet earth.

SCS 4. *(p. 8)* All Angels' Church, New York, 31 July 1976.

SCS 6. *(p. 12)* St Xavier School, New York, 9 July 1975.

SCS 7. *(p. 13)* St Xavier School, New York, 23 July 1976.

SCS 8–34. *(p. 15)* This interview with two Boston journalists on 22 March 1975 was unpublished.

SRI CHINMOY SPEAKS

BOOK 2

PART I

SCS 35. *Finding a genuine spiritual Master*

When one is ready, when one is sincerely ready in his spiritual life, either he will go to his Master or the Master will come to him. In India we say that when the student is ready, the Master is bound to come.

When one is thirsty, one goes to fetch a drink from the kitchen or from a pond or somewhere where water is available. Again, there is another way. When the child is crying for milk, the mother comes no matter where she is. If the child is crying in the living room and the mother is in the kitchen, the mother comes running to feed the child. When a seeker is really crying, it is God's bounden duty to bring someone to feed the spiritual child. In the human life, somebody is there to take care of the child, either the mother or the sister or somebody in the family. In the spiritual life also, if one is really crying, the Guru has to come from somewhere. No sincere prayer will remain unanswered. God's main business is to please us, to make us happy if He sees that we want the right thing.

There are many, many, many false Gurus, but it is very easy to recognise them. If a Guru says that he will be able to give you God-realisation in one night or ten days or in one month or two months, then he is a false Guru. If the Guru says that you have to give him some set fee for each lesson, and that if you give him a certain amount of money he will be able to give you realisation, then he is a false Guru. It is like a prescribed course. Twenty lessons you will get and after twenty lessons if you do not realise God, then the Guru will say that you are insincere. This is absurd.

Again, even a beginner can easily recognise a genuine Guru. If a beginner sees someone giving out Peace, Light, Bliss and

Purity through his eyes and through his consciousness, then he can be sure that this is a true Master. But although that Master is genuine, he need not be the seeker's own Master.

How can a beginner or anybody know who is his Master? When you see a Master, if you get an inner thrill all of a sudden, then you know that this is your Master. When a child sees his mother after a long separation, he simply jumps with joy. And the mother also gets tremendous joy when she sees her own child after a long time. In the spiritual life it is the same. When a Master sees his spiritual child, outwardly you can't see it, but inwardly his heart is flooded with joy. When Sri Ramakrishna, the great Master, saw his dearest disciple Vivekananda for the first time, he was inwardly thrilled.

The Master will always know who his real spiritual child is, but he does not tell because he may be misunderstood. If the Master tells a seeker, "You are my disciple," then immediately the seeker will think, "Perhaps there is some motive behind it. What does he want from me?" But if the disciple makes the commitment himself, then if ever the disciple wants to leave the Master, the disciple cannot blame the Master. That is why wise Masters always tell the seekers, "You accept me first; then I will decide whether or not to accept you. Let us accept each other mutually. Then, if ever you feel the necessity to leave me, you can leave me freely."

The seeker must judge each Master for himself. In this world everything is comparative. A seeker may get a little joy when he sees one Master. He may get much more joy when he sees another Master, and he will get the most joy from some other Master. The seeker has to give a mark to each Master. I am a Master. Some of you who are seeing me may give me ten, some may give me sixty or seventy, some may give me eighty. Those who are my disciples, those who have accepted me, should give me ninety-nine or a hundred; but those who are not my disciples may give me a zero. They are not making a mistake. I am not meant for them and they are not meant for me. They are the judges. They give marks to each Master according to the joy, the thrill, the inner ecstasy they feel. The Master who gets the highest mark from the seeker is the right one for that seeker.

But this does not mean that you have to go from one Master to another in order to see which one is yours. If you see a Master for the first time and you are able to give him ninety or a hundred out of a hundred, then you do not have to go and see twenty Masters more. If you are lucky enough to see your own Master first, then you don't have to roam all over the world to see others.

In this connection I wish to say that it is most essential to have only one Master. If you have really accepted a Master, then you should have only him. Why? There is a Goal, which we call the Golden Shore, and each Master has a boat of his own in which to take his disciples there. If today you stay in this boat and tomorrow you jump into another boat, you will not reach the Golden Shore. If you keep one foot in this boat and one foot in another boat, you will fall into the sea of ignorance. All genuine, God-realised Masters are absolutely right. You just have to choose one Master and then follow him.

In school you learn many subjects under the guidance of many teachers. Each subject has a different teacher. But God-realisation is only one subject, self-discovery is only one subject; and for that, one teacher is more than enough. Those who say that each Master has something special to give are right; but that speciality you don't need. You need only to realise God. And when you realise God, you get all the unique qualities of all the spiritual Masters. Yes, I have something which perhaps my disciples will say is special. And the disciples of other Masters will say the same about their own Masters. But I wish to say that this speciality is next to nothing in comparison to God-realisation. When you realise God with the grace of a Master, you see that you are flooded with Light.

So please follow one path, one Master; stay in one boat. And then, once you reach the Goal, you will see that you have got everything. But on the way, if you constantly change from one boat to another with the hope of getting special things from everyone, then you are only delaying your progress.

SCS 36. *Love, service and transformation*[5]

How do we love the world? We love the world with our inner peace. How do we serve the world? We serve the world with our inner joy. How do we transform the world? We transform the world with our inner faith.

Outer peace is a mutual compromise. Two individuals or two nations find no better way to bring about some harmony; therefore, they resort to compromise. There is no inner satisfaction here, but just because the two individuals or two nations have to stay together on earth, they feel that there is no other way. If they have to live on earth, then they have to resort to compromise. But inner joy, inner satisfaction, inner peace remain a far cry.

Inner peace is mutual sacrifice. This sacrifice is founded upon conscious awareness of one's reality. In this sacrifice, the one finds fulfilment in the many and the many find fulfilment in the one. On the strength of their inner oneness, two individuals on the outer plane make a sacrifice. But when they dive deep within, they feel that there is no such thing as sacrifice. It is the supreme necessity in both of them to please, satisfy and fulfil each other.

Outer joy is nothing more than pleasure, pleasure-life. This pleasure-life is followed by depression and frustration-life; and what looms large in depression and frustration is destruction.

Inner joy is spontaneous satisfaction. This satisfaction we discover in the heart of universal oneness. In order to have inner joy we have to give up the desire-life and enter into the domain of aspiration-life. Only in aspiration-life can we discover the heart of universal oneness.

Outer faith is nothing more than a rope of sand; it crumbles in the twinkling of an eye. With outer faith we cannot sing the everlasting song of the Absolute Supreme. Only in everlasting things can the Absolute Supreme sing His transcendental, universal Song.

Inner faith is our divine conviction. Inner faith makes us realise that we are of God, that we have a Source and our Source is God. Inner faith also makes us realise that we are in God and we are for God. When we discover that we are of God, we feel that our life has meaning. Our life has made a promise to God, and our human life, both individual and collective, must fulfil that promise. What is that promise? That promise is to manifest God here on earth in God's own Way.

We are in God. What does this mean? It means that we have accepted God's cosmic *lila*, His divine Game. We want to participate in His cosmic Game. God the eternal Player invites us and inspires us to participate in His cosmic Game and we want to play in the Game. While playing the game we will enjoy peace, bliss and satisfaction in boundless measure.

We are for God. What does this mean? It means that we have become supremely chosen instruments of God and He is manifesting Himself in an unprecedented manner in and through us. He is manifesting His Divinity, His Eternity, His Infinity and His Reality in and through us on earth.

Each human being has three natures: the animal, the human and the divine. The animal in us is nothing short of immediate destruction. The human in us is give and take, or possess and be possessed. The divine in us is self-giving, and self-giving eventually is transformed into God-becoming. The divine in us grows, glows and flows. When it grows, it grows into the transcendental Consciousness, the transcendental Height. When it glows, it covers the length and breadth of the world and finds its existence in the entire universe. When it flows, it flows in Eternity. At that time, Eternity and the divine Love flow together.

Transformation, service and love. What is transformation? Transformation is the unlearning of the things that ignorance has taught us. This ignorance had a favourite student. That student is the physical mind, not the higher mind or the illumined mind. The gross physical mind has taught us quite a few things which we now want to unlearn. The sooner we can unlearn the teachings of ignorance, the sooner our transformation, the transformation of our entire being, will take place.

Service. Whom do we serve? We do not serve the human in others or the human in ourselves. We serve the divine in others, the Supreme in others. And the Supreme in others is the same Supreme who abides in us. When we serve the Supreme in others consciously, soulfully, devotedly and unconditionally, we feel a kind of expansion. In this expansion we feel that we are no longer just for ourselves, but for all. United we are singing, playing and dancing in God's Garden.

The human in us does not use the term "service"; it immediately uses the term "help". But when the human in us thinks that it is offering help, the divine in us knows that this is a mistake. The divine in us serves the Supreme, the Absolute Supreme. The Absolute Supreme does not need help; He has and He is everything. He is Infinity, He is Eternity, He is Immortality. But when we serve Him, our humility grows, our spontaneous divinity grows. We feel that we are tiny drops in the ocean, insignificant, infinitesimal drops. But when the drops enter into the ocean, when even the tiniest possible drops lose their personality and individuality, they become the infinite ocean itself.

So it is through our service, devoted service, that we consciously grow into the Vast, into Infinity's Light and Delight.

Love. Why do we love? We love because our Source, He who created us, has taught us one supremely significant thing: love. This is what He has taught the soul in us, and the soul in us tries to bring this teaching always to the fore. The Supreme is the only teacher and He teaches only one subject, and that subject is love. He has infinite Love and He is infinite Love. Just because He is all Love, eternal Love, He is our dearest, He is our sweetest, He is our All. And because we want to love Him for the sake of love alone, without asking Him for any recompense, He feels that we are His chosen instruments.

Love is the greatest power, the most powerful power in us. But it is divine love that is most powerful, not human love. When a seeker enters into the spiritual life, he feels within and without a flood of love. And when he feels this love, he consciously tries to dedicate himself to the Source. He sees and feels that he is becoming consciously and constantly the perfect embodiment of God the eternal Truth, God the eternal Light and God the eternal Delight.

Each individual seeker is God's conscious representative on earth. A seeker is he who knows that ignorance-life is not the answer. Aspiration-life, which is the life of love divine — love of God, love of truth, love of light — can be the only answer. A seeker may not be consciously aware that he is infinitely higher than those who are unaspiring. Even if he is aware of what he is and who he is, he may not fully manifest what he has and what he is within. For the manifestation of his inner divinity, he has to aspire, constantly aspire, and become the ceaseless, ever-mounting flame. Right now the flame is within him, but there shall come a time when he shall grow into the flame itself. Once the seeker becomes the burning, glowing and illumining flame, the Absolute Supreme manifests Himself in and through this ever-mounting flame. And in this ever-mounting flame the seeker discovers not only his self-transcendence but also God's Self-transcendence. He and his eternal Beloved together are transcending, constantly transcending the height of Eternity's experience and Eternity's realisation.

SCS 37. *O my Inner Pilot*[§]

O my Inner Pilot, do grant me the highest boon: love. I wish to love You devotedly and soulfully because You are always my All.

O my Inner Pilot, I wish to love the world because You are its only real reality.

O my Inner Pilot, I wish to love myself because in and through me You want to reveal and manifest Your Dream-Boat, Your Consciousness-Sea and Your Reality-Shore.

O my Inner Pilot, it is such temptation to criticise and chastise the world. It is such temptation to steer the world-boat to an uncharted shore, to a nowhere-shore. It is such temptation to demand the world's ultimate surrender. It is such temptation to beg of You to please me in my own human way, since it is simply impossible for me to please You in Your own Way even for a fleeting second.

O my Inner Pilot, if I ever do what I want to do, then my name will be changed to selfishness, strangling selfishness. Selfishness is nothing but fruitless loneliness, loneliness is another name for stark frustration and frustration helplessly changes its name to utter destruction.

O my Inner Pilot, I have a tiny world of my own. Here the teeming and increasing demands of my raving vital torture me, my little world. I know I shall not be able to save myself, save my world, on the strength of my love for You. I know my love for You is a tiny drop; its capacity is incapacity itself. But again, out of Your infinite Bounty I know You will save me and guide me to my destined Goal. But O my Inner Pilot, I am tired, I am exhausted, I am practically dead. I beg of You, I implore Your infinite Bounty, to expedite Your Hour. O my Inner Pilot, do save the "I-ness" in me, save it and illumine it so that it can claim You as its very own — as the other divine members of my inner family rightly, devotedly and soulfully claim You as their very own.

O my Inner Pilot, my outer life, which is my mind, desperately needs Your Peace. My inner life, which is my heart, badly needs Your Patience. Your Peace I shall eternally treasure because I know that Your Peace is my ever-increasing success. Your Patience I shall eternally treasure because I know that Your Patience is my ever-fulfilling progress.

O my Inner Pilot, I have all along talked to You. I have talked and talked and promised to give You everything that I claimed as my own — everything, that is, but one thing: my ignorance-life. I have talked and talked and You, my Inner Pilot, have always listened to me. Now, my Inner Pilot, I wish to reverse the game. I wish to listen to You. I do not merely want to hear You but also to listen to You. To hear You is to offer my human ear: in one ear and out the other. But to listen to You is to offer You my divine heart, which exists only to please You in Your own Way at every moment. O my Inner Pilot, do grant me that heart that listens to You at every moment, the heart that is eagerly waiting throughout Eternity only to obey You, only to listen to You and please You in Your own Way. O my Inner Pilot, give me the heart divine.

O my Inner Pilot, You have given me countless opportunities and I have misused all these countless opportunities. At every moment You have showered Your choicest blessings on me in the form of opportunities, but the ignorance in me has not permitted me to use Your opportunities soulfully, devotedly and supremely. Now I wish to reverse the game. Now I wish to give You the opportunity, the constant opportunity, to play Your cosmic Game in and through me. Your opportunities I have misused; I have failed. But I wish You to exercise Your opportunities in and through me. You play Your role in and through me. I leave my heart's door wide open. Let me become from now on only an ever-mounting cry, an open heart, an open room in which You can play Your cosmic Game, in which You can sing Your cosmic Song, in which You can dance Your cosmic Dance.

O my Inner Pilot, Your creation is vast, infinite. You have created countless worlds, but I know for certain that You have two most affectionate creations: your daughter and your son. Your daughter is our Mother Earth and Your son is our Father Heaven.

O my Inner Pilot, I wish to serve Your daughter, our Mother Earth. I wish to offer her my soulful contribution, which is my heart's ever-mounting cry.

O my Inner Pilot, I wish to offer my soulful contribution, my soul's illumining smile, to Heaven, our Father Heaven. I wish to add my smile to Father Heaven's ever-illumining Smile.

O my Inner Pilot, constant hunger tortures my Mother Earth: hunger for perfection in her children. I wish to offer my devoted service to satisfy her hunger, so that her children, my brothers and sisters, can see the face of perfection.

O my Inner Pilot, do give me the capacity to offer my dedicated service to feed my countless brothers and sisters in my Mother Earth.

O my Inner Pilot, do grant me the capacity to serve Your son, Father Heaven. Let Father Heaven accept my gift of dedicated service, so that when he feeds the hunger of Mother Earth, I can be the dedicated, life-giving, soul-offering reality inside the sumptuous feast that Father Heaven will offer to Mother Earth.

O my Inner Pilot, You have given me many, many things, countless things since I first saw the light of day. But two things I see play their role most powerfully and significantly: my earth-bound body and my Heaven-free soul. My earth-bound body always reminds me of my obscure past, of my precarious present and of my absolutely uncertain future. My past tortures me, my present deceives me; but my future will illumine me.

O my Inner Pilot, You have also granted me a Heaven-free soul. My Heaven-free soul constantly blossoms inside me like morning jasmine, emanating its perfume, its redolent, earth-illumining, soul-fulfilling and Heaven-satisfying fragrance. The soul, the Heaven-free soul, reminds me of what You eternally are and what I, in the world of my inner heart, eternally am: the Eternal Now.

O my Inner Pilot, do grant me only one more boon. Your first boon was love; the second and last boon I ask from You is the Eternal Now, where You and I can grow, glow and flow. Again, there shall come a time when I shall say, "We shall grow, glow and flow together." Finally, there shall come a time when I shall not say "you and I" or "we", but only "I": not the human I, not the ego, but the Universal I, which is the Transcendental I.

SCS 38. *Religion, spirituality and yoga*[§]

Religion is the house, spirituality is the living room, yoga is the prayer and meditation room. The house is beautiful, the living room is meaningful, the prayer and meditation room is fruitful.

When seekers come to the house, they feel a divine vibration. If they are really sincere seekers, they will look for the living room. Otherwise, they will eventually go away from the house. Only sincere seekers feel God's presence in the house. It gives them tremendous joy, so they want to see God and speak to Him. For this they enter into the living room, where they try to lead a divine life. And from there, when they begin to feel the necessity of fulfilling their aspiration in a most significant way, they enter into the prayer and meditation room in order to achieve satisfaction in their inner life. For they feel that only seeing God and speaking to God is not enough. They feel that it is of utmost importance to pray to God and meditate on God so that they can be divinely and supremely satisfied. They cry to God in their prayer and meditation room for boundless Peace, Light and Bliss so that they can fulfil God on earth. They meditate on God so they can manifest His perfect Perfection in and through themselves.

Human religion and divine religion. Human religion says, "God is everywhere." Divine religion says, "God is everywhere, I don't deny it. I fully subscribe to this view. But I want a living God with whom I can talk and mix at every moment. I want to feel Him. I want to see Him. I want to speak to Him. I want a living God." This is the soulful need of divine religion.

Human spirituality and divine spirituality. Human spirituality says, "God is above, in the highest realm of consciousness. He is only in Heaven. Here in this world of imperfection God is not to be found, not to be seen, not to be expected." Divine spirituality does not see eye to eye with human spirituality. It says, "God is everywhere. He is in the highest plane of consciousness and, again, He is in the lowest plane, in the lowest chasm. He is everywhere. If God is not here on earth, then I do not need that kind of God. My God is within, He is without, He is below, He is above. He is everywhere. He has to be with me, even on earth, one hundred per cent of the time." Divine spirituality does not care for the God who stays only in Heaven.

Human yoga and divine yoga. Human yoga is all about the body, the perfection of the body and the perfection of the physical consciousness. In human yoga the body is all. If the body can live without food, then the body is perfect. If the body can live without sleep, then the body is perfect. If the body can walk on water without sinking, or walk on fire without being burned, then the body is perfect. But divine yoga is totally different. Divine yoga wants the real, integral perfection of the body and the soul. It feels that each limb has to aspire to receive light from above. The physical has to be a perfect receptacle. The capacity of receptivity must grow inside the physical along with the growing capacity of the soul. In divine yoga, perfection lies in receiving light from above and also in bringing to the fore the Light, Peace and Bliss that are inherent in the soul.

The divine yoga says, "The smile of the soul has to be manifested here on earth, but first the cry of the body, vital, mind and heart have to reach the highest transcendental Source." The union of the soul's manifestation-smile and the body's aspiration-cry is what the divine yoga needs. Aspiration for the Highest and manifestation of the Highest are what the divine yoga needs. When we aspire, we discover how we shall consciously reach the Light, Peace and Bliss which we eternally need; and when we manifest, we feel that we are offering the Highest to all of God's creation.

Here on earth we practise religion, spirituality and yoga in a human way. Religion says, "I am great. Why? I am great because I can exercise God's Justice. I can punish the rest of the world in accordance with the Will of God. I am great because I can tolerate the world. The world is full of imperfections, the world is constantly rejecting and misunderstanding me, but in spite of that I can tolerate the world. Also, although the world is unforgivable, I have the capacity to forgive the world; therefore, I am great."

Spirituality says, "I am good. I try to love mankind. Although mankind and I have countless limitations and imperfections, according to my power of receptivity and capacity I try to love mankind. I am imperfect and the world is imperfect, but with all my imperfections I try to love the imperfect world as my own, my very own; therefore, I am good."

Yoga says, "I do not know whether I am great or good. But whether I am great or small, whether I am good or bad, I am what God wants me to be and I will become what He wants me to become. I do not want to be caught by the snares of either greatness or goodness. I want only to be the devoted, dedicated, soulful and self-giving instrument of God."

Religion speaks to the sleeping world: "Wake up! Can't you see that God is standing at your door waiting for you? He has come to you out of His infinite Bounty. It is high time for you to wake up."

Spirituality speaks to the awakening world: "Look, look! Your Eternal Friend is waiting for you. Look at Him, smile at Him, talk to Him. He is your Eternal Friend."

Yoga speaks to the awakened seeker: "Why are you such a fool? Why can't you recognise your own self, the real in you? The highest in you, the real Reality in you, is right in front of you. Claim yourself. Claim unreservedly and wholeheartedly what you really and eternally are."

Religion says to the seeker, "O seeker, I can tell you who God is. I can tell you all about God in unmistakable terms."

Spirituality says to the seeker, "O seeker, I can do something more for you. Religion says it knows who God is, and it can tell you all about God. But I can tell you where God is. I can show you where He is and what He is doing. I will be able to establish a free access for you to God."

Yoga says to the seeker, "O seeker, I cannot only tell you about God and show you where God is, but I can make you another God."

Religion tries to do the right thing precisely because it is afraid of God. It loves God, but it is afraid of God and does not want to displease God in any way. It tries to please God because it feels that by pleasing God it can fulfil itself.

Spirituality feels that it is its bounden duty to please God precisely because God is its Source, its perennial Source, and eventually it has to go back to the Source and claim the Source as its very own.

Yoga knows and feels that God is omnipresent. On the strength of its oneness with God, yoga feels that it can do nothing but please God in every way, at every moment.

Each individual human being has religion in him, spirituality in him and yoga in him. When he uses his religion-power, he is blessed with God's infinite Greatness-Light. When he uses his spirituality-power, he is blessed with God's infinite Goodness-Power. When he uses his yoga-power, God blesses him with what He has and what He is. What He has and what He is far transcends His Greatness-Light and His Goodness-Power. It is something beyond human comprehension. It transcends both greatness and goodness; it is a Reality which perfectly houses God's ever-transcending Height and God's ever-manifesting Vision-Delight. It is something a yogi grows into and eventually becomes.

scs 39. *Retardation*

Some people are retarded because they have done something wrong in a previous life; it is the law of karma. But others are retarded simply because they have been attacked and now they are helpless. That is to say, in some cases a person has violated the cosmic law; in some cases the person has not violated any law but undivine cosmic forces have attacked him.

If someone has done something wrong, then he will meet with the consequences: an eye for an eye, a tooth for a tooth. In the case of mental retardation, the punishment is the person's lack of progress. Time is a factor. If one is prevented from making progress, is this not punishment? It is like this: a child is running a fifty-yard dash and someone prevents him from finishing. The actual punishment is that he is delayed, for eventually he will run and touch his goal.

A retarded person doesn't even know what his punishment is. Here the cosmic forces are kind; they hide the good things. Here, "good" means things that will tempt him, things that others enjoy, but he cannot; otherwise, his suffering would be beyond his capacity, beyond his imagination. He would be terribly frustrated. It is like an operation. Sometimes, you know, it is necessary for a doctor to make some part of you numb or senseless before an operation. Doctors use chloroform or something else, because that is the only way a person will be able to undergo a very serious operation. If they didn't use chloroform, then there would be too much pain for that particular person to bear. So the person has to be lifeless. If life were there, he would create a scene.

We have to know that the real soul is not unhappy, but at some point the vital has captured the soul. It is like the vibration in a house. Although this house may have a good soul, the vibration of the house may be ruined. If the vital comes and ruins the vibration of the being, then the soul's capacity remains fast asleep. The soul cannot do anything with its potential. When we say the soul is sad, we mean that the vital has taken possession of the soul and covered the possibilities of the soul. It is like the sun when the sky is dark and raining; the soul is eclipsed. When the sun is covered by clouds and is not performing its usual function, what good is it to us at that time?

Again, there is always something to pick a person up and carry him to his destination after he has been wounded and that something is Grace, Compassion. A retarded person may come back deaf, blind or crippled, or he may be retarded again in his next life — a crippled soldier of the Divine. But with the Grace of a spiritual Master, a retarded person can come back as a normal person. If Grace intervenes the law of karma has to surrender to evolution. We are evolving when we consciously or unconsciously are doing the right thing. But if we do something seriously wrong, our progress stops there and we are caught by wrong forces that take us away from the path of Truth. Eventually though, we have to follow the path of Truth because deep inside us is the soul, the sea of Truth.

It can happen on rare occasions that if a person has a very large heart, he may take incarnation with a serious defect such as retardation in order to lessen someone else's bad karma. If the mother has done something very wrong and the daughter is most kind and sympathetic, the daughter may say, "Let me take it," or they will each take half. If the mother has to suffer, say, for twenty years, in that case the daughter may take ten years of it and the mother will only have to suffer ten years.

The soul may or may not have the consent of the Supreme to do this, because the soul doesn't ask the Supreme's permission for every little thing. In the case of the soul, the lifetime during which it takes on the karma is just like a minute in the Supreme's Eye, so the Supreme doesn't interfere. This experience, according to the Supreme, is not even as much as a pinch in the soul's life, although for us it may be unbearable.

scs 40. *Serving others*

First of all we have to become spiritual ourselves, and only then can we try to raise the consciousness of others. If we *are* spiritual, then we have to become more spiritual. If we have a little light, then we have to acquire more light. As soon as we come out of our house, we are facing a destructive world; we are entering into the battlefield of life. While in the battlefield we have to be prepared to fight against our enemy. Here our enemy is ignorance.

Just because we are sincere, just because we are following the spiritual life, we feel that we have considerable ignorance within us. So first we try to conquer our own ignorance — the limitations and bondage we have inside us — and then we come into the world and try to fight the ignorance of others. But actually we do not fight; we only try to illumine.

In the ordinary world when we see an opponent, we try to conquer him by hook or by crook. We try to destroy that person and show our supremacy and then only do we feel that we are satisfied. In the spiritual life, we feel that everything is part of God; so we don't have to destroy our opponents, only we have to illumine them. Unless and until they are illumined, we are not totally satisfied. Here is the difference. In the spiritual life, unless and until we have illumined the world at large — the world around us and before us — we are not satisfied.

Now, in order to do that, we have to prepare ourselves. We prepare ourselves by feeding the soul. If you have to fight against someone, you strengthen your body. You take exercise, you eat properly and in this way you strengthen yourself. As you feed the body in order to be strong physically, so also you have to feed the soul in order to strengthen your inner being. And how do you feed the soul? You feed the soul by aspiring. Aspiration is the real spiritual exercise. When we aspire we energise our being, our entire inner existence.

So every morning before we enter into the world arena, we energise ourselves through prayer and meditation. Before we leave our house and go outside, we pray and meditate to strengthen our inner existence so that we can brave the buffets of life. It is from inside that we come out.

If you want to help the outer world, early in the morning during your meditation you can offer goodwill. If you feel that your near and dear ones are not at all spiritual, then it will take a long time to help them with their problems in the material world. But if they are spiritual, it won't take much time. The cure depends on their disease and the amount they are suffering.

You have to know that when the morning dawns, the divine within you comes forward and you see what kind of life you are leading. If you have good thoughts, divine thoughts, then immediately you get a kind of inner joy and inner cheerfulness. But if you have undivine thoughts, jealous thoughts, suspicious thoughts, then immediately you feel miserable.

If you have a good thought, you have to feel that it is coming from a good world. And if you have a bad thought, you have to feel that it is coming from a bad world. When you have a thought, consciously or unconsciously you are entering into a world. Now, if it is a divine thought, then you can bring your dear ones into this divine world with you.

From your aspiration, from your prayer, from your meditation, you create a world of your own. It is not that you are in the world of fantasy. No! It is the world of reality. As you aspire you enter into a higher world, a broader world. In that world you can embrace your near and dear ones and the entire outer world. It is on the strength of your own achievement, your own realisation, that you accept the world and change the face of the world. The higher and deeper you go, and the stronger you become, the sooner you are in a position to change the face of the world.

Let us go back to the world of Light and Delight, where there is no death, only Immortality. This is the world that our soul came from. Let us become one with the soul and fly with the wings of the soul. This world is within us, inside the inmost recesses of our heart, where Light and Delight are constantly playing.

scs 41. *Spiritual dryness*

In the spiritual life, a seeker should know that he cannot always eat the most delicious food. Once he has eaten something delicious, this does not mean that every meal from now on will be most delicious. It is possible, but only if he is very rich and has an excellent cook. If he is not rich and if he does not have a good cook, he will not be able to have most delicious food every day. In the spiritual life, it is also the same. One must have inside him a seeker who is most sincere, and constantly sincere. When people accept the spiritual life, for five days, for five months, for five years they are sincere. But to be sincere at every moment is something else.

You may think, "Oh, I am following Guru's path." Yes, that is true, but to be sincere every day and every hour and every moment is a different thing. In each day there are twenty-four hours. Seven or eight hours we sleep and then five or six hours we waste talking or mixing with others. On spirituality we spend just two hours. And even during these two or three hours sometimes we are not sincere. For two minutes we are sincere and the rest of the time we are daydreaming and building castles in the air.

There is a constant battle going on in us between the heart's inner cry and the mind's constant or conscious rejection. When sincerity plays its role constantly, we remain inside the heart. But sometimes the heart loses. When the heart loses in the battlefield of life, it is all a barren desert.

Just because you are experiencing night, you cannot say there will be no day for you. There will be. But if you want to remain in day all the time, then you have to do two things. The first thing is to use your imagination-power. Imagination is something most important in the spiritual life. Today something is all imagination; but tomorrow this very thing becomes inspiration and the day after tomorrow it becomes aspiration. And the following day it becomes realisation. With your imaginative power, think how you used to meditate on the heart centre one year ago or two years ago. Immediately you will be able to go back and catch the bird that used to fly so well in the psychic sky. As soon as you feel that you have reached the stage where you were two years ago, offer your gratitude to the Supreme. So, first use your imagination-power and then use your gratitude-power. In this way you are bound to get back in your day-to-day life the capacity you once had to concentrate, meditate and contemplate on your heart.

Once you have achieved something, you are bound to get it back; only it is a matter of time. But you can expedite your progress through constant inner cry, through imagination-power and gratitude-power. Again, if you have not got something, that does not mean that you are not going to get it. But if you once had some inner treasure, it is always infinitely easier to get back that treasure.

scs 42. *Surrender to the Guru*

When you surrender to the Guru, it is like entering into his room. If you stay in his room, naturally he will feed you. If you stay with your friend, how will your friend eat without giving you anything to eat? Is it possible if he is a real friend? He has allowed you to come into his room to stay with him. Since he is drinking Peace, Light and Bliss, will he not allow you also? Naturally he will. But your problem is to call him your friend, your eternal friend, and then to beg him to allow you to enter into his room. Once you are allowed to enter, naturally he will share with you when he eats.

Sometimes people ask a spiritual Master, "If I surrender to the Guru, how do I know what he is going to do?" I tell them,

"If you do not make the surrender, then how are you going to know?" If you do not touch water, you will not know what water feels like. Only if you touch water do you get a feeling of what it is. If you touch a wall, immediately you feel the consciousness of the wall; the consciousness that is inside the wall will give you an immediate feeling. When you make a conscious surrender to the Guru, that means you are touching his consciousness. He is the tree. You have touched, let us say, the foot of the tree or you have touched some of the branches and leaves.

The moment you make surrender to your Master, you have established a free access to him. You can say that one part of your body is making surrender to another part. Let us say my feet are not yet illumined, but my heart is illumined. Now, if my feet are wise enough they will say, "The heart is illumined. Let us surrender to the heart and become one with the heart." In the spiritual life, surrender means conscious oneness.

In the ordinary life, when one surrenders to someone, it is like a slave making surrender to the master. The master will use him according to his sweet will: "Sit down! Stand up! Go there!" In the spiritual life the Master cannot do that because if he is a real Master he knows perfectly well that he is only an instrument who is executing the Will of the Supreme. If you surrender to an ordinary human being, he lords it over you in his own way. But for the spiritual Master it is a different matter. He knows that he is not receiving your surrender. Somebody else, the Inner Pilot, is receiving your surrender, and the spiritual Master is at the mercy, at the command of the Inner Pilot, who is the real Master.

So the moment you make the surrender and touch the Master's soul, you will know how he will guide you. If you don't enter into him, if you don't touch him inwardly, then you will never know. But in the spiritual life, you should not worry about how he will guide you. That is his business. How he will take you to God is his problem; your problem is to give yourself, to make the surrender. You have to jump into a boat. It is the problem of the boatman to pilot you. Your business is to enter into the boat and it is the business of the boatman to carry you through inclement weather to the goal.

scs 43. *We learn*[8]

We learn. We learn from sorrow. We learn from sorrow how to purify our emotional vital. We learn from sorrow how to be watchful, careful and soulful. We learn from sorrow how to widen our hearts and how to heighten our lives.

Our emotional vital is unlit, obscure, impure and unaspiring. When we live in our emotional vital, there comes a time when sorrow and suffering knock at our door. Then we try to purify, sanctify and illumine the vital and make it a perfect instrument of God.

When we are watchful, we do not allow the world around us with its teeming imperfections to enter into our being. When we are careful, we do not allow anything undivine to grow within us. When we are soulful, we are safe both in the outer world and in the inner world precisely because the divine in us takes full care of us. The divine in us protects us, perfects us and immortalises us. When we are soulful, in the inner world we can sing the song of perfection and in the outer world we can dance the dance of satisfaction.

When we widen our hearts, we enter into the Universal Consciousness. When we widen our hearts, we expand ourselves. The finite in us grows into Infinity and the Universal Consciousness becomes part and parcel of our aspiring existence. When we heighten our lives, we grow into the Transcendental Consciousness. This Consciousness constantly transcends its own height. The Transcendental Consciousness is not and cannot be a static consciousness. It is always proceeding, climbing high, higher, highest. It is always transcending its own supernal heights.

We learn. We learn from joy. We learn from joy how to love God, how to serve God, how to fulfil God unconditionally in God's own Way. When we are happy, we give everything that we have and everything that we are. It is in our soulful self-giving that we eventually become perfect prototypes of our Inner Pilot, the Absolute Supreme. From joy we come to discover what we eternally are: God's Golden Dream. We are His Dream; we are His Dream-Boat. Again, it is in and through us that He will manifest His Reality-Shore. Either He will carry us to the Golden Shore of the Beyond or He will carry the Golden Shore to us. From joy we learn how to become God-seeds and God-fruits. When we become God-seeds, Heaven treasures us. When we become God-fruits, earth treasures us.

We learn from Heaven; we learn from earth. From Heaven we learn how to smile divinely and compassionately. From earth we learn how to cry ceaselessly and soulfully. From Heaven we learn that God is all Beauty. From earth we learn that God is all Duty. From Heaven we learn why God is, where God is. From earth we learn who God is, how God is.

Why is God? God exists to satisfy Himself divinely and supremely. His divine Satisfaction is far beyond the domain of our mind; the mind will be sadly baffled by it. But the heart, on the strength of its identification with God, can and will realise what God-Satisfaction is. God-Satisfaction is the Nectar-Life in God's Silence-World, in God's Sound-World.

Where is God? God is where His children are. God is all-where in His creation. God is the Creator; again, He is creation itself. In Silence-Life He is the Creator. In Sound-Life He is the creation. He is at once the Creator and the creation.

Who is God? God is eternally our Beloved Supreme and our Lover Supreme. When we aspire, when we cry from the inmost recesses of our hearts, when we grow into the burning flame that climbs high, higher, highest, at that time God becomes our Beloved Supreme. When we consciously, devotedly and unconditionally participate in God's cosmic Drama, Him to satisfy, Him to fulfil, Him to manifest in His own Way, at that time God becomes our Lover Supreme.

How is God? God is fine; God is happy. He tells the seeker in us that He is eternally happy because He feels that it is through His happiness and His happiness-life that He can create, preserve and immortalise His creation. There is no other way. He cannot be otherwise. Only through joy can He create, preserve and immortalise His creation.

We learn from the unreal in us. The unreal in us tells us that we were nothing, we are nothing and we will be nothing. We came from ignorance, in ignorance we dwell and, at the end of our journey's close, to ignorance we shall return. We learn from the real in us that we are everything. Not only are we everything to ourselves, but we are everything to the Supreme Pilot. The real in us tells us that we came from Delight, in Delight we grow and, at the end of our journey's close, into Delight we shall retire.

Then the real in us goes one step ahead. It tells us that our life has no end, our life-march knows no halt. It tells us that life is an eternal journey. There is no final destination. The real in us tells us something more. It tells us that when we reach any destination, that destination becomes the starting point for the next day's journey. Today we are at the starting point. Tomorrow we reach our destination. The day after tomorrow that destination becomes the starting point for a higher goal, a more fulfilling goal. There is no absolute Goal. The Goal is always transcending its own supernal heights.

We learn from man; we learn from God. Man has only one message to offer us: "The future is all darkness. The future is ruthlessly frightening. There is no certainty, there is no reality in the heart of the future. Stick to the past, live in the past, for you know about the past. No matter how deplorable the past was, the past is the only reality. Don't look ahead. If you look ahead, you are bound to notice the dance of destruction. Stick to the past." God has a different message, and this message we must try to learn from God. God tells us: "There is no such thing as future, children. My sweet children, there is only here, there is only now, there is only here and now. Try to grow in the immediacy of today. Try to live in My Vision-Boat and My Reality-Shore. Like Me, try to remain always in the Eternal Now. Grow in Me, glow in Me, flow in Me. The Eternal Now is the only reality. He who aspires discovers the reality of the Eternal Now."

SCS 44. *You do not know, he does not know, I do not know*

[Sri Chinmoy was introduced to the audience by Ken Pillar, head of the Yoga Centre.]
Sri Chinmoy: I am extremely grateful to you and your wife for having given us the opportunity to be of devoted, dedicated service to the Supreme in you. Ours is a path of service. Whenever we get an opportunity to serve the Supreme in His children, we feel it is our bounden duty to do so. So it is I who have to be extremely grateful to the seekers here and especially to you and your wife.

You do not know, he does not know and I do not know. Do you know who God is? Does he know who God is? Do I know who God is? No. You positively do not know God, he unmistakably does not know God and I absolutely do not know God. Why don't we know God? You do not know God because you love your body-consciousness infinitely more than you love God's Body, His Reality-Consciousness. He does not know God because he loves his own vital pleasure, his vital self-indulgence, infinitely more than he loves God's Universal Vital. I do not know God because I love my mind, my doubting mind, my judging mind, infinitely more than I love God's transcendental, universal and eternal Mind.

Let us know the difference between God's Body and your body. Over the years you have reached a certain height, let us say five feet eight inches. Here your height has come to an end. But God's Height is endless. He is infinitely tall. In your case, you have reached your maximum height. In God's case, He is eternally growing because He has discovered the secret of Self-transcendence. He knows what Self-transcendence is, so He is constantly transcending His own inner and outer Height.

Let us know the difference between God's Vital and his vital. His vital is like a tiny drop and God's Vital is like the infinite ocean. In his case, he cherishes and treasures this tiny drop. He feels that it is special. He feels that he does not have to increase the size of the drop; he does not have to grow into a larger drop. No, he is self-sufficient. But in God's case, although He is an infinite ocean, He still feels the necessity of increasing His own Infinity. Always God wants to grow, glow and flow. There is constant flow in God's movement, constant, everlasting Life.

Let us know the difference between my mind and God's Mind. My mind is like a tiny streak of light and God's Mind is like the vast sun. But it is not like the star sun. The star sun, according to the scientists, has already lost some of its warmth and power and in the future it will lose even more. Who knows, in the bosom of Eternity it may even disappear. But the inner sun, which God is, will perpetually shine. And not only will it shine, but it will offer to humanity — to God's creation — Light, more Light, abundant Light, infinite Light. God the inner Light, the inner Sun, will perpetually shine and illumine the ignorance and inconscience of the world.

You do not know where God is. He does not know where God is. I do not know where God is. You do not know where God is precisely because you live in the temptation-world. He does not know where God is precisely because he lives in the indulgence-world. I do not know where God is precisely because I live in the thought-world.

You do not know, he does not know, I do not know. But there are some people who have discovered who God is and where God is. In the ordinary life, some people have got their Master's degree and Ph.D., whereas there are many who have not got even a high school diploma. In the spiritual life also, just because we do not have something, that does not mean that others cannot have that very thing. They can have it and a day will dawn when we will all have it. Right now those who have seen and realised God and who are in constant communion with God tell us something quite significant and momentous. They tell us, on the strength of their own realisation, who God is. They tell us that God is our own yet-unrecognised infinite capacity. They also tell us that not only do we need God, but God also needs us equally. We need Him to realise our own height. He needs us so He can manifest Himself on earth in and through us. For self-realisation we need Him; for God-manifestation He needs us.

These God-realised souls tell us something more: they tell us where God is. They tell us that God is everywhere, but there are two places where He is noticeable most of the time. These two places are inside our heart's mounting cry and inside our soul's descending smile. Just as a person stays during the day in his living room and kitchen and at night retires to his bedroom, God also distributes His Presence. When we are soulfully crying for Him, He presents Himself inside our mounting cry. And when we are soulfully smiling, He grants us His Reality in a visible form in and through our soul's smile.

These God-realised souls also tell us that the first and foremost necessity is peace of mind. If we do not have peace of mind, God-realisation will always remain a far cry. How can we have peace of mind? There are a few ways. If we decrease our earthly needs and increase our heavenly needs, then we can get peace of mind. Also, if we do not expect anything from anyone or from anything except from God, then we can have peace of mind. As long as there is expectation, human expectation, earthly expectation, we cannot have peace of mind. Again, we cannot have peace of mind by positive or negative renunciation. Only by affirmative acceptance can we have peace of mind. We have to accept the world, we have to accept the real Reality of God in the world. With our inner cry, with our aspiration, we have to create receptivity inside our body-consciousness so that we can welcome God the Supreme Beloved with His boundless Light and Delight.

In order for us to realise God, we also need purity, especially in our emotional vital. When we purify our emotional vital, we see and feel God's Presence. Then we have to establish clarity in the mind. When we establish clarity in the mind, we will be able to see God very intimately. Then we have to commune with God all the time. In order to commune with God all the time, we have to create the supreme necessity for this inside our heart. This necessity has to be our psychic necessity. When we have created a psychic necessity to commune with God all the time, we shall without fail see God, talk to God, grow into the very image of God and consciously participate in God's cosmic Drama as devoted and unconditional instruments of God. At that time we shall feel that God is not only there in Heaven but also here on earth.

God is where His children are. His children are the exact prototypes of His Reality; therefore, wherever we are, God is. But in order to realise this supreme truth, we have to return what we have borrowed from this world: darkness, ignorance, bondage, limitation, imperfection and death. We borrowed these things because we felt that they would considerably help us, but now we have come to realise that they are real obstructions. So these things we must return. And the things that we eternally have in the inmost recesses of our being — Peace, Light, Bliss, Truth — we have to increase. We have to bring them to the fore, for they are the real Reality of our existence. Things that eternally *are* we have to claim and offer to the world at large. If we do this, you will know who God is and where God is, he will know who God is and where God is and I shall know who God is and where God is.

scs 45. *Does evil exist?*

Sri Chinmoy: From the strict spiritual point of view there is no such thing as evil. Only when we remain in the world of relativity, in the ordinary human consciousness, do we say that this is evil and this is divine. If we go deep within, we see that there are a few things with less light and there are a few things with more light. Things that have little light or practically no light we call evil. And things that have considerable light we call divine. Each individual has divinity within him. But his divinity has not come to the fore and fully manifested itself. Each individual also has undivine qualities to some extent. His undivine qualities can be transcended, illumined, perfected and transformed into the divine qualities that he already has.

When we use the term "evil", our mind immediately looks down upon the reality and has a superior feeling. But if we say something right now embodies light in infinitesimal measure, then we get the opportunity, the inspiration, the aspiration to transform it into something divine. So the best thing is to say a limited light is operating in the existence or the reality which we call evil. Then we will try to transform the limited light into abundant light.

scs 46. *What is pure emotion?*

Sri Chinmoy: Pure emotion is an enlarged, expanded conscious-ness of our reality. In pure emotion, we feel that we are God's children and therefore we cannot wallow in the pleasures of ignorance. There are many things we cannot do when we have pure emotion. How can I torture you, or how can I in any way show my superiority to you if I have pure emotion? When we have pure emotion, we are the Universal Consciousness. Since God is universal, we are also universal, because we are His children. So pure emotion is self-expansion, an expansion of our reality.

But impure emotion always binds us. It takes us to the pleasure-life, which is filled with frustration, and what follows frustration is destruction. In the pleasure life we bind others. When we try to bind, we ourselves are bound. But when we try to offer pure emotion, we are liberating ourselves and expanding today's reality. When we have pure emotion, the reality that we all know is increased, its light is increased, its power is increased.

SCS 47. *How can we make spiritual progress?*

Sri Chinmoy: There are two ways. One way is to cry like a child, soulfully. When the child cries for milk or something else, immediately his mother comes and offers the thing that is needed. But his cry has to be sincere. In the spiritual life also, we have to cry soulfully and constantly so that we can hear the dictates of God, our Inner Pilot. This is one way.

Another way is to take help from someone who can increase our inner cry or who can show us how to listen to the dictates of the Inner Pilot. So one way is to go deep within; we cry and cry. And the other way is to take help from someone who can help us increase our own inner cry.

SCS 48. *When should a child start meditating?*

Sri Chinmoy: A child should start meditating the day he can utter a syllable. The day the child can say a word, at that time the mother should teach the child the word "God". Right from the beginning, the parents can instruct the child that it is not they who are responsible for his life, but God. The mother will not always be there, but there is someone who will always be there and that person is God. The mother has to direct the child to the right person, to the Source. She has to let him know that there is someone in him, for him and around him all the time, and this person is none other than the Supreme.

Also the mother can pray to God on behalf of the child. The prayer will be most effective when the child is asleep, for at that time the child's soul comes to the fore. When the child is awake he cries and makes noise; at that time he is not in his soul. When the parents have unruly children, disobedient children, they should meditate beside the children when the children are asleep. Most of the time, their children's inner divinity comes to the fore during sleep.

scs 36. *(p.44)* White Plains, New York, 11 July 1975.

scs 37. *(p.48)* Greenwich, Connecticut, 25 July 1975.

scs 38. *(p.51)* Syracuse University, Hendricks Chapel, 26 October 1975.

scs 43. *(p.63)* Southampton College Theatre, Southampton, New York, 12 July 1975.

scs 45–48. *(p.71)* Ellicottville, New York, 13 July 1975.

SRI CHINMOY SPEAKS

BOOK 3

scs 49. *Concentration, meditation and contemplation*

In concentration we focus our attention on a particular subject or object and do not allow our mind to roam. Thought-waves must stop in concentration. We are like a bullet entering into something divine, or we are like a magnet: we are pulling the object of our concentration towards us. This is concentration.

Then comes meditation. Here we try consciously, soulfully and devotedly to enter into something vast. Right now vastness is something we imagine with the mind. But if we can feel the reality of vastness inside us, if we can feel the existence of the vast ocean or the vast sky inside us, then we will find ourselves growing into this vastness. Meditation means our conscious growth in the infinite. In meditation, the mind becomes calm and silent and we consciously allow ourselves to be nurtured and nourished by Infinity itself. Meditation is our conscious awareness of the Vast, and from this point of our meditation we grow into the Vastness itself.

Contemplation is the third and last rung in the spiritual ladder. In our ordinary life we say that the knower and the known, the Creator and the creation, the Player and the instrument, the lover and the Beloved are different things. But when we learn the art of contemplation they become one. At that time, the Creator and the creation, the Player and His instrument, the Dancer and the dance, become totally one. Here dream and reality become totally one. Right now I separate myself from my action. If I am the doer, then I am separating myself from the action; and if I am the action, then I hope that the doer in me will do something to please me. But when we contemplate we see that the doer and the action go together.

So contemplation is the message of inseparable oneness; meditation is the message of vastness; and concentration is the message of alertness. First we become alert and one-pointed; then we enter into the Vast through meditation; and from the Vast we become one with Infinity.

SCS 50. *Consciousness*

What we call matter is not really inert or totally unconscious. Spirit is always there in matter. We see matter all around. The physical world is all matter, but Spirit is deep inside matter fast asleep. Spirit has to be awakened inside matter. Matter is the sister, Spirit is the brother. Sister and brother always go together. Or we can say Spirit is the husband and matter is the wife. Matter without Spirit does not exist. Similarly, Spirit without matter cannot function. Matter needs Spirit in order to have its life. Spirit needs matter in order to make its manifestation clear, visible and tangible. When Spirit starts functioning in matter, matter gets life.

Consciousness is the Light of the Supreme. It exists in Spirit, it exists in matter, it exists in life, it exists everywhere. Without Consciousness nothing can come into existence, nothing can grow, nothing can be manifested on earth. If you have true Consciousness, this Consciousness will be backed by Existence and, at the same time, by Bliss.

Consciousness is the connecting link, the golden link between our heart's ascending inner cry and God's descending Smile. The individual consciousness is divided, but the Universal Consciousness can never be divided. In your individual consciousness, early in the morning you can cherish pure thoughts, then in two hours' time you can be subject to undivine, impure thoughts. This happens when you live in your own individual, personal consciousness. But if you enter into the Universal Consciousness, then it is all Peace, Light and Bliss in boundless measure. There you cannot separate consciousness into pieces.

Again, when consciousness operates in the physical, the gross physical, it has very limited capacity and opportunity. But when it operates in the soul, it has boundless capacity because the soul is all freedom, whereas the body is all limitation and bondage.

The highest state of Consciousness is all Light, all Delight. When you enter there, you see that you came from infinite Light and that you are offering infinite Light to the world at large. This state is normal, absolutely normal. When you realise the highest state, at that time you feel that this is some thing that you badly needed. When you enter into that plane, when you see God, you feel that it is absolutely normal, something more normal than your own eyes and nose. As soon as you realise the highest state, you will feel that from time immemorial this highest state was at your beck and call. Right now you are not searching for it, or you are searching for it at a wrong place. But the day you discover it, you will see it is like your own everlasting friend.

The highest state is something beautiful. Right now you see a beautiful child and say, "Oh, this is the most beautiful child I have ever seen on earth." But when you enter into your own highest state, you will feel that your own inner beauty is infinitely more beautiful than the most beautiful child on earth. And it is not your imagination; it is reality.

Right now you may feel that you are very impure and that somebody else, a saint or a spiritual person, is very pure. But when you enter into your highest state of consciousness, there you will see that your own purity is infinitely greater than the purity of the saint. Previously you felt that he was the purest being, but in the highest state you are dealing with Infinity.

Because we are in the finite, our vision is very limited. We can see fifty or sixty metres and then we are like a blind person. But when we enter into the highest state and our Third Eye opens, we can see the past, the present and the future. But we do not use our Third Eye in order to enjoy. No! Once we see darkness in someone, we try to help that person. If we see ignorance in someone, we try to illumine that person. We do not look at the situation of others with a feeling of superiority or enjoyment. We do not get enjoyment from the fact that someone else is still in a low state of consciousness and we are in a higher state of consciousness. No, we only are happy that we are in a position to serve him at that moment, that we have the capacity. There was a time when we did not have the capacity, in spite of our best intentions. But now we have the capacity, so we utilise it.

Once we enter into the highest state, we look at Mother Earth as part and parcel of our own being. Here on earth, when we are superior to someone, we either show compassion or we ignore the other person. But when we enter into the highest plane of consciousness, we feel that those who are unrealised are part and parcel of our being. We have to help them. We have to illumine them. And the moment we serve them, help them, fulfil them, at that time we feel that we are entering into the highest plane of Delight.

scs 51. *Ego and freedom*

Suppose you have a shop and in the shop you are employing quite a few workers. You pay your workers a salary, but one of them wants more money, so he revolts. This is what happens in the ordinary world. In the spiritual world it is also like that, but in a different sense. God is utilising us and the freedom he gives us is our salary. Here we get no money or cash; we get our freedom. He has given to each one limited freedom. Now, what do we do? We do not create within us the capacity to increase that freedom. No, we fight to get more freedom by hook or by crook, by adopting foul means. God has given us limited freedom and one day God will give us infinite freedom. But for that we have to prepare ourselves. We have to go deep within; we have to pray, we have to meditate. Freedom here means freedom from ignorance, freedom from bondage, from limitation, from imperfection, and from death.

But we don't exercise our freedom in that way. We use the limited freedom God has given us to strike someone, to punish someone. It is just like a knife someone has given us. With that knife we can cut fruit and share it with others; again, we can use that knife to stab someone. We can misuse our freedom; and each time we misuse our freedom, ego comes in.

Now, limited freedom is not bad. But we are never satisfied with what we have. From one possession we go to two, from two we go to three, and so on. We are always trying by hook or by crook to get more. We have thousands of desires. We exercise our power of freedom in a destructive manner, not in a creative manner. But although desire wants to be rich overnight, let us say, still desire is afraid. The desire-thief in us wants to be as vast as the ocean, but when somebody carries him or drags him in front of the ocean and tells him to jump into the ocean, he becomes frightened to death. Desire wants vastness and, at the same time, it is frightened to death when others come and tell it, "Become vast."

But if we aspire, at that time nobody will ever have to bring us in front of the sea. We ourselves will come and jump into the sea and start swimming. First ego came and made us want to become something vast. But inner courage we did not have. When we have aspiration, at that time we have inner courage. We know that we will not drown, but on the contrary, we will be illumined.

Desire comes from our self-imposed, self-styled authority. We can do this; we can say this. But the moment we say, "No, we are only instruments; we are not the doers," then ego vanishes. When we say, "God is the Doer; I am just His instrument," then ego disappears. But if we feel that we are the doers, ego comes into existence. Since we are spiritual seekers, we have to feel all the time that there is a higher reality that is acting in and through us. Then there can be no ego.

Once one realises the soul, he will not have the so-called human ego. He will say, "I am God's son. How can I do anything wrong? You are God's son. How can you do anything wrong?" He is saying that it is beneath his dignity and others' dignity to make friends with ignorance. Here his ego is not speaking. It is his divine personality, not his human personality. It is his divine awareness, his universal oneness that is coming forward. When he says "you", at that time he feels that it is his own life that he is speaking of; and when he speaks of his own life, he feels it is your life that he is speaking of.

After a person has realised the soul, at that time he becomes one with his friends, his relatives, his brothers and sisters. At that time, there is no ego. It is all oneness. When he says, "How can you do this? I don't do this kind of thing," it is not his superior feeling. It is only an injection of inspiration and encouragement. He is only trying to convince you that you are something really divine, something really great, something immortal.

The Christ said, "I and my Father are one." Ignorant people will say, "Oh, look what kind of ego he had." But he became one with his Almighty Father; that is why he said this. When we realise our soul, at that time it is only our oneness with others that is speaking. There is no ego there. It is only the song of oneness in infinite forms and shapes.

SCS 52. *Ego and the Transcendental Self*

There are two "I"s. One is the ego that says, "I, my, mine; my family, my brother, my sister, my home." That is the little "I". The other "I" is the Transcendental Self, the Universal Consciousness which houses everyone. The ego does not house anybody. It only claims and possesses: "This is *my* father. This is *my* sister." But the Universal Consciousness or the Transcendental Self does not claim anything in that way. It houses everybody as its very own.

In an ordinary family, when one member tries to possess another, he feels that without the other person he is totally lost; or he feels that if that person does not take light from him, the other person will be totally lost. In the ordinary life, when the ego operates, we feel that we are indispensable. We feel that we know better than everybody else and we are responsible for everything. We feel that everybody needs us. This is the ordinary ego.

But the Transcendental Self houses the entire cosmos and offers liberation or freedom to each individual soul. The Transcendental "I" says like the Christ, "I and my Father are one." Here the Father is not an ordinary human being, but the infinite Self, the infinite Reality. This "I" identifies consciously with Infinity. This "I" is the Inner Pilot within us.

The big "I", from the highest spiritual point of view, is always extending itself. Even when we realise the Truth, we feel that there is no limit to our Truth. There is a goal. Yesterday, we felt that the goal was a far cry. But today we come and touch the goal and then we feel that the goal which we have touched is not the Ultimate Goal. It becomes the starting point for tomorrow's goal.

When we are consciously expanding, we drink in ecstasy, nectar. We expand like a bird spreading its wings. But we are not possessing. When we try to possess something, we try to possess by hook or by crook. But this spontaneous expansion of our consciousness is like a mother spreading her arms around her children. There is no possessive feeling. It is a spontaneous feeling of one's own extension. Right now I am raising my hand. Gradually, gradually I am extending it and stretching it. It is my own reality that I am extending. I am not possessing anybody or putting anybody under my control. I just feel that on the strength of my aspiration, I am extending my own inner reality. I am spreading my wings far, farther, farthest.

God is everything. He is omniscient, omnipotent, omnipresent. But He Himself is transcending His own Beyond. He is in the process of transcending His own Infinity. Now it is beyond our mind to grasp Infinity, but when we identify ourselves with the Lord Supreme we see Infinity and realise that it is to be found in the ever-transcending Beyond. Today's Beyond is always our goal. And tomorrow when we enter into the Beyond, we feel that this Beyond is ever transcending its own reality.

So what we call the Transcendent is always extending itself. When we expand, we transcend. This is happening in the inner world constantly. Consciousness is always expanding. When it is a matter of the physical body, once you attain your height you will not grow. I am 5'8". I will never be tall. But if I meditate, my consciousness will easily expand. There is no limit to our progress in the inner world.

In the inner world we are dealing with aspiration. In the outer world we are dealing with desire. Desire has a limit; it cannot go very far. But in the spiritual world, when we deal with aspiration, we are dealing with Infinity and Eternity. And there is no end to Infinity; there is no end to Eternity.

scs 53. *Evil*

In the beginning there was only Silence and Light, infinite Light. Then each individual was given a limited amount of freedom, but we misused that limited freedom. God gave us limited freedom but we misused it to such an extent that we created, in some ways, our own world of ignorance, inconscience and undivine forces. Like a cow we are tied to a tree with a rope and given a little freedom. But the cow runs around and thrashes and destroys everything in reach.

The evil force is in our mind, not inside our aspiring heart. The mind wants to taste the whole world infinitesimally, piece by piece. The heart wants to embrace the whole world as a unit. The heart feels that the whole world belongs to it. But the mind says this is mine, that is yours. The more the mind can separate, the greater joy the mind gets. Evil is a sense of separativity. When there is union, there is no evil; but when there is separation, at that time evil starts. If we have goodwill, love, a feeling of oneness, then instead of destroying the world, we shall try to embrace the whole world.

It is the same old story: disobedience. If we obey the law, the inner law, then nothing happens. But when we disobey the inner law, evil comes into existence. If we properly use our freedom, then we go towards the Divine, towards the Light. But if we misuse it, then we become anti-divine; we become a hostile force. It was not God's intention that there should be undivine forces, hostile forces. No! But many things happen in this world, in the creation, that are tolerated. It is one thing for something to be fully sanctioned and another thing to be just accepted or tolerated. Parents sometimes have bad children. Now what do they do? Disobedient, naughty children they just tolerate. We are all God's children. Some are good, some are bad. But God did not intend to have a bad creation.

God is omnipresent. That means that God is everywhere; He is in good and He is also in so-called evil. For us a tiger is an undivine force. A tiger comes and wants to devour me, so I feel the tiger is an undivine force. But inside the tiger is also God's existence. Everything is in the process of evolution towards greater God-manifestation. But no matter what stage of evolution a person or thing has reached, God is still inside that person or thing.

Right now I am drinking distilled water. It is good water. But water can also be dirty, filthy, impure. God can be found inside impure water as well as inside pure water. But I won't drink impure water because I know it will harm my body. Even though God is there, I won't drink impure water.

Here we are all spiritual people; we are meditating together. Bad people won't come here. Because of our evolution, we are trying to see God at a particular level of consciousness. God is in bad things also, but we don't want to go back to the animal kingdom and the lower realms of consciousness to look for God.

scs 54. *Now* [8]

Now. N-O-W. "N" represents necessity. "O" represents oneness. "W" represents when. When must we feel the supreme necessity of discovering our conscious, constant and inseparable oneness with the Absolute Supreme? Now! Now is the time to see, now is the time to feel, now is the time to do, now is the time to become. Now is the time to discover what we eternally are.

What are we supposed to see? Beauty within, beauty without.

What are we supposed to feel? Peace within and peace without.

What are we supposed to do? Love the Real in man: God. Serve the real in God: man.

What are we supposed to become? God's perfect instruments.

What are we supposed to discover? God's Silence-vision and God's Sound-reality.

If we have been living in the body-consciousness, now is the time for us to find a new place to live. From now on, let us live in the vital, the vital that builds and not the vital that destroys. If we have been living in the vital, now is the time for us to find a new place to live. From now on, let us live in the mind, the mind that believes and not the mind that disbelieves. If we have been living in the mind, now is the time for us to find a new place to live. From now on, let us live in the heart, the heart that expands and not the heart that contracts. If we have been living in the heart, now is the time for us to find a new place to live. From now on, let us live in the soul, the soul that longs for the manifestation of God-Reality on earth and not the soul that does not care for the manifestation of God-Reality. If we have been living in the soul, now is the time for us to find a new place to live. From now on, let us live in the Supreme God: the Supreme God who tells us that He needs us just as we need Him, and not the Supreme God who tells us that He does not need us, whereas we do need Him. As a matter of fact, the real Supreme God tells the seeker that He needs him infinitely more than the seeker needs God. "How is it possible?" the seeker asks. God's immediate answer is at once divinely simple and supremely convincing. He tells the seeker that, at times, unfortunately the seeker makes friends with fear, doubt, anxiety, jealousy, insecurity and other undivine forces. Therefore, it is not possible for the seeker to be always conscious of the infinite Truth that abides in him. It is not possible for him to be conscious of his infinite potentialities, infinite possibilities and infinite inevitabilities. The seeker does not know what he actually is.

But in God's case, precisely because Infinity, Eternity and Immortality are at His express command, He knows what man actually is. Man is Infinity's heart, man is Eternity's breath, man is Immortality's life.

Now is the time for each genuine seeker to develop an eternal God-thirst and God-hunger. With his eternal God-thirst and God-hunger on earth, he will transcend what he is not: ignorance-night. And with his eternal God-thirst and God-hunger in Heaven, he will descend to earth to offer God-satisfaction in life and God-perfection in life.

Through the sweep of the centuries each spiritual Master of the highest rank has offered something unique. Four thousand years ago Sri Krishna offered his supreme message to mankind, to the world at large: "Whenever *dharma*, the code of inner life, declines and unrighteousness prevails, He, the Consciousness Infinite, incarnates Himself in human form in order to transform the wicked propensities in us and fulfil the divine Reality in us."

Then the Lord Buddha, two thousand five hundred years ago, descended with a most special message: "The Middle Path". Do not wallow in the pleasures of the senses and, at the same time, do not resort to austerity: neither sense-gratification nor sense-mortification. Each seeker has to strike a balance by following the middle path. The transformation of our lower self and the manifestation of our higher self must take place at one and the same time, but without resorting to sense-gratification or sense-mortification. This was the Buddha's message.

Two thousand years ago the Christ, the Saviour, descended into the earth-arena. His supreme message was: "I am the way, I am the Goal." Here "the way" represents aspiration and "the Goal" represents salvation. It is through aspiration that one eventually attains the highest salvation. Today's aspiration transforms itself into tomorrow's salvation.

I wish to mention another spiritual Master of the highest order. His name was Sri Chaitanya. His message was purity and love — purity in love, love in purity. If one achieves purity in love and love in purity, then one divinely enjoys Delight, which is our Source, our perennial Source.

Thousands of years ago, the Vedic Seers of the hoary past offered a significant message: "From Delight we all came into existence; in Delight we grow; at the end of our journey's close, into Delight we retire."

Sri Ramakrishna came with a most significant message. His message to humanity was, "Cry, cry like a child to the mother. A child's heart can easily conquer the Mother's Love, Compassion, Divinity and Immortality. Cry, cry like a child, an innocent child. The Mother Supreme is bound to grant you the illumination of the highest Height."

Then came Sri Aurobindo, with the message of life divine, with the message of nature's transformation. Here on earth the physical body has to be transformed, here on earth the message of Divinity must be manifested. The transformation of human nature and the purification of all the limbs must take place here on earth, so that Immortality can find its due place in the physical frame.

Since then, many spiritual Masters here in the West and there in the East have offered their light to the aspiring humanity. Each spiritual Master has something to contribute to the world at large according to his own realisation, according to his own receptivity and according to the world's receptivity.

Out of His infinite Bounty, God has given me the opportunity to be of service to the aspiring mankind. We have a path of our own and this is the path of love, devotion and surrender. For the followers of our path, the supreme necessity is love, devotion and surrender: love divine, devotion divine and surrender divine.

The love that binds and blinds is human love. The love that expands and illumines is divine love.

Devotion in the physical is nothing short of attachment. When we are devoted to the sense-world, the ignorance-world, it is not devotion but attachment. When we use the term "devotion", it has to be applied only to the Divine in us, to the Supreme Reality in us. We are devoted to a higher cause, to a loftier ideal.

Human surrender is the surrender of a slave to his Master. Divine surrender is the surrender of one's own unlit, obscure, impure reality to one's own fully illumined, fully divinised, fully perfected reality. Here the lower in us surrenders to our own higher reality. It is not a surrender thrust upon us, it is not a surrender forced upon us. It is a surrender based upon our feeling of inseparable oneness with our own higher Reality-existence. The finite in us cheerfully, devotedly, soulfully and unconditionally surrenders to the Infinite in us. The raindrop surrenders to the mighty ocean and thus loses its individuality and personality and becomes the vast ocean itself. Likewise, we who are now in the finite consciousness, bound in the finite consciousness, will one day be totally freed and liberated, and we shall realise the eternal Freedom-Reality, which in the inner world we eternally are.

scs 55. *When I am asleep, who is it that sees my dreams?*

Sri Chinmoy: When you are asleep, one of your inner beings can see your dreams, or the aspiration accumulated in your inner life can watch your sleep, or the Divine Grace and Compassion which wants to manifest itself in and through you can watch your sleep. There is no hard and fast rule that one being or one person or one inner reality observes the sleep state or the dreams that you are having.

scs 56. *Can you say something about the overcoming of fear?*

Sri Chinmoy: Fear is one of our most troublesome difficulties; fear is extremely hard to overcome. But we do conquer fear on the strength of our oneness. When we establish our oneness, we always conquer fear.

A child has established his oneness with his father. The father is perhaps six feet tall, stout and strong. But the father does not create fear in the child's existence; the child is not at all afraid of his father. Why? Precisely because he has established his oneness-reality with his father. Therefore, there is no necessity on his part to be afraid of his father.

The creation which is around us is frightening us, threatening us. It is causing unnecessary fear in our mind or in our earthly existence. Why? Precisely because we have not yet established our oneness-reality with the world around us. If we pray and meditate soulfully, we establish a free access to the inner reality, which pervades the entire outer world. For a seeker, the paramount thing is to dive deep within and discover the road that leads to the all-pervading oneness-reality. On the strength of our inner cry, which we call aspiration, we climb up and reach the high, higher, highest state of consciousness, where it is all oneness. Where there is oneness, inseparable oneness, there cannot be even an iota of fear. Fear looms large when the sense of separativity looms large. Fear exists just because we want to remain separated, consciously or unconsciously, from the all-pervading Reality which we eternally are.

Fear most of the time is in the mind and not in the heart. The aspiring heart knows how to establish its inseparable oneness with the reality that is within and without. But the doubtful, suspicious and sophisticated mind finds it difficult to see eye to eye with the reality that is blossoming right in front of us. The mind suspects the reality before it. And there even comes a time when the mind, to its wide surprise, doubts its own judgement. At that time the mind feels a tremendous sense of dissatisfaction. Once it was the judge and now it has become a victim to its own judgements. But the heart, right from the beginning, tries to identify itself with the reality around it. And on the strength of its identification with the reality, it absorbs what the reality is and what the reality stands for. So if we live in the aspiring heart, the heart that cries for the all-pervading oneness-reality, the torture of fear can easily come to an end.

scs 57. *What does the soul do when it goes up to God's plane of existence?*

Sri Chinmoy: The soul is the spark, the soul is the conscious representative of God. God is at once Silence and Sound. In His highest state of Consciousness, He is Silence; and when He wants to manifest Himself He manifests through Sound. The soul, like a bird, flies up and reaches the highest Height. Then it brings down the message of Light, Truth, Beauty and Perfection and tries to manifest these qualities on earth. The bird flies from one branch of the Reality-tree to another. Then it comes down gradually, steadily, unerringly and offers the fruits that it has collected from above. So the soul goes up to achieve the highest Truth, Light, Peace and Bliss. The same Divinity, same Reality, same Consciousness, Light and Bliss the soul then offers to aspiring mankind when it descends to earth.

SCS 58. *At what time should we focus on the heart and at what time should we focus on the third eye?*

Sri Chinmoy: Now, there is no specific time when the seeker has to focus his attention on the heart or on the third eye. The third eye is the eye that sees the past, present and future all at once. The heart feels the reality, the omnipresent Reality, and omnipresent Divinity, all at once.

If someone is a genuine seeker, he will see that he has two hearts. One heart is just a muscle located right inside the chest. The other heart can be found in his aspiration, in his mounting flame. The other heart is the Universal Heart, which houses the entire universe. This divine heart of ours is the Universal Reality which perfectly houses everything that is in God's entire creation. It is composed of both God's ever-transcending Vision and His ever-manifesting Reality. If it houses the entire universe, it also houses the third eye as well. The third eye offers us cosmic vision, but this cosmic vision is perfectly housed in the Universal Heart. So if one knows how to focus all his concentrative power on the divine heart, then he is at the same time concentrating on the Vision aspect of reality, which he longs to know or manifest on earth. If the seeker concentrates on the heart, he will get everything that he wants, far, far beyond his expectations.

scs 59. *Is there any difference between meditation and self-hypnosis?*

Sri Chinmoy: Yes. When we meditate, we become a perfect channel through which the Reality above us can flow. Here we surrender entirely to God's Will. "Let Thy Will be done": This is the acme of meditation. We bring down God's boundless Peace, Light and Bliss on the strength of our soulful meditation, and this Peace, Light and Bliss operates in and through us according to our capacity of receptivity.

But when we enter into the realm of self-hypnosis, we try to impose on our subconscious plane certain ideas or even ideals. We convince ourselves this is what has happened or this is what is going to happen. We try to bring to the fore, either from the subconscious world or from the inconscient world proper, thoughts which are not predominant or which have not yet come to the fore. We unconsciously or subconsciously bring up these ideas and make ourselves feel that these are realities which we once upon a time lived or which we are going to live in the near or distant future. So in the subconscious mind, formulated ideas or ideals operate.

But when we soulfully meditate, we go far beyond the realm of the thought-world. Here nature's Dance comes to an end. All thought-waves cease and we see reality in its pristine form.

scs 60. *Realisation and reincarnation*

The soul can easily go from one plane of consciousness to another. It is like visiting relatives in another place. The soul is not a stranger there. But can the soul make progress in these other worlds? No! Progress means evolution; and in the case of the soul, evolution means the manifestation of Divinity. This manifestation must take place here on earth while the soul is in the physical. And here, while the soul is manifesting the Light, the entire being is evolving. Each individual has to realise the Highest here on earth and not in Heaven. Only here can God-realisation take place, and in no other plane of consciousness.

God's creative Vision created this world and God has special concern for us because we try to realise Him and manifest Him on earth with our limited capacity. Other beings in other worlds have got something and they are satisfied with what they have. But we are not satisfied. When we live in the desire-world, we want to have more, more, more material satisfaction; and when we are on a spiritual level, we want to realise God, reveal God and manifest God. God has special fondness for human beings because in other worlds the inhabitants don't suffer like us. So when somebody is suffering, even if he is guilty, a kind of special compassion or grace flows from the inner world.

Many minor cosmic gods do not have the realisation that some human beings have. The realisation that the Christ had, the realisation that Sri Krishna and the Buddha had, is simply unique. It is incomparable. That kind of matchless realisation the minor cosmic gods do not have. Today the soul is for God-realisation, tomorrow it is for God-manifestation. Realisation and manifestation can take place only here on earth. That is why each time after a few years' rest the soul takes on the physical sheath again.

The manifestation of Divinity cannot take place in one incarnation. Even to do one ordinary thing, just to fulfil a desire, it may take us ten, twenty, thirty years or more. So the manifestation of Divinity, which is a much more difficult task, takes quite a few incarnations for each individual. God will never allow us to remain unsatisfied, but we have to know what kind of satisfaction we are speaking about. If it is the satisfaction of our ego, then God is not going to grant it. Today He may boost up our ego; tomorrow He may not feed our ego. But when it is the inner satisfaction, heavenly satisfaction, divine satisfaction that we want, then naturally God is going to offer it to us even if it takes many, many years.

We start our journey with aspiration and when our aspiration reaches the end of its journey we realise God. First God aspired in and through the stone life and then He came into the plant life. There He aspired again. Then He came into the animal life and from the animal life He came into the human life.

Before we entered into the spiritual life we acted like animals. Jealousy and destructive forces, doubt and many, many negative things we cherished and treasured. Then we tried to reject these forces, but when they tried to enter into us we were scared to death. But we prayed to God and meditated on God and eventually we were able to threaten these negative forces when they tried to enter into us. We made them feel that they had nothing to do with us, that we belonged to some other world. So we can observe here in one incarnation the role that quite a few previous incarnations have played in our lives. In order to progress and realise God, one has to go through reincarnation. This is the only way. God wants us to continue playing His cosmic Game until He sees that we are playing the Game extremely well. Until we have realised God, God will not allow us to retire. And even after realisation, He may still not give a person relief. He may want that particular soul to continue to work for Him on earth.

Reincarnation means what? It is only a series of years and then death comes into the picture. We feel that there is a break, but it is not true. When we aspire we see that there is continuous life; only we take a short rest when death enters into the picture. On the strength of our inner aspiration we feel that there is endless Life, eternal Life. We are now waves of the Eternal Sea.

SCS 61. *Sleep and the dream world*

We can learn much from our dreams, but we have to know from which plane a dream is coming. If it comes from the vital plane, the lower vital plane, then we have to discard it. If we have a dream that somebody is killing us or that we are killing someone, it is absurd to pay attention to it. The lower vital is also a plane of consciousness and dreams from this plane are unimportant and useless. But if the dream comes from the intuitive plane, from the psychic plane, from the higher mind, from the overmind, from the illumined mind, then we have to give it importance. If we see that we have the capacity or the need to help someone in his meditation or elevate his consciousness, then to that kind of dream we have to pay proper attention. In this case, today's dream is tomorrow's reality; dream embodies reality.

The dreams that come to us from a higher plane, good dreams, divine dreams, we have to treasure and try to expedite. We shall try to transform these dreams into reality. We have to create new life within us all the time, but not in the dreams that try to destroy us or destroy others.

A human being is the king of destruction. One day I will destroy the whole world. Then, when I am in a divine mood, I will love the whole world, I will serve the whole world, I will fulfil the whole world. But we have to remain always in a very high state of consciousness. The Christ comes, the Buddha comes, Sri Krishna comes. They come to love the world, to inundate the world with peace. Again, there are others who come into the world to create destruction in themselves and in others. As spiritual persons, as seekers, we shall try to create peace. That should be our dream. We will invoke peace from above and then offer peace to mankind. So our higher dreams, divine dreams, are most welcome, but destructive dreams, lower vital dreams have to be discarded.

Right now it is difficult for us, impossible for us to know if we are dreaming. We feel that it is all reality. Then, when we get up we feel it was all dream. But if we are spiritually developed, while having the dream we will see it is all dream. It is just like a magic show. While watching the show, at the same time we are also seeing the reality. We are seeing the magic and we are wonderstruck. But we know it is magic, not reality. If we watch closely a coin trick, immediately we see which is the false coin and which is the real one. From a distance the false coin looks real; when we are far away it is difficult to distinguish. So the deeper we go, the clearer it becomes to us whether we are having a dream or whether we are in the world of reality.

When we sleep, sometimes our highest consciousness continues to operate and sometimes it does not. There is no hard and fast rule. It depends on whether God wants the high consciousness to operate while we are fast asleep or whether God wants the high consciousness to sleep while the physical is taking rest. It entirely depends on God's Will.

There are many seekers who meditate every day and then sleep at night. Just because they have meditated during the whole day, God is pleased with them and God says to them, "My children, you have worked very hard. During the day, you have prayed, meditated. Now I have other instruments that can most powerfully help you. Now there are other forces that can work on your behalf."

At that time, He asks the higher Self or the higher beings to operate and help the seekers who during the day prayed and meditated. But if during the day we don't pray and meditate, God will never ask the higher beings, the higher forces to work for us. It is absurd. Only when the Inner Pilot is pleased with the seeker will He ask the higher forces to help when the person is asleep.

SCS 62. *Yoga and self-giving*[5]

Dear ministers, dear God-lovers, dear truth-lovers, dear oneness-lovers, I am extremely grateful to you for you have given me the golden opportunity to be of service to the universal reality-oneness in you. I have not come here in the capacity of a teacher. I have come here in the capacity of a friend, a brother of your heart and soul. You are teachers and I also happen to be a teacher. I feel that we are all truth lovers, peace lovers, harmony lovers and oneness lovers. I belong to a school and you belong to a school. To my deepest satisfaction, I see that our schools have basically the same principles: love and service. I feel from deep within that the Unitarian Church is all love and all service. The school that I belong to has the same basic message to offer: love and service. But mine is not a specific religion. My teachings are for humanity as a whole, for the real in every man is his heart's oneness, universal oneness.

I come from India. My teaching is founded upon the Sanskrit word, "Yoga". The significance of this word is spiritual oneness. This oneness cannot be established by talks. You and I have given hundreds of talks, but oneness can be established only by self-giving. Self-giving is truth-becoming and God-becoming. Yoga is oneness with the highest Truth, which is totally free from religious, political, racial or geographical boundaries. This Truth is also the goal of the Unitarian Church. If your goal and my goal are identical, then I am perfectly safe in the heart of my spiritual brothers and you are also safe in the very depth of my heart.

I wish to share with you some of the things which I teach to my students. You may call them my disciples, my followers, but to me they are like members of my family. We form a small group and we belong to one boat, the boat that is carrying us to the Golden Shore of the Beyond. This Beyond can be a vague term or it can be a living reality. We need only to realise that there is a goal. Before we reach that particular goal, we call it the world of the Beyond. But once we reach that goal, we feel that it is nothing but a new starting point for an ever-transcending goal. Each day in the inner world we try to reach our goal. Sooner or later we do reach it. But when we reach our goal, we feel that that very goal is nothing but a starting point for a higher goal.

We feel that God the ultimate Truth is also in the process of eternal Self-transcendence. He is infinite, He is eternal, He is immortal. We all know this, although we often try to bind Him. But He does not want to be bound and He does not want to bind us. The higher and deeper we go, the more we feel that God Himself is always transcending His own Reality and that we who are His conscious, chosen instruments are also doing the same. Each day we aim at a new goal and each day, consciously or unconsciously, we arrive at a new goal. Each day we look forward to something new, something more fulfilling, something more satisfying.

We call our path the path of love, devotion and surrender. Basically, it is a path of the heart, and from my own inner knowledge, inner aspiration, I feel that yours is also absolutely the same. What we want is universal oneness, founded upon love and peace. We are doing the same thing; we are in the same boat. We have adopted different names and different forms but in reality we have the same spirit, same goal, same soul, same awakening.

I came to the West at the express command of my Inner Pilot. Each time I see an individual, I try to see my Inner Pilot inside that individual. And each time I get an opportunity to be of service to an individual, I feel that my life on earth is blessed with some purpose, some significance, some reality. So I have not come here just to give a talk. I have come to make you feel that I am of you and I am for you in the Heart of the Absolute Supreme. We are like a rose or a lotus growing inside the Heart of the Eternal Reality. Each individual is a petal, and petal by petal the flower is blossoming. We are getting ready to be placed at the Feet of the Absolute Supreme, for He needs us as we need Him.

It is our misconception that tells us that God does not need us but that we only need Him, like beggars. No, we need Him, but He needs us more. How can we say that He needs us more than we need Him when we are so weak, so helpless, so meaningless, so insignificant? It is precisely because He knows what we are. We are exact prototypes of His all-embracing, all-fulfilling Reality, although we do not know it. We are helpless and hopeless because we are earth-bound; we treasure and cherish doubt, consciously or unconsciously, and then we forget our Reality, our Divinity, our Immortality. But He knows that we are of Him and for Him; therefore, He constantly reminds us of what we are and teaches us how we can feel in the inmost recesses of our hearts that we are of Him and for Him. The philosophy that we are studying and the school that we belong to teach us one truth: it is by self-giving that we eventually grow into the very image of God.

There is a message unparalleled in Indian history. This message tells us that today we are crying to realise God, tomorrow we shall realise God and the day after tomorrow we shall do something more: we shall become consciously aware of the truth that we are not only of God and for God but we are God Himself in the process of realisation and manifestation. This God you can call anything you want to: infinite Light, infinite Energy, infinite Bliss, infinite Peace, Infinity's self-expanding, self-transcending Reality. This is what we all are in our highest.

Again, I wish to say that what you are doing and what I am doing is the same. The truth that we embody we are consciously, soulfully, devotedly and unconditionally trying to place before mankind. We are human beings. Some of us are fully awakened, others are in the process of awakening and still others are still asleep. We are trying to knock at the door of those who are awakening or still asleep. We believe in God's Hour. God's Hour has struck for us to knock at the heart's door of the seekers who can run with us fast, faster, fastest towards the Goal. And that Goal is universal love, oneness in realisation, oneness in revelation, oneness in manifestation.

SCS 63. *I think that some of us might be interested to know what your view is of the thinking of Dr. Radhakrishnan, who was probably the best known philosopher of Hinduism in the rest of the world. Has his thinking made an impact on your religious philosophy?*

Sri Chinmoy: To be very frank with you, not in the least, although I have the greatest respect for Dr. Radhakrishnan. While he was still alive, I received three letters from him here in New York encouraging me in my philosophy and in my inspiration to the young generation.

As far as I know, Dr. Radhakrishnan was a philosopher, a thinker. Now, Indian philosophy is founded upon Indian religion and Indian religion, which we call *dharma*, is founded upon Yoga. But Yoga is something that one has to practise. It is not theoretical. It is more than practical; it is a living reality. At every moment we have to live it and practise it in order to grow into the very image of that reality.

Dr. Radhakrishnan knew about this reality only in its theoretical aspect. In his practical life, unfortunately, he did not practise it. Anybody can speak on philosophy, on truth, even on the ultimate Truth, but if that particular person does not live those truths, then we feel that there is a yawning gulf between the reality that he understands or believes in and the reality that he embodies. Dr. Radhakrishnan knew the reality, but he did not embody it. I may know you, but if I don't enter into you and become part and parcel of you, I will not get all the knowledge, wisdom, light, reality and peace that you embody. Dr. Radhakrishnan's approach to what we call reality was theoretical, not practical. He could speak on reality in faultless terms. But he did not embody that reality.

In the case of Sri Ramakrishna, Swami Vivekananda, Sri Aurobindo, Ramana Maharshi and others, they not only knew the reality but also grew into the reality itself. For them it was a living reality. You could not separate that reality from the man. In Dr. Radhakrishnan's case, he was the man and reality was somewhere else; whereas the real spiritual Masters grew into inseparable oneness with the reality that they knew. My experience is of the second type. Being a seeker, I wanted to experience and grow into the reality, not learn about the reality on an intellectual level.

SCS 64. *Your practice of Yoga seems to be distinct in some way from the practices of other teachers. When people come to you to be disciples, on what basis do you accept them? What do they have to do in terms of Yoga? In what way is your path distinct from the paths of others?*

Sri Chinmoy: Thank you. When a seeker comes to me for guidance, the first thing I do is concentrate on that particular seeker and see if he is meant to follow the path of love, devotion and surrender. If I see that he can do well on our path, I accept him. When I do not accept a seeker, it does not mean that he is not sincere. Far from it. But each individual must follow the proper path for him. There are paths of the mind and there are paths of the heart. Some people are devoted to the mental approach, while others are meant for the heart approach, the psychic approach. The seekers whom I am unable to accept may be sincere, absolutely sincere, but they have to know that they can make faster progress if they follow another path or another Master. At the end of our journey, my Inner Pilot will not ask me how many millions of seekers I have brought to Him. He will ask me whether or not I have brought the seekers that He wanted me to bring to Him. The number is not important. If

I try to take someone who is not meant for our boat, then He will be displeased with me.

Ours is the path of the heart. The heart means oneness. As soon as I see you, if I feel oneness with you, then you are meant for me and I am meant for you. But if I try to analyse and scrutinise you and want to know how much wisdom you have or how much capacity you have, then at every moment I will be subject to suspicion, doubt and various wrong forces. So when I look at a seeker, the first thing I see is whether the seeker is really in the heart and for the heart. I go deep within for guidance from my Inner Pilot to see if that particular seeker is ready to follow our path. If a seeker wants to follow the path of the heart, then there is every possibility that he will fit in with our path, which is divine love, divine devotion and divine surrender.

Human love, we know, is an express train whose destination is frustration and frustration is immediately followed by destruction. But divine love is a local train. Slowly and steadily it reaches its destination, which is illumination.

Human devotion is just another name for attachment. We are usually not conscious of it, but eventually there comes a time when we see that it is nothing but unconscious attachment. Divine devotion is our oneness-cry to the higher reality, our feeling that there is a purpose for our lives and our need to establish our deepest oneness with that purpose.

Human surrender is the surrender of a slave to the master. It is forced, fearful and resentful surrender, not spontaneous, loving and devoted. We surrender to our boss because we feel that if we don't, he will dispense with our services. This is forced surrender. But divine surrender is totally different. Here the finite becomes fully aware of its oneness with the Infinite. When a tiny drop surrenders its limited existence and enters into the ocean, at that time it gets the message of Vastness, Infinity.

This surrender is spontaneous, natural and cheerful. It is divine surrender, surrender to our highest reality, of which right now we are not conscious.

This is the essence of our path. In our ladder of divine consciousness there are three rungs: love, devotion and surrender. With divine love we start. Then we go to devotion and then to surrender. When we make our surrender, we feel that there is no end to our surrender. Each time we surrender soulfully and cheerfully, we reach a specific goal. But that goal is not the ultimate Goal; that goal is only the starting point, because we are pilgrims walking along Eternity's Road.

scs 65. *If you were to accept a seeker who was meant for you, would he be practising or following certain specific exercises?*

Sri Chinmoy: In my case, I do not give much importance to the physical part of Yoga, the postures and breathing exercises. I give all importance to the mental discipline and vital discipline. This we get from our practice of concentration, meditation and contemplation. If you go to an Indian village, you will see many, many village boys who will be able to perform hundreds of difficult physical exercises. But perhaps they are millions of miles behind us in God-realisation or Truth-realisation.

The exercises do help to some extent. If you are wanting in physical fitness, then you will not be able to meditate well. But we should not give too much importance to physical fitness. The boxers, the wrestlers, the athletes of the world are physically extremely fit. But in terms of peace of mind, those who meditate will be much better off than they are.

Physical postures and exercises are like the kindergarten class. You can easily skip it and go directly to primary school. Concentration, meditation and contemplation are the higher courses. One can easily start with concentration. Concentration paves the way for meditation, and meditation paves the way for contemplation.

When we concentrate on a particular subject or object, we focus all our attention on it. We try to place in front of us the tiniest possible object or the tiniest possible thought; then we concentrate, we penetrate. The minutest thing that we can possibly imagine will give us the best result. If we keep a flower in front of us and concentrate on it, we try to enter into the fragrance of the flower, into the essence of the flower.

When we meditate, we do just the opposite of concentration. At that time, we enter into something vast. When we meditate, we try to feel inside us the vast sky, the vast ocean or the infinite universe. We try to expand our consciousness as far as possible.

When we contemplate, at that time we become consciously one with Reality. In contemplation the divine lover and the Supreme Beloved become one. When we contemplate on something, we feel that very thing as our own reality. We become both the object and the subject of our contemplation. The lover and the Beloved become one. Right now we see God as somebody else or somewhere else. But when we approach Him through contemplation, we see that He is also approaching us. Now we are seeking the Reality, thinking that it is something other than ourselves. But when we contemplate, we will see that what we considered Reality is running after us, because we are the Reality itself.

SCS 66. *I was going to ask what part Hatha Yoga had in your discipline, but you have already answered my question.*

Sri Chinmoy: Discipline is a very significant word. It is necessary to have discipline. But just by having a certain amount of discipline we cannot say that we are on the road to self-discipline. If we take ten or fifteen minutes daily to keep our body fit, then early in the morning when we try to meditate, we will not have a stomach upset, a headache or some other ailment. In this way, physical discipline helps us. But just by becoming physically strong we cannot become spiritual. We know so many people who have excellent physical discipline, but they are not for truth, not for peace, not for reality. It is the spiritual discipline that is important to a seeker.

scs 67. *You mentioned two paths, the mind and the heart. I was wondering if they were mutually exclusive or is a combination possible?*

Sri Chinmoy: The ultimate goal of both paths is the same. The only thing is that if we take the mental path, our road will be long. When we follow the mental path, we often cherish doubt, because the mind tells us that by doubting someone we will remain a few inches higher than that person. Doubt makes us feel superior.

I have come here as a seeker. If you remain in the realm of the doubting mind, at this moment you may think of me as a good person, but before I leave this place you may think of me as a bad person. A few minutes later you will ask yourself whether you were right in your assessment. Then you will start doubting yourself. The moment you doubt yourself you are totally lost. By thinking that I am a bad person or that I am a good person, you don't lose anything. But the moment you start doubting your own assessment you are totally lost.

If you follow the path of the heart, your inner feeling will tell you whether I am a good person or a bad person, and that feeling will last inside your heart for days, for weeks, for months. It is a question of identification. Once you identify with me, my entire reality is yours.

I wish to say that the body, vital, mind and heart all belong to one family: the family of the soul. The body, instead of remaining lethargic, must become dynamic. The vital, instead of remaining aggressive, must become expansive. The aggressive vital wants the entire world to remain at its feet. Like Napoleon and Julius Caesar, it wants to conquer the whole world. But that vital we don't need. We want the vital that will expand and spread its wings like a bird.

The mind that suspects, the mind that doubts, we don't want. We want the mind that has the eagerness, the thirst for universal knowledge. We want the mind that is eager to learn from everyone and from everything. We need the mind that has the sincere thirst to know something that is illumining and fulfilling. The seeker has to know which kind of mind he utilises. If it is a sincere and searching mind, then there can be a close connection between the aspiring heart and the mind. But if it is a doubting and suspicious mind, then we see that there is a yawning gulf between that mind and the aspiring heart.

SCS 68. *I find that search and doubt are part of the same thing, that part of searching is doubting. I am not sure of your meaning of doubt.*

Sri Chinmoy: Unfortunately, you are using the mind. Suppose there are three individuals walking by. You will see three human beings right in front of you, but will feel a kind of affinity with one of them and not with the other two. The one you feel drawn to is meant for you. You have already established your oneness in the inner worlds. It is the same when you are looking for a teacher. There may be three teachers in front of you, but the presence of one of them is going to give you more joy. That particular teacher is meant for you, not the other two. You don't have to ask anybody which teacher you should follow. You already have an inner identity, an inner oneness.

Here there are so many seekers. With one, perhaps, you have more in common; you have a stronger bond, a feeling of oneness. With the others, you may not have that feeling. All this comes on the strength of inner identification. When you use the heart, immediately you feel something, and this feeling is the reality within you. But if you use the mind to find a teacher, you won't know which will be best qualified to teach you. Has he studied Indian philosophy? Has he practised spirituality? Has he practised Yoga? Many questions will arise in your mind, and these questions will either be given satisfactory answers or not. Even if you are given satisfactory answers, still you may doubt them. But if you use the heart, immediately you get the answer to your questions and the inner assurance that the answer is right.

SCS 69. *I think one of the reasons I, as well as other people, experience this doubt is because there are so many bad teachers in the world.*

Sri Chinmoy: You are absolutely right. There are false teachers. But just because there are twenty bad teachers who are deceiving themselves or deceiving others, I can't say that you are also a bad teacher. That is why we are given the opportunity to choose. There are twenty spiritual Masters and you are given the choice. You say, "How am I going to know that I am choosing the right one?" The answer is that the one who gives you the utmost joy, whose very presence gives you joy, is the right one. He has already established his oneness with you in the inner world. In the inner world your soul has a free access to his soul's reality. Any teacher who does not give you the same joy, the same delight and feeling of oneness, is not meant for you. You follow the one whose very presence gives you immediate joy. This is where the heart plays its role most satisfactorily.

scs 70. *I am not sure how truthful it is to say that we are all doing the same thing, that we all have the same goals. You are saying we shall convert the individual and there will be a better United Nations, a better America, a better India. I think we say that we convert the individual, but also we must convert groups of individuals; we must change institutions and change society. And I don't perceive that you are in the same boat about personal religion and social religion.*

Sri Chinmoy: To be very frank with you, I do not follow any religion. Our path is not a religion at all. Ours is only the message of oneness. As your faith believes in universal brotherhood, if I understand correctly, irrespective of sect, irrespective of nation, irrespective of race, so also do we believe that all are God's children. For us there is no caste, creed, sect or nation that is more important than others. We are all members of the same family. Ours is not a religion at all. Ours is a path which anyone can walk along. But you have to live in one particular house, one particular religion. You cannot live in the street, and I cannot live in the street. You can live wherever you want to, but you will walk along the street with the rest of us when you want to get to a particular place.

Let us do the first thing first. If we are bad people, we will not feel the necessity of having a better world. Only when we become good people will we be able to work divinely and soulfully to change the world in God's own Way. My students are trying to change themselves and, at the same time, those of them who work here at the United Nations and in other places are working in and for the world as well.

SCS 71. *I think people would say that the way in which you choose to discover yourself is not good for people because it tends to turn them inward, so their attention is more exclusively on themselves rather than on making the kinds of changes that have a significant impact on large numbers of people. And by concentrating on one's own fulfilment and self-discovery a lot of other things that are of greater need to the world are neglected, in a sense.*

Sri Chinmoy: I fully understand. The thing is that if I do not know who I am and what I stand for, how am I going to be of any use to mankind? I have to have some inner conviction first that I am of the Source and I am for the Source. Reality is within as well as without. My highest Reality I can bring to the fore by entering deep within. If I do not do this, what can I offer to mankind, or how can I make humanity feel that I am of them and I am for them?

Real spirituality does not mean entering into the Himalayan caves and remaining closeted. Far from it! Ours is the path of acceptance. The spiritual path that we are following demands the acceptance of the outer world.

I don't ask my students to enter into a room and remain there meditating for hours. I don't ask them to retreat to the Himalayan caves or the mountains. I tell them to mix with humanity and share what they have with humanity. The only thing is that inside they have to have something to share. If they don't have something better than what the rest of humanity has, then what are they going to share?

We are not satisfied with our own lives or the lives of others right now. We want to change the face of the world for the better. But if I have no capacity, then how can I be of service to you? And to develop capacity, I have to dive deep within and establish a free access to the highest Source. I have to attain some inner peace and light and have something worthwhile to offer humanity. Only then can I become a perfect instrument of that Source and be of service to earth in the best possible way.

SCS 72. *Once they have looked within, then what do your people do socially for the world?*

Sri Chinmoy: When we go deep within, we feel peace, joy and love. Then, when we mix with the world, people see and feel these things in us. Before we meditate, people will see something in us, and right after meditation they will see something else. Inwardly they will see and feel something; they can't name it but they can see it. And that very thing, is it not our dedicated service? Before we entered into meditation, we were absolutely unaspiring, useless people. But afterwards, others will look and look and look. They will see something pure, divine, illumining. Is that not our dedicated service offered through our prayer and meditation?

You can go to the United Nations Church Centre on Tuesdays. Before we enter the chapel to pray and meditate, you can look at us; or you can even take a picture. Then, when we come out, you can look at us or you can take another picture. Then you will see and feel the difference. You are inwardly seeing something in us, and that seeing is nothing but becoming. When you compare the feeling you get from an individual before prayer and right after prayer, you will see that right after prayer he will give you more joy. Before your secretary enters into the chapel, look at her. When she comes out, you will see that she is a totally different person. The peace, the joy, the light that she receives from her prayer and meditation will inspire you inwardly or outwardly.

If we see a saint, immediately his face gives us inspiration. If we see a good person, his very presence gives us inspiration. Since we are all trying to be good people, each of us is offering inspiration to others. If we mix with bad people, with thieves or hooligans, immediately our consciousness descends. Even when we mix with ordinary unaspiring people, our consciousness descends. But the very presence of a seeker who is aspiring to become good and do good will elevate our consciousness. Nobody has to convert us; we are automatically transformed.

So after we have prayed and meditated, people see something in us. It is like a divinely contagious disease. This is just the beginning of our service to mankind.

scs 73. *Is there another kind of Yoga that is specifically for service?*

Sri Chinmoy: That is Karma Yoga; that is also part of our path. I have achieved something in the inner world. Now I go out and give talks and hold meditations at various places. In this way I offer my dedicated service to mankind. If we can inspire one person to lead a good life, that is our service.

scs 74. *Is there any difference between prayer and meditation?*

Sri Chinmoy: They lead to the same goal, but there is a slight difference between prayer and meditation. When we pray, at that time we feel that our Eternal Father is listening to us. Prayer goes upward. But when we meditate, at that time we feel that God is talking to us and we are listening. Meditation goes outward. So prayer is when we talk to the Father, and meditation is when the Father talks to us.

scs 54. *(p. 86)* University of Maryland, October 18, 1975.
scs 55–59. *(p. 91)* Questions and answers following *Now*.
scs 62. *(p. 99)* Lecture before Ministers of the Unitarian Universalist Church, Community Church, Manhattan, 3 December, 1975.
scs 63–74. *(p. 103)* Questions and answers following *Yoga and self-giving*.

SRI CHINMOY SPEAKS

BOOK 4

PART I

SCS 75. *Love me or hate me, but don't ignore me*[5]

The Irish have a saying, "Love me if you will; hate me if you must; but for God's sake, don't ignore me." I wish to address this saying to God. There are three significant ideas here: to be loved, to be hated and to be ignored. I wish to discuss these from the spiritual point of view. "Love me if you will." Where human love is concerned, sometimes we expect love because of what we have done and sometimes we receive love without making any actual effort to be loved. And, of course, sometimes we don't get the love that we feel we rightly deserve. In the spiritual world, it is not like that. God is constantly standing right in front of us with His all-fulfilling Love. He is All-Love; He cannot be otherwise. Very often an ordinary human being has to make a conscious effort to try to love others. But in God's case, He does not have to will or desire to love us. Love is God's very essence. It flows from Him eternally. An ordinary person sometimes feels that he is wanting in the capacity to love others and he tries to cultivate this divine quality in himself. But if a person is already endowed with a few divine qualities, then the love which is most essential in our human world and in our divine world, he will have in boundless measure.

God's Dream and God's Reality go together. He does not separate His Dream from His Reality. If, in His Dream, love looms large, then we can rest assured that in His Reality also love looms large. God's potentiality and His expression go together. Love itself and its power of expression can never be separated in God's case. And those who are consciously aspiring to be godlike will have this capacity. Divine love and the expression of this love will be one and simultaneous. Love is the quality and the expression of love is the capacity. So the quality and the capacity can both be achieved if one soulfully aspires for a better and more fulfilling life. "Hate me if you must." God can never, never hate us. A man who has even a little wisdom cannot hate his fellow beings. Why? Because he knows the reasons that one hates another. One reason is that an individual feels inferior. Another reason is that an individual is afraid of someone. A third reason is that a person feels that his oneness with the other person is not complete; his real identification with the other person is lacking and there is a feeling of division. That is why he starts hating.

But how is it that sometimes one hates oneself? It is quite possible. Sometimes you get angry with yourself. You have done something wrong or you wanted to do something wrong; that is why you hate yourself. You want to do something, achieve something, but unfortunately you are not able to accomplish this. That is why you hate yourself. What do we actually observe in this hatred? We observe that our soul is separated from the physical mind and physical consciousness.

When we are living in the soul, we realise that we are not the doer. We are only an instrument. Also, when we live in the soul, we do not care for success. We care only for progress. It is our job to listen to the dictates of the Inner Pilot. Then it is up to Him whether He gives us the experience of success or failure. So if we live in the soul, we can never hate ourselves. Only we love the divine in us, the Supreme in us, who is also in the world.

If we care most for the soul, then when the soul comes to the fore, it acts like a pilot. The outer physical being can easily be shaped and moulded by the light of the soul. We cannot do it the other way around. From the physical we cannot take light and transform the soul. That is absurd. But very often we think that if we go deep within with our physical capacity or vital capacity or mental capacity, then a time will come when the soul and the physical, the vital and the mental will meet together and together establish the divine Truth on earth. But it is not possible. It is the soul that has to be brought forward and it is the light from the soul that has to inundate the body, the vital, the mind and the heart. From inside we have to come outside; from outside we can't go inside. That is wrong. "Don't ignore me." Who ignores whom? It is when there is no love, no hatred, no concern — when there is nothing between us and someone else — that the question of ignoring others arises. But we have to know that God can never ignore us. He Himself is manifesting in and through us, so He cannot ignore us. When God knows that we are His instruments, His chosen instruments, how can He ignore us? We are His children. He cannot ignore us just as we cannot ignore our eyes, our hands, our feet. Nor can we ignore God, for He is our higher part. God is man yet to be realised; man is God yet to be manifested and fulfilled.

scs 76. *How can one bring harmony into one's inner being when there is conflict in one's life?*

Sri Chinmoy: In order to acquire harmony, one needs peace of mind; and in order to acquire peace of mind, one has to pray most soulfully. How does one pray soulfully? One prays most soulfully when one offers gratitude to God, the Inner Pilot, or to the Light that makes him feel the necessity of harmony. Harmony has to be invoked, and if one properly invokes harmony one is bound to get peace of mind. And if one gets peace of mind, there will be harmony in what he does and what he becomes. Even in his outer movements there is bound to be harmony. We are wanting in harmony in our outer life only because we do not have an iota of peace of mind. When the mind has peace, then there is always harmony in one's whole being.

scs 77. *What is the best cure for our human frustration?*

Sri Chinmoy: The best cure for human frustration is a state of consciousness which never expects anything from anyone, even from oneself. We should act only because God wants us to do something. We should feel that we are His instruments and that He is working in and through us. When we act or speak only to please God in His own Way, without expectation, then only will we cease to experience frustration.

The moment we expect things, we are bound to be frustrated. Expectation always creates frustration. If the individual has a desire and this desire is fulfilled, he is then satisfied for a few days. However, even if the desire is fulfilled, he will not be satisfied for very long because other desires will come and destroy his satisfaction. This moment a fleeting desire is satisfied, but the next moment another desire is not satisfied. And it goes on like this forever.

But if we feel our oneness with everything in God's creation, then we become inspired. That does not mean we will become lethargic and wallow in the pleasures of ignorance. Far from it. Only we shall feel that we are not the doer and that someone else is acting in and through us. If we feel that we are not the doer, then we will not have expectations. If we can think of ourselves as divine instruments, we will feel that God is having an experience in and through us. And whether this experience takes the form of success or failure does not matter. It is only the experience that is important. In our human life, we feel that if we are successful, we have everything; and if we fail, we have nothing. In the divine life, we feel that we neither lose nor gain; we only rediscover what we are. We are not concerned with the results of our actions; we are interested only in rediscovering our birthright of Eternity and Immortality and bringing to the fore what we are. Everything that God has and everything that God is, is in us. So why do we have to expect anything? We expect only because we have separated ourselves from the divine Light. If we know how to rediscover within ourselves infinite Peace and Light, then we don't have to expect anything; we only have to claim these qualities as our very own.

scs 78. *Could you speak on accepting guidance from highly advanced beings who are not on earth, but possibly in some other dimension?*

Sri Chinmoy: There are many good beings in the inner world. If you have access to the good beings, then definitely they will be able to help you and guide you to God-discovery and God-realisation. But again, there are some inner beings that may not be spiritual at all. Sometimes they pretend to be spiritual, like false teachers, and if the seeker depends on them and listens to their dictates, he can make serious blunders. But if the seeker has someone in the inner world who is guiding him and really taking him to God-realisation, then he is very fortunate. It depends on the being that he is in touch with.

scs 79. *How can one be certain of following God's Will?*

Sri Chinmoy: We can easily know if we are following God's Will or if we are motivated by our own desires and propensities. When we do something, if we can offer the result of our action with the same joy, the same cheerfulness, whether it is success or failure, then we know we are following God's Will. If we are not disturbed if we fail and if we do not expect to be extolled to the skies if we succeed, if we can take each action as an experience that the Supreme is having in and through us, then it is God's Will we are carrying out.

scs 80. *Interviewer: I would like to ask if you feel only spiritual joy is genuine in this life? Do you deny the existence of physical joy?*

Sri Chinmoy: No, we do not deny the existence of physical joy. But we feel that if the physical joy becomes an expression of the spiritual joy, only then will it be lasting. Otherwise, it has no backbone, let us say. If there is no real source, if there is no reality behind the physical, then the physical joy cannot last. The Vedic Seers, Indian spiritual figures, came to realise that it is from Joy that we have come into existence; it is in Joy that we exist; and at the end of our journey's close it is to Joy that we return. But the source has to be spiritual joy, that is to say, God. If God expresses His Light in and through the body, then only will the joy be lasting. Otherwise, if we discard the inner Light, the God-Light, and only care for the physical joy, which is sense-pleasure, then there can never be abiding satisfaction. Right after we indulge in sense-pleasure, we get the experience of frustration; and frustration is followed by destruction. But if the physical becomes a conscious instrument of the spiritual, if the spiritual joy is being expressed through the physical, then the joy lasts.

scs 81. *Interviewer: Joy both physical and spiritual very often emanates from an appreciation of beauty. Now, how are we to recognise beauty and the validity of beauty? John Keats wrote that "Beauty is truth, truth beauty; — that is all ye know on earth, and all ye need to know."*

Sri Chinmoy: Right. He also said that "A thing of beauty is a joy forever." We have to know that there is a vast difference between the physical beauty and the spiritual beauty. When we see physical beauty, earthly beauty, we immediately want to possess it, grab it. Even when we look at beauty with our naked human eyes, while we are appreciating it, we try to devour it. So appreciation is immediately followed by destruction. We see a flower which is so beautiful and we immediately want to touch it. But when we touch it, the life-force, the life-principle of the flower goes away. When we touch physical beauty, immediately we destroy the essence of the beauty there. But when we touch the inner beauty, the spiritual beauty, at that time we become part and parcel of the beauty itself. We grow into the beauty that we touch.

When we say that physical beauty is skin-deep, there is much truth in this. But inner beauty, the beauty of the soul, is infinite, because in the inner world we are always growing; we are always singing the song of self-transcendence. In the physical everything is limited. Somebody is beautiful, but he can be more beautiful. Somebody is tall, but he can be a little taller. The physical beauty that we notice in human beings or in nature is always limited. But inner beauty comes from the soul and the soul is the direct representative of God, who is all Beauty. Since the soul derives beauty from God directly, the soul's capacity to express beauty is limitless.

So beauty is truth when we speak of inner beauty. The outer beauty is also truth; but it is temporary and transitory because it fades away. A flower, after one day, fades away. Physical beauty is truth; undoubtedly it is a form of truth, but its capacity is very limited. But inner beauty, which is limitless, is eternal.

scs 82. *Interviewer: Can we turn now to the subject of music? Do you see music as something related to spirituality?*

Sri Chinmoy: Yes, I do feel that music has a special role in the spiritual life. Next to spirituality is music. Again, if I have to be sincere, as spirituality encompasses music, so do the higher types of music, soulful music, encompass spirituality. It is through music that the universal feeling of oneness can be achieved in the twinkling of an eye. Thousands and thousands of people come to listen to one person who will play for an hour or so. Now, what is he doing? Through his music he is entering into the heart and soul of the audience. For an hour he is showing his capacity; that is to say, he is bringing down some Light from above. Music is not just playing on an instrument. No, music is receptivity to something higher, something from the higher world. First the musician receives it and then he offers it to the world at large. In an hour, thousands of people can feel it as their very own. So music has the opportunity, the capacity, to claim the universe as its very own.

scs 83. *Interviewer: Reading about your background, I see you entered a place called an ashram. Can you tell me something of your experience there?*

Sri Chinmoy: It is a spiritual community. I stayed there twenty years and I prayed and meditated most sincerely. I also participated in sports, because I saw the necessity of having a fit body. The message of the spirit must be expressed in and through the body. Here we are on earth, in the physical body, and the Light we receive from our meditation must be expressed through the physical. The body-consciousness must not be neglected. The higher messages that we get from our meditation must have a channel for expression and the body is that channel.

scs 84. *Interviewer: In this sense, is some kind of punishment of the body necessary? You know, in the rigorous observance of a fitness regime?*

Sri Chinmoy: It is not actually punishment. True, we feel it is better to wear out than to rust out. But actually, we do not wear out. The only thing is that if we don't utilise the body, we don't know how much capacity it has. The body needs exercise. If we do not take exercise, we do not know how much we are capable of achieving. If we do not eat, we do not know how much we can eat. The capacity of the body remains fast asleep. But when we take exercise, we allow the body or we encourage the body and inspire the body to play its role in the Cosmic Game.

scs 85. *Interviewer: What were your particular interests in the sporting life there?*

Sri Chinmoy: At that time, I was very fond of athletics: running, jumping and throwing. Also, I was a good football player. But now I am so hesitant. Scotland is excellent, excellent in sports, especially in football. Scottish people play football extremely well.
Interviewer: Oh, that's very kind of you to say so. Now that you have mentioned Scotland, perhaps we shall come to a Scottish lady who is sitting beside us. *[Speaking to her]* In fact you run and organise the Centre in Glasgow?
Disciple: Yes. We call it the Sri Chinmoy Centre and we practise meditation under Sri Chinmoy's guidance. There are ten or twelve of us at the moment and we meet twice a week to meditate. We also make crafts and hope to have a store where we shall sell the things we make.
Interviewer: So there is some kind of practical outlet for this awareness and consciousness of what you are doing?

Disciple: Oh, yes. We are very close. We don't live together, but we do meet very often. We have a theatre group that puts on plays that Sri Chinmoy has written. We also have a choir.

Interviewer: Sri Chinmoy, thank you very much for talking to *Radio Clyde* and I hope your stay in Scotland will be a happy one.

Sri Chinmoy: Thank you so much for your most interesting and significant questions. I am so grateful to you. This is the only way I and my students can be of service to mankind. If we had not accepted the world, we would not have met together today. I would have remained in the Himalayan caves and you would have remained in Scotland.

Interviewer: Thank you very much.

PART IV

SCS 86. *Canada tree-planting*[§]

O aspiration-dawn of Canada, you will succeed, you will proceed, you will become, you are. You will succeed. The universal earth-cry you will embody. You will proceed. The transcendental Heaven-smile you will reveal. You will become. Infinity's all illumining Vision you will become. You are. Immortality's Oneness-Reality you eternally are.

O aspiration dawn of Canada, there is a special reason why we are planting this divine tree here in Ottawa. Ottawa is the capital of Canada. The capital is the heart. Inside the heart is the soul. Inside the soul is God-promise. A few minutes ago I was told that this divine child of ours is going to live for two hundred fifty years. We shall not be on earth for two hundred fifty years, but from Heaven we shall offer our love-light and our gratitude-life to this divine child of ours. The physical in us will pass behind the curtain of Eternity. The spiritual in us, the eternally Real in us, will remain here with this child of ours. Aspiration-dawn is Eternity's treasure and Immortality's pride.

It is my fervent wish that the disciples in Ottawa come to visit this divine child of ours once a month for fifteen minutes and pray for this child divine who will, in the course of time, bring us boundless joy, glory and divine pride. Also, I wish that disciples from all parts of the world, when they visit Ottawa, make it a special point to come to this place and offer their aspiration-dedication to this child of ours.

I offer my heart's deepest gratitude to the government of Ottawa for granting us this unique opportunity to be of service to the soul and body of Canada. Finally, I wish to offer my most soulful blessingful gratitude to Don. You have been a chosen instrument, a supremely chosen instrument, for this divine journey. A tree represents aspiration. Aspiration-dawn is the ever-transcending soul and goal. When I climb up high, higher, highest, either I carry Don or I bring down the Nectar-fruit to offer to him and all his spiritual brothers and sisters, to all our spiritual children.

SCS 87. *A true seeker*[§]

A true seeker does not make complaints, for he knows that each complaint of his is a blight, a spot, in the Heart of his Beloved Supreme. A true seeker is he who does not criticise the world around him, for he knows that each criticism of his is a blight in the Heart of his Beloved Supreme. A true seeker wants a world of perfection. This world of perfection he will find only through his oneness, his ultimate oneness with the world within him, the world around him. Each time he complains, each time he criticises, he fails in his own purpose. It was his own promise, when he was in the soul's world, to serve the aspiring mankind. This was the solemn promise he made to the Supreme, the Pilot Absolute. It is not through criticism, not through complaining that he can bring about world peace and world harmony. It is through acceptance of earth-reality as such. It is through constant self-giving, which eventually grows into God-becoming. Today's self-giving is tomorrow's God-becoming.

A true seeker does not try to influence the world, for he knows that to influence the world is to ask the world to see the reality the way he himself sees it or the way he wants to see it. A true seeker wants only to inspire the world. When he inspires the world, he feels that he is giving the world ample opportunity to see the reality in its own way. Here there is no imposition. Here there is no direct or indirect insistence that the reality be seen in a certain way.

A true seeker is always ready to serve the Supreme Beloved in each individual. First he tries to serve the Supreme according to the world's receptivity. Then, after he himself makes considerable progress, he tries to serve the world the way the Supreme wants him to serve the world. While he is a beginner, while he himself is making progress, he feels that it is his bounden duty to help the world accelerate its own progress and success the way the world wants to achieve progress and success. But there comes a time when he feels that he has to see the success and progress of the world the way his Inner Pilot wants him to see it.

A true seeker is nothing short of a lamp-post. This lamp-post offers its glow not only to the fellow travellers who walk along his path, but also to those who walk along other paths. He offers light and travellers walking along other paths are able to receive and achieve the light that he offers. His life is for all; but again, for those who want to be in the same boat he is in, he feels that he has extra responsibility. They are his fellow travellers, journeying to Infinity's Shore.

A true seeker knows what divine authority is and he knows what divine responsibility is. To him, authority is not the power that lords it over the world; authority is the recognition of the illumining and liberating, transforming and immortalising reality as world-power. To him, responsibility is not an unwanted burden. Each responsibility is an added opportunity to serve the Inner Pilot in an inimitable way, in God's own Way. He feels that each responsibility is an opportunity to add to his soul's reality and he knows that he can increase this opportunity. How does he increase it? He increases his opportunity by creating happiness. Happiness increases opportunity. And what is happiness? Happiness is a quality of the soul. This quality of the soul we notice and grow into only when we see that the Vision-world and the reality-world can become one.

The Vision-world is God's Silence-world; the reality-world is God's sound-world. The seeker comes to realise that either he has to climb up from the body-consciousness to the soul's loftiest height or he has to bring the soul's loftiest height down into the gross physical world. When he climbs up, he lifts up humanity's consciousness and places humanity's consciousness in the lap of Divinity. And when he brings down Peace, Light and Bliss from above, he feeds humanity's age-long hunger. But whether he carries humanity up the tree or brings down the fruits, he offers Divinity the golden opportunity to transform, to shape and to mould humanity's life-breath the way the Eternal Pilot wants humanity transformed, illumined, perfected and fulfilled.

A true seeker has discovered the truth that his Pilot Supreme is not only the Highest but also the lowest. The magnitude and the infinitude of his Beloved Supreme is the reality precisely because the Supreme's Love-power has become the Universal Consciousness, the Transcendental Consciousness, the Infinite Consciousness, which is expanding at every moment; and also because He is smaller than the smallest, tinier than the tiniest. The Beloved Supreme is the reality just because He can become Infinity and just because He can become the finite, the infinitesimal drop. The true seeker feels a one-pointed inner urge to see the Infinite in the finite and to see the finite in the Infinite.

When a true seeker aspires, he sees that it is the real in him that aspires. The unreal in him just waits for the opportunity to be transformed at God's choice Hour. The unreal in him cannot aspire; only the real in him can aspire. What is the real in him? The real in him is happiness, delight. What is the unreal in him? The unreal in him is the suffering that he creates for himself. How does he create suffering? He creates suffering by mixing with the unreal in himself. The unreal is his desire-world; the unreal is his thought-world. Each desire is a world of its own; each thought is a world of its own. The unreal in him is sorrow. When he mixes with sorrow, with desire, with suspicion and doubt, when world-suffering assails him and he identifies himself with world-suffering and with his own suffering, at that time he sees darkness within, without, below, above. But when he identifies himself with inner happiness and outer happiness, at every moment he transcends his own reality. At every moment he dances with the reality of self-transcendence.

Instead of staying in the unreal — in the desire-world, in the thought-world — a true seeker wants to live in the aspiration-world and the will-power-world. His aspiration-world tells him, "Not this, not that, but something beyond this, something beyond that." And what is it that is beyond this, beyond that? It is his constant inner flame, the flame that at every moment achieves satisfaction. Again, at each level of satisfaction he feels an eternal hunger to achieve higher satisfaction. This hunger is not simply a cry for the world of truth and reality which has given him his present satisfaction; it is a ceaseless cry for Light, abundant Light, infinite Light. A true seeker cries for satisfaction and when satisfaction dawns, he cries for higher satisfaction. He is not like an ordinary human being in the desire-world who can never be satisfied. The seeker *is* satisfied, but at the same time he still wants to go higher. The true seeker's satisfaction in crying for a higher world, a higher reality, is his spontaneous inner growth. An iota of satisfaction can please him; but he feels that the greater his satisfaction, the greater the opportunity he will have to manifest the Divinity within him. It is not that from dissatisfaction he is going to satisfaction; but from satisfaction he is growing to higher satisfaction. From God's aspiration-world he is climbing to God's realisation-world. And inside the realisation-world he tries to see God's manifestation-world, God's Perfection-world.

A true seeker is he whose name is always synonymous with devotion. A true seeker has discovered the truth that it is his devotion that can fulfil the Divine in him, the Supreme in him. In his devotion, God's perfect Perfection and God's continuous Satisfaction loom large. His devotion is not the devotion of a man touching somebody else's feet. His devotion is speed, the fastest speed of his own aspiration-reality and God's Compassion-Reality. When his aspiration-reality and God's Compassion-Reality are bridged by his own inner cry, which is nothing else but his devotion, at that time he sees the world of the Eternal Now as his own, very own. He sees that there is no past, no future; there is only one Eternal Now, only one Eternal Life, only one Eternal Love. What he has and what he is, and what God has and what God is, are nothing but the Eternal Now. Here he sows, here he grows. Here he is God the seed; again, here he is God the fruit. In the Eternal Now, God's Self-Transcendence-Reality and his own life-liberating, life-immortalising reality abide.

scs 88. *How can one know God when he is carrying on his day-to-day earthly responsibilities?*

Sri Chinmoy: He has to know that what he is calling responsibility is not something thrust upon him; it is something necessary in his life. Responsibility is something very painful. Human beings don't want to be responsible for anything. But necessity plays a role of paramount importance. If someone feels it is a supreme necessity to take care of the members of his family, to do everything that is needed in his family, then he is doing absolutely the right thing. At that time God is acting in and through him.

If an individual takes his tasks as a responsibility, then he is shouldering a heavy burden. On his shoulders he is placing a very heavy burden. But if he takes his life as a supreme necessity for God-realisation, God-revelation and God-manifestation, then no matter what he does, what he says or what he becomes, there will always be satisfaction, abiding satisfaction. Here it is an inner urge that he is fulfilling. It is not that from the outside world somebody has forced him to do something and he is doing it. He is under no compulsion to do it unwillingly. If we accept life as the supreme necessity to love God and serve God in mankind, then we can satisfy ourselves and we can satisfy the rest of the world in the midst of multifarious activities.

If we take life as a necessity, then there is all joy; we do the needful in order to derive happiness. But if we take the world as something foreign to us, as a stranger who is not part and parcel of our life and with whom we have not established our oneness, then naturally anything that we do we will feel was done either under compulsion or because we have a big heart. But if necessity prompts us, then we are not showing any kind of compassion; we are only trying to bring to the fore the oneness-reality that we have within us by loving and serving the human beings around us.

SCS 89. *I experience shame, fear and guilt. How can I overcome this?*

Sri Chinmoy: You find fear, shame and guilt standing between you and your true surrender to the Supreme. Please think of the Supreme as your most beloved father, mother, brother, sister. Also think of Him as someone who is more than prepared to do everything for you unconditionally. No matter how many mistakes you commit or how many wrong things you do, the Supreme will purify, illumine and perfect you.

You may ask, "If there is someone who is so kind to me, why can't I offer Him these faults on the basis of my oneness?" You say you have doubt, fear, shame; but I wish to say that He is more than willing to accept them as His own. What you have can easily be accepted by Him. If you fear that He will not accept these things because they are not divine, you are making a deplorable mistake. You must offer Him whatever you consider your very own, whether divine or undivine. In your case, all the negative qualities that are standing in your way can easily be surrendered if you are constantly and consciously sincere. If you are sincere, then I assure you that your sincerity will help you in establishing oneness with His boundless, unconditional Concern, Compassion, Forgiveness and Oneness-Light. Very often, human beings observe something but do not give importance to it. But if you give importance to God's Concern and Love, you will feel the results in your life of aspiration.

scs 90. *Could you speak about patience?*

Sri Chinmoy: Patience is something that lengthens time. Now we are living in earthbound time. That means our time is very limited. We have bound it with our limited life of ignorance. We should take patience as something that extends our time limit. We want to become a long-distance runner. While we are running, the goal seems far away and we want to reach it in the twinkling of an eye. But if we do not put a limit on the amount of time it should take us to reach our goal, if we don't bind it, then the light of patience is working in and through us. Patience is our conscious surrender to the Hour of God. We want to reach our goal just because God wants us to reach it, and God selects the Hour. Then, when we do reach the Goal at God's choice Hour, we have to know it is the realisation of our patience.

scs 91. *What is the best way to control emotions?*

Sri Chinmoy: If we use the term "control", then we will encounter difficulties. In this world we cannot control anything; only we shall try to illumine everything. If we try to control unruly children, they disobey us more than they would have done otherwise. A child is naughty, mischievous. If the mother tries to control him, she does not succeed. Only if the mother can throw light into his daily needs or into his life of reality can she transform his life. What will happen then is that he will not find any satisfaction in his mischief; he will get joy only when he leads a better life.

In the spiritual life, when we try to control anything, that particular thing gets new strength, like elephant strength. When we try to control something, we focus attention on that particular object or subject. When we focus attention without the soul's light, very often our opponent gets strength. If we pay attention to someone undesirable, he bothers us more than before. So we do not try to control anything; we try only to do the right thing. First things first. Instead of entering into the emotional life, we try to enter into the world of light.

Early in the morning, instead of entering into the vital or the emotional world, we try to enter into the soul. Then from the soul we get boundless strength. Since our goal is the light of the soul and not the life of indulgence, we shall always try to pay all attention to the soul's need, to our life of aspiration. If our goal is situated to the north, we shall look only towards the north and not towards the south. If we cry for truth and light, automatically our need for pleasure-life and indulgence-life goes away from us. What we actually want is love, light and truth, so let us pay all attention to these things and ignore everything else that takes us away from our real life.

SCS 92. *Guru, how can I learn to speak to the Supreme during the day all the time?*

Sri Chinmoy: You can speak to the Supreme at every moment just by remembering one thing, and that thing is your silent inner cry. Always you have to cry in silence, inwardly. The moment you cry in silence, you are bound to feel His Presence inside you. And if you feel His Presence inside you, you will be able to speak to Him. You can do your office work, enter into your household activity, speak to your friends; you can do everything, you will do everything. But while talking and working and mixing with people, try to feel an inner cry. Nobody will know what is happening inside your heart. They will only know what is in your mind. You are telling them something and they are hearing you. But what is happening inside you, only you will know. Easily you can do more than one thing at a time.

While you are driving the car, you are watching the road and your hand is on the steering wheel and you are pressing the gas pedal. How many things you can do at once! Similarly, while you are talking to people in the outer world, you can easily cry inwardly in the inner world. So if you can cry in the inner world constantly, you are bound to speak to God.

PART VI

SCS 93. *Love human, love divine, love supreme*⁵

Dear seekers, dear sisters and brothers, I wish to give a short talk on love. Love is most significant in our human life, in our earthly existence. Love is life, life is love.

Love human, love divine and love supreme. Human love wants to possess and be possessed by the world. Divine love wants to establish its inseparable oneness with the world and then it wants to divinely enjoy this oneness. Supreme Love transforms human love into divine love and blesses divine love with boundless joy and divine pride.

Fear and doubt quite often torture human love. Cheerfulness and confidence increase and support divine love. Perfection and satisfaction fulfil Supreme Love. This perfection is continuous progress and continuous self-transcendence. This satisfaction is something that each individual needs in his eternal journey towards the ever-transcending Reality-Height.

Human love is nothing but incapacity. If we dive deep within human love, then we see clearly that it is weak and impotent. Divine love is capacity. Slowly and steadily it wins the race. There comes a time when human love becomes transformed into divine love. When divine love wins the race, it is not filled with pride. It shares its success cheerfully and soulfully with the transformed human love. Supreme Love, out of its infinite bounty, grants divine love the boon of transforming humanity and, at the same time, living in the boundless immortal Consciousness. Supreme Love is the endless Reality which always transcends and the immortal Vision which always illumines the earth-consciousness and Heaven-consciousness.

Human love craves for a satisfactory result. Then, when it does not get a satisfactory result, it is doomed to disappointment.

It sinks into a chasm where it finds something quite unknown, a stranger: despair. Despair soon is devoured by frustration and this frustration eventually devours human love itself.

Divine love makes a soulful attempt at reaching the goal. It does not pray for or long for the result as such. Its aim is to make a soulful attempt and then it leaves everything in the blessingful care of the Supreme Pilot. It says to the Inner Pilot, "It is up to You to give me success or failure, which is only an experience. I wish to please You, O Supreme, in Your own Way." This is divine love.

Supreme Love unconditionally gives and gives. What does it give? Compassion in infinite measure, Love in infinite measure, Peace in infinite measure. It depends on the individual to receive its boundless Compassion, Light, Peace and Bliss according to his soul's receptivity. According to his life's progress, the individual receives these immortal treasures from above.

Human love says to the world, "I love you; therefore I have the supreme authority to strike you and punish you if and when necessity demands." Divine love says to the world, "I love you; therefore I feel that it is my bounden duty to perfect you so that you can become a perfect instrument of the Supreme Pilot." Supreme Love says to the world, "I love you; therefore I feel at every moment a constant necessity in My cosmic Vision and in My cosmic Reality to claim you as My own, very own. I also wish for you, too, to claim Me as your own, very own, at every moment here on earth and there in Heaven."

Slowly, steadily and gradually human love decreases; and finally it dies. Slowly, steadily and unerringly divine love increases in the aspiring humanity; and then it flies. Compassionately, ceaselessly and unconditionally Supreme Love always remains the boundless sky. From there it guides and illumines the aspiring humanity and illumining divinity.

A doubtful mind, a suspicious mind, an insecure mind is quite often visible in human love. A soulful heart, a climbing heart, a glowing heart is always visible in divine love. A fruitful life, within and without, is eternally visible in Supreme Love.

Imagination reigns supreme in human love. With imagination human love starts its journey and at its journey's end again it sees imagination. It sees the soul, the body, the vital, the mind, even the goal itself as imagination.

Conviction paramount, conviction illumining, conviction fulfilling always reigns supreme in divine love. This conviction is the soul's Reality-Light that illumines the entire world. It is this conviction that divine love offers to the seekers of the absolute Truth. This conviction is the treasure-reality which, at the beginning, belongs to the Ultimate Source and which the Ultimate Source offers to the soul to share with aspiring mankind.

Compassion eternal reigns supreme in Supreme Love. This Compassion is the Supreme's highest Power, deepest Peace and brightest Light. He offers His infinite and immortal Reality to us unconditionally and we receive it according to our inner capacity and our outer receptivity.

Love of the limited self, the very limited self, is another name for human love. Love of the entire world is another name for divine love. A cheerful, beckoning Hand the Supreme offers to divine love for earth's illumination, salvation and perfection. Love of the limited, unaspiring, desiring, binding and blinding human in us and the unlimited, eternally aspiring, self-giving divine in us is another name for Supreme Love.

In the process of evolution, each individual starts with animal love, love that destroys. Gradually this animal love makes progress. It receives an iota of light and changes its consciousness. Then it goes into human love, which is the song of possession, the song of doubt and insecurity. Eventually this doubtful existence is transformed into faithful existence; this life of insecurity becomes a life of security and confidence. For human love grows into divine love, which feels its identification and oneness with God's entire creation. Divine love is finally transformed or given the golden opportunity to grow into Supreme Love, which is Infinity's Perfection and Eternity's Satisfaction. This is how each individual walks along Eternity's road to reach the ever-transcending and ever-fulfilling Goal.

scs 94. *What role does music play in religion?*

Sri Chinmoy: Music plays a considerable role in religion. Music is a most convincing instrument to help religion play its role. A great musician can add to the inner cry of the person who practises a religious life. And if the musician himself believes in God wholeheartedly, then his music can be of tremendous help to his own religious practice.

Again, from the core of religion, one can bring illumining spirituality to add the living reality of God to his music. So a musician can help religion with his own search for higher beauty, the all-pervading Beauty and Light. And again, religion can come and help the musician who wants to play devotional, spiritual, illumining and God-manifesting music on earth.

scs 95. *I am an artist and I was wondering if there is any way to use my painting or music to inspire my consciousness.*

Sri Chinmoy: When we paint, we have to become one with the inner painter. When we sing, we have to become one with the inner singer. Outwardly, we may be very expert in music, but if we do not have the capacity to become one with the inner singer, then our singing will not be soulful.

Inner life is realisation; outer life is expression. First we realise, then we express. If you know that there is an inner painter who has realised the Truth, the Reality, and that this inner painter is trying to reveal the inner Truth through the outer painting, then your painting becomes a form of meditation. We can meditate twenty-four hours a day during all our multifarious activities provided we know that there is somebody doing the thing for us. If we feel that we are doing the work ourselves, with our ego, with our pride, with our personal effort, then there is nobody inside for us. But if we feel that the thing that we are doing is being done by somebody else, the divine part of our being, then it is all meditation, it is all expansion of consciousness, it is all fulfilment of our life of aspiration.

scs 96. *Whenever I have to perform, I become nervous and I end up performing badly. Is there anything I can do about this?*

Sri Chinmoy: Feel that you are not performing in front of fifty people. Just think that there is only one person listening to you and imagine that that person is an idiot. No matter how badly you sing, no matter how bad your throat is, just think that that person is infinitely inferior to you. Or think that he is a child of only two years old. This is the human way. But the divine way is to see immediately the Supreme before you. If you see the Supreme and feel that you also are the Supreme, then how can one Supreme be afraid of the other Supreme? There is only one Supreme. If you bow down to the Supreme inside each individual in the audience, then immediately you become one with each individual. Then you will not be afraid. Because you do not feel your oneness, you are afraid. But if you are one, then you don't feel afraid. This is the divine way.

In Jamaica, West Indies, someone once told me a funny story. "We went to a conference and the lecturer stood up and said, 'Ladies and gentlemen, two persons were supposed to deliver the speech. It was all decided. But my best friend has disappeared, so I am going now in search of him'. God had told him that He would inspire him and that he should not be afraid. But when he came up to the stage, God was not visible anymore. So he forgot everything and said, 'This is unfair. My friend has deserted me, so I am going to look for him'. He left the platform."

SCS 97. *What does it mean to be spiritual?*[§]

What is spirituality? Spirituality is a divine subject. Anyone can study this subject; this subject is open to all. This subject is at once theoretical and practical. If one wants to see God only in Heaven, the spirituality is theoretical. If one wants to see God not only in Heaven but also on earth and everywhere, then in his case spirituality is practical.

Spirituality is an inner cry for the Source. Spirituality is an inner cry, an inner decision and an inner determination for perfection. Perfection is not a fixed standard. It is continuous progress. Perfection is the seeker's divinely surrendered self-expansion in God's illumining Satisfaction and fulfilling Manifestation. Perfection is self-transcendence. Perfection is the act of piloting Eternity's Boat in Infinity's Sea towards Immortality's Shore. Perfection is self-giving. Perfection is the flower which grows into a God-nourishing fruit.

Napoleon says, "Ability is of little account without opportunity." Surprisingly enough, spirituality is both ability and opportunity. Ability is an inner and outer oneness with God's Vision. Opportunity is an inner and outer oneness with God's manifestation.

What does it mean to be spiritual? To be spiritual is to be normal, natural and spontaneous. To be spiritual is to be simple, sincere and pure. To be spiritual is to be a lover and server of truth and light. To be spiritual is to become a chosen and perfect instrument of God. To be spiritual is to become a God-representative on earth. To be spiritual is to become a liberator of humanity.

What does it mean to be spiritual? It means we long for God-discovery. It means we long for perfection in our body, vital, mind and heart. It means our old friend, desire-night, is no longer with us. It means we have a new friend: aspiration-day.

A spiritual person is he who loves God, not because God is great, not because God is good, but because God alone *is*.

How do we become spiritual? We become spiritual by loving, by serving and by surrendering.

Whom do we love? We love man in God. Whom do we serve? We serve God in man. To whom do we surrender? We surrender to God the transcendental Vision, God the universal Reality and God the eternal Will.

Why do we love? We love because love is life. Why do we serve? We serve because service is perfection. Why do we surrender? We surrender because surrender is satisfaction.

How do we love? We love soulfully. How do we serve? We serve devotedly. How do we surrender? We surrender unconditionally.

A spiritual person sees only one thing: God's Beauty. A spiritual person feels only one thing: God's Responsibility. A spiritual person becomes only one thing: God's Compassion-Light. God tells the spiritual person only one thing: "You are My Satisfaction."

You are spiritual; that means God comes first in your life. You are spiritual; that means God is the only reality in your life. You are spiritual; that means God is your heart's constant choice and God is your life's constant voice.

He is a great seeker who feels that God loves him. He is a greater seeker who knows that he loves God. He is the greatest seeker who knows that God and he love each other. God loves man because man is God's creation. Man loves God because God is man's salvation, liberation, illumination and realisation. God is man's salvation from sin-consciousness. God is man's liberation from bondage-life. God is the illumination of man's darkness-existence. God is man's realisation; and realisation is self-discovery and God-discovery. Let us cry and cry within. Then ours will be self-discovery. Let us smile and smile without. Then ours will be God-discovery.

scs 98. *What is the difference between spiritualism and spirituality?*

Sri Chinmoy: Spiritualism includes mediums and seances and all this. But in spirituality, true spirituality and Yoga, we only think of God, meditate on God and love God; we try to transform and divinise our own nature. Real spiritual people will get boundless Peace, Joy, Love and Bliss from within. But those who practise spiritualism and are deeply involved in the so-called spirit-worlds will never get these qualities.

scs 99. *What is Christian spirituality?*

Sri Chinmoy: Real spirituality is everywhere the same — in India, in America, in Milan. Everywhere spirituality is the same. Real spirituality means Yoga. Yoga means oneness with God. Now this oneness we establish in two ways. In the West we give more importance to prayer. In the East we give more importance to meditation. In Christian spirituality, prayer comes first. In Indian spirituality, meditation comes first. I believe that the realisation which the Christ had, our Krishna also had. But the Christ spoke so much of prayer, prayer, prayer, whereas our Krishna emphasized meditation, meditation. But when realisation comes, the Goal is the same. To come to the Goal I can take one road, you can take another road; but the Goal remains the same.

SCS 100. *What is the difference between a spiritual group and a religious group?*

Sri Chinmoy: If it is religious, then it becomes to some extent narrow-minded. But if it is spiritual, there is a cosmopolitan view. Spirituality encompasses all religions, no matter which religion or denomination one belongs to. But religion cannot house spirituality in that way. If somebody is religious, naturally he has some spirituality. But if he becomes a staunch follower of a particular religion, he may not like other religions. He may find everything wrong in other religions. He feels that his religion is by far the best. But if one becomes spiritual, really spiritual, he will give due value to all religions. A follower of a particular religion may not, or need not, or cannot, accommodate all religions as true. But if one follows spirituality, then he will feel that all religions are true, that all are good, that all are fulfilling God's Mission according to their capacity.

SCS 101. *Is it possible to distinguish between Jesus the man and what is referred to as the "Christ-Consciousness"?*

Sri Chinmoy: The conflict is in the seeker's mind, not in the seeker's heart. If you think of the Christ as a human being who lived on earth for thirty-three years, then you are mistaken. If you think of the Christ as the representative of the Absolute Father on earth, birthless and deathless, then you are absolutely right. However, if you feel that the Christ is the only Saviour, again you are making a deplorable mistake. We know that this world has existed for more than two thousand years. Sri Krishna and Lord Buddha both lived more than two thousand years ago. We must realise that the Christ-Consciousness, the Buddha-Consciousness and the Krishna-Consciousness are all manifestations of the same Absolute. The Christ, the Buddha and Sri

Krishna are not on isolated planes of consciousness, apart from the Absolute. On the one hand, they represent the Absolute; on the other hand, they *are* the Absolute. Here on earth they represent the Absolute, but in Heaven they actually are the Absolute.

If you have faith in a particular spiritual Master, that Master will help you realise the Absolute, from which the Christ-Consciousness, the Buddha-Consciousness and the Krishna-Consciousness have come. So if you wish to follow our path, I wish to say we are able to take you to the Christ-Consciousness, which is all-pervading and all-illumining, but we are not able to take you to the Jesus-consciousness. If you think of Jesus as the son of Joseph, as a human being like us, that is not the Christ-Consciousness. But if you want the all-illumining and all-fulfilling Christ-Consciousness, it does not matter which path you follow. Whichever path you follow will take you to the one destination, which you can call the Christ-Consciousness, the Buddha-Consciousness or the Krishna-Consciousness. There can be no conflict in Truth. If you really cry for the Truth, you will eventually realise it.

SCS 102. *How does a spiritually illumined being illumine evil?*

Sri Chinmoy: There is no such thing as evil and good. There is only lesser light and greater light. An illumined being will know where there is light in boundless measure and where there is only a small amount of light. What has very little light, others will call evil, or darkness, or destruction; but he will simply call it lesser light. Just because he is in touch with the infinite Light, he will be able to bring down the infinite Light where the infinite Light is wanting. If there is an iota of light, he will bring down more light; if there is abundant light, he will bring down boundless Light. This is what he will do.

scs 103. *Prayer and meditation are the same thing?*

Sri Chinmoy: Prayer and meditation are the same thing. When we pray there is somebody to listen to us, and that Someone is God. I pray, "God, give me Peace, give me Light, give me Bliss." My prayer is going up to God. But when we meditate, we become calm and quiet and we feel Peace, Light and Bliss descending. In prayer we are going up to get this, and in meditation we are bringing it down through our aspiration. It is the same thing whether we get it here or we get it there. Through prayer we feel that we go to God. Through meditation we feel that God comes to us. But it is the same thing, absolutely the same. I say that when we pray, we speak and God listens; when we meditate, we listen and God talks. Praying means that I am talking and somebody is listening. Who is listening? God is listening. And when I meditate somebody is talking. Who is talking? God is talking and I am listening.

scs 104. *How can I quiet the mind?*

Sri Chinmoy: There are many ways, but I will tell you the two main ways. First, you can repeat a specific mantra or you can say "God" or "Supreme" as slowly and quietly as possible. While repeating this, please feel that God's divine qualities are entering into your mind; do not simply repeat like a parrot. Each time you repeat "God" soulfully, feel that a divine quality is entering into your mind. When this happens, the Power of God's Light is bound to silence the mind.

You want to silence your mind because it is acting like a restless monkey. Restlessness comes because of darkness; darkness and restlessness are inseparable. Restlessness is due to your lack of receptivity to light. There are two places where light is available: above the head and inside the heart. When the mind is illumined, restlessness is transformed into tranquillity. When you can bring down light or carry it from the heart into the mind, at that time the mind becomes calm and quiet.

scs 105. *How can a seeker clear the confusion and know which path is the correct path for him?*

Sri Chinmoy: As a student you come to a school and see the teacher and the students. If they satisfy you, if you feel an affinity with them, then you go to that particular school. Similarly, you come to a spiritual Master and see his students and hear about his path. If you feel an affinity with the path, then it is meant for you. When you see a Master, if he gives you intense joy, if you feel he can easily solve your problems or has the capacity to illumine you, if you experience a feeling of oneness, then undoubtedly he is your Master. If you don't feel an affinity with the Master and his students, it doesn't mean that you are insincere. No, you *are* sincere, but he is just not the Master for you.

scs 106. *My own spiritual background has taken me into different paths of meditation: Buddhism, Zen and other forms. I feel myself centred in all these particular areas, but am I really splitting myself by consciously practising more than one type of meditation?*

Sri Chinmoy: Spirituality is only one subject. It is not like history, geography, science and mathematics, for which you need different classes. It is only one subject, and for that it is advisable to walk along one path. The Goal is one and it is at one particular place. If we constantly change our roads, then our progress will naturally be slow. Today we prefer one road and tomorrow we feel that there is another road which can take us to the Goal faster. So we are only changing from one road to another and not making progress on any road. Each path is right in its own way. No path is faulty. But we have to know which path suits us, which path satisfies us most. Once we discover the path of our soul's choice, if we walk along that path only, we will reach our destination sooner than otherwise.

scs 107. *The* Bhagavad-Gita *talks about purification. How can I be purified?*

Sri Chinmoy: How can you be purified? You can purify your existence, your inner and outer life, just by feeling deep within yourself a living flower, a burning flame and an incense stick that is burning all the time. The incense, the flower and the candle flame symbolise purity. If you can feel within yourself, for example, a beautiful flower, a rose or lotus or any flower that you cherish, then you are doing the right thing. Today it is imagination; but if you continue imagining for five days or ten days or a month or two, then you are bound to see and feel the flower within you. First you may feel it, then you are bound to see the existence of the flower, and then automatically the fragrance and the purity of the flower will enter into you to purify you.

We have to feel that we have within us all the divine qualities. If we feel that we don't have them, then it is almost impossible to get them. If we feel that God is within us, for that reason one day we shall see God face to face. But if we think that God is not within us, that He is somewhere else, then we will never see God. If we want to achieve something in our life, first we have to feel that we have that very thing within us. And because we have not yet discovered it, we have to use our imagination-power to help bring it to the fore.

Also, we have to feel that we are God's children. Now we can't feel it. We have done many things wrong and to say that we are God's chosen instruments is a self-mockery. This is what we feel. But if we continuously say, "No, we are God's chosen children. Deep within us is divinity. God is there, only we have covered Him with our ignorance," then we are bound to bring our inner divinity to the fore. So try to have that kind of feeling. You have to feel that God is within you, purity is within you; only you have to reveal it. How do you reveal it? You reveal it by imagining within yourself the things that you see around you as pure — flowers, incense, candles — and then automatically one day you do become purified.

SCS 75. *(p. 119)* Puerto Rico, 27 January 1970.

SCS 76–79. *(p. 122)* Questions and answers following *Love me or hate me, but don't ignore me.*

SCS 80–85. *(p. 125)* On 29 June 1974, Sri Chinmoy and one of his disciples appeared on *Radio Clyde*, a radio interview programme in Glasgow, Scotland. A transcript of the broadcast follows.

SCS 86. *(p. 130)* On 18 November, 1974, Sri Chinmoy planted a young oak tree in Federal Parkland in Ottawa, as an offering to the soul of Canada. What follows is a transcript of Sri Chinmoy's remarks at the planting ceremony.

SCS 87. *(p. 131)* St. Xavier Auditorium, New York, 2 July 1975.

SCS 88–92. *(p. 136)* Questions and answers following *A true seeker.*

SCS 93. *(p. 141)* State University of New York, at Purchase, 18 February 1976.

SCS 94–96. *(p. 145)* Questions and answers following *Love human, love divine, love supreme.*

SCS 97. *(p. 147)* St. Paul's Chapel, Columbia University, New York, 25 February 1976.

SCS 98–107. *(p. 150)* Questions and answers following *What does it mean to be spiritual?*

SRI CHINMOY SPEAKS

BOOK 5

scs 108. *Spirituality*

Dearest seekers, we are all spiritual people precisely because we are seeking. For this reason, I wish to give a short talk on spirituality, and then I shall welcome spiritual questions as a form of my dedicated service to each of you.

Is the spiritual life an act of giving? Yes, it is. What precisely do we give? We give our bondage-night and ignorance-day. To whom do we give them? We give them to God. What else do we give to God? We give God, or rather, we reconfirm to God our soul's promise that we made millions of years ago. What was that promise? Him we shall realise unreservedly and Him we shall fulfil unconditionally.

Is the spiritual life an act of receiving? Yes, it is. What precisely do we receive? We receive God's Grace and we receive God the Grace. What is the difference between God's Grace and God the Grace? The difference is this: God's Grace shows us God's Face with form and without form; and God the Grace tells us that we are not only eternal, infinite and immortal like Him, but also equal and perfect. We have made friends with ignorance; therefore, we are not conscious of what we truly are. But God and we are inseparably one: this is what we learn from God the boundless Grace.

We should know something about God with form and God without form. God with form is often questioned by the dark human mind. God without form remains always a far cry for the proud and unaspiring human mind. The dark, unaspiring human mind does not want to see God in God's own Way, whereas the loving and aspiring heart tries to see God in God's own Way. God with form is accessible to those who love God with their heart's inmost feelings. God without form is also accessible to those who love God in the inmost recesses of their hearts.

Is the spiritual life an act of becoming? Yes, it is. What precisely do we become? In the process of evolution each individual becomes another God. When? At God's blessingful, choice Hour.

How do we know that a certain individual is spiritual? If we say that he is spiritual because he often talks about God, we may be making a deplorable mistake. People can talk about God day in and day out but never follow the true spiritual life. If someone feels that there is a world of Peace and Bliss unlike this world of ours, and that he belongs to that world, does it mean that he is spiritual? No. He may be building castles in the air, or he may be enjoying some mental hallucinations. If we say that someone is spiritual because he gives up his friends, his relatives and the members of his family and enters into a Himalayan cave to become a recluse, then we will be mistaken again. Spirituality does not demand that we live the life of an ascetic; it does not ask us to give up our near and dear ones. Far from it.

So how do we know whether or not an individual is spiritual? We know that an individual is spiritual only when we notice a certain amount of purity in his body and surety in his soul. What do we mean by the body's purity? The body's purity is the divine capacity for endless God-receptivity. And what do we mean by the soul's surety? The soul's surety is the soul's conscious and constant oneness-perfection with the Absolute Supreme. The soul's surety is the soul's conscious and constant oneness-satisfaction in the Absolute Supreme.

Some people are of the opinion that spirituality and divinity are very close to each other, that they are adjacent to one another — two loving, faithful, soulful and fruitful neighbours. They are absolutely correct. But I wish to add one thing. The nature of spirituality and the nature of divinity are similar. What both of them embody is God's boundless creation and what both of them reveal is God's infinite Compassion. But if we observe spirituality and divinity very minutely, then we do observe a subtle difference. Spirituality is God's Self-expansion and divinity is God's Self-perfection. While expanding Himself, God perfects Himself; and while perfecting Himself, God transcends Himself. Therefore we can safely say that spirituality and divinity are complementary.

The question is often asked whether each and every person on earth can be spiritual and divine, or whether spirituality and divinity are the monopoly of only a few selected individuals. Spirituality and divinity can be claimed by each and every individual, providing each and every individual has a sincere need for spirituality and divinity. Spirituality is not the sole monopoly of any individual. Each and every individual can practise spirituality, provided he wants to cry — cry for the ultimate Truth, the transcendental Height, the immortal Delight.

How does one become spiritual and divine? One becomes spiritual and divine by studying the inner life. One has to spend time on inner studies. When we study other subjects, we go to school and learn from our teacher. To learn spirituality and divinity, we go to the inner school. In the inner school, God is the only Teacher.

God the Teacher always asks us to be simple, sincere, humble and pure. Only then will He be able to teach us. If we are wanting in simplicity, sincerity, humility and purity, then God will not be able to teach us. What does God teach us? He teaches us how to become His perfect instruments on earth. He teaches us how to take part in His cosmic *lila*, the Game eternal. He also teaches us how to fly and how to march, how to fly with His ever-transcending, infinite Vision and how to march with His ever-progressing, boundless manifestation. God grants us

His Vision-Reality and His Reality-Vision at the end of our journey's close. God's Vision-Reality is God's eternal Greatness-Height and God's Reality-Vision is God's eternal Goodness-Depth.

Our Teacher, God, tells us that we cannot enjoy double-dealing. In secret we make friends with desire-night and in public we make friends with aspiration-day, aspiration-light. God says He cannot accept this double-dealing precisely because He has an aversion to this double-dealing. With our desire-night we try to bind God and have God please us in our own way. With our aspiration-light we try to love God and serve God in God's own Way.

Why do we love God? We love God because He is all Beauty. Why do we serve God? We serve God because He is the only Reality: the Reality that we long for, the Reality that we want to grow into, the Reality that is all satisfaction, Eternity's satisfaction. What we all need here on earth and there in Heaven is satisfaction: satisfaction in God's own Way.

scs 109. *God-Reality*

God's Reality operates on two different planes. One Reality operates in the desire-world; the other Reality operates in the aspiration-world. The ordinary human mind operates in the desire-world and it is here that it wants to see God. The mind feels that satisfaction can be achieved only when it is satisfied the way it wants to be satisfied. The mind wants the Reality to please it the way the mind wants to be pleased. The mind wants the Reality, but for its own purpose. "I want this and if I get it, then only will I be pleased." This is the truth of the mind.

In the aspiration world, the heart is of paramount importance. The heart wants the Reality, not to fulfil itself, but so it can become part and parcel of the Reality. It wants the Reality so it can enjoy the Light and Delight of the Reality. It wants the Reality because it gets joy from the way Light and Delight operate in and through the Reality. The heart wants the Reality to satisfy the Reality the way the Reality wants to be satisfied. The heart wants to get satisfaction on the strength of its oneness with the Reality.

The mind wants to derive satisfaction by maintaining a sense of separativity. The mind does not want to unite. The mind says, "You stay where You are, and let me stay where I am. Only come to me whenever I want You or need You. But that doesn't mean I have to surrender to You all the time. Stay wherever You want, but I wish You to be at my beck and call." The heart, however, says to the Reality, "I am at Your Feet; only allow me to be where You are. I want to stay at Your Feet. If You want to kick me out, I am ready to be kicked if that gives You satisfaction. If You want to place me inside Your Heart, place me there; and if You want to keep me elsewhere, do that. Only please Yourself, please Yourself in Your own Way." So naturally the heart, on the strength of its oneness with the Reality, is pleasing the Reality. This is what a seeker of the absolute transcendental Truth must try to see, feel and grow into.

The mind does not accept the Reality's existence but it wants to fulfil itself by taking help from the Reality for its own purpose. But the heart wants to fulfil itself only by pleasing the Reality in its own way. Again, today's doubting mind may tomorrow become a searching mind and the day after tomorrow it will become a self-giving mind. It is not a hopeless case for the mind. But right now, at the present stage of our evolution, the mind is doubting and suspecting the Reality, while, at the same time, it wants to derive utmost satisfaction from the Reality. The mind suspects the Reality and, at the same time, the mind is always like a beggar waiting for the Reality to satisfy it. But the heart is all oneness with the Reality.

scs 110. *The positive approach towards progress*

It is unnecessary to go through the negative aspects of life: doubt, fear, anxiety, jealousy. If I have to go to light and if my aim is to arrive at light, why is it necessary for me to go through darkness? If my goal is situated to the north, why should I go to the south first and then come back towards the north? It is absurd. But the only thing is that in the spiritual life very often it is not always sunlit. If you follow the path of surrender, constant surrender, divine surrender to the Will of God, then it becomes a sunlit path. But since we cannot make constant and conscious surrender to the Will of God, very often we run into difficulties. Our mental sky is overcast with clouds, with fear, doubt, anxiety, worries and so forth. When these undivine forces threaten us or delay our progress, we fight them with our inner faith, our inner determination, our courage and mounting aspiration. If we feel that we have to go through the negative forces and feed them in order to go beyond them, we are mistaken. If we feed the snake within us and feel that one day the snake will leave us, we are making a deplorable mistake. The snake will bite us and kill us. Undivine forces are nothing but snakes or ferocious tigers within us. So if we feed the tiger within us, do you think the tiger will be pleased with us and say, "Since you have fed me for a long time, let me give you freedom. You go."? No, it is not like that.

So always we have to run towards light, if light is our goal. If perfection is our goal, then we have to run towards perfection. By staying in imperfection and waiting for imperfection to release us from its prison, we will never reach our goal. For a sincere seeker, it is always advisable to accept the positive aspect of life, to feel, "I am God's child. I shall aspire. I shall try to grow into the very image of God." This is the positive approach.

God is in everything. God is in light; God is in darkness, too. But we are trying to transform darkness into light. God is in filthy water; God is also in pure water. So we have to use the power of discrimination. If we drink filthy water, poisonous water, we shall die. Then again, if we drink pure water, we shall quench our thirst.

In the spiritual life, always we are trying to discriminate good from bad and stay only with good. Then there comes a time when we don't want to leave bad aside; we want to transform bad into good, darkness into light. But by staying with darkness, we won't be able to change darkness into light. If we stay in light, we not only have the possibility, but the assurance, the guarantee, that eventually we will be able to transform darkness into light. If I stay for many years in an illumined room, then my whole being will be illumined and flooded with light. At that time, when I enter into the unlit room, that room will automatically be lit by my very presence.

So we try to go to light first and then from light we come into darkness. Otherwise, no matter how many years we stay in darkness, we will not be able to see the face of light. True, God is in everything; in darkness also there is a little light. But God's living Presence is more vivid, more encouraging, more inspiring, more illumining in certain things. God is in animals. And once upon a time, if we believe in reincarnation, we must say that we were all animals. But right now consciously we are aspiring. In the animal life we were not aspiring consciously, so we will not go back into the animal kingdom, even though God is also there. No. We are now in the human world. Here we are trying to go one step ahead; that is to say, we would like to establish the divine world, the Kingdom of Heaven. If we can bring down light from above, then only is there every possibility and assurance that, in the long run, we will be able to transform our human life, which is half animal, into the divine life, and the negative aspects of life into higher and more fulfilling realities.

scs III. *Human confidence and divine confidence*

There is a great difference between human confidence and divine confidence. When it is human confidence, like Julius Caesar we shall say, "I came, I saw, I conquered." But when it is divine confidence, we will say, "I came, I saw and then I became inseparably one." In human confidence there is always a feeling of superiority. I am one inch higher than you, so I can lord it over you or guide you or mould you the way I want. But divine confidence is not like that. Divine confidence is the recognition, acceptance and inner assurance of oneness. And this oneness is guided, moulded, shaped, fulfilled and immortalised by a higher reality, the highest Reality, which is the Supreme. When we have divine confidence, we feel that we are God's instruments and that God is guiding us, moulding us, shaping us. But when it is human confidence, there is no God; there is only you and I, and I am one inch higher than you; therefore I can dominate you and fulfil myself in my own way.

God-realisation is my birthright. It is my birthright because God needs me to manifest Himself in and through me. Our work is shared. I need God to realise the Highest and God needs me to manifest His Reality. In divine confidence, we share our capacity, we share our necessity. I am doing my respective job, whatever is asked of me, and God is doing His job, whatever is asked of Him. So I have confidence because I know I am of Him and for Him, and He is of me and for me. And God has confidence in me because He knows that from His Silence He has created me. I am His creation. If the Creator and the creation do not become the obverse and reverse of the same reality, then the Creator will not feel satisfaction. For the creation is like

God's mirror. He looks into the mirror, His own reality, and if He does not see Himself in what He creates, then He can never be satisfied. I as an individual have to become an exact prototype of His Reality. That is what God wants.

So divine confidence is our acceptance of the divine reality which is within us, as our very own. I am of God and I am for God; I am of Light and I am for Truth. This realisation is founded upon my feeling of universal oneness. I am not one inch higher or lower. In human confidence there is always a competitive spirit. I compete with someone and if I win, then I dominate. With divine confidence I do not compete, I do not challenge. I have become one with the reality that he has or is or he represents, for I am also the same reality. Inside us there is only one Reality and that is God Himself singing the song of universal oneness and the song of constant self-transcendence.

A sincere seeker always has confidence. He has confidence that in and through him God is going to manifest Himself. This is not his pride that is speaking. It is the necessity, the God-Necessity that he embodies. God has made him the fulfilment of God's own Necessity.

SCS 112. *Responsibility human and responsibility divine*

Most human beings enjoy self-imposed responsibility, and when they see that responsibility, they say it has been thrust upon them. But, as spiritual people, our responsibility is to listen to the dictates of the Supreme twenty-four hours a day. He may say, "This moment you don't have to pray and meditate. Just go and give away all the dollars that you have in your pocket or do some selfless service: clean the street." In that case, we do it. If He asks, definitely we will go and give spiritual comfort to patients in the hospital who are dying. Many things are very good, but we have to know whether a particular good thing is meant for us to do. The Supreme perhaps wants to utilise somebody else to do that very thing. Perhaps He wants to fulfil Himself in and through that other person. Our idea may be very good, very spiritual, but we are standing in God's way.

If we are not spiritual in the purest sense of the term, whatever we know from the mental point of view, we do. We live up to morality. But far above morality is real spirituality, which means listening to the dictates of the Supreme twenty-four hours a day, all the time. We have to play the role that we are intended to play. Suppose the Supreme wants us to play the role of a slave and we want to play the role of a king. If we take the part of the king because we feel that this part is most meaningful, most fruitful, then the Game will not be successful; it will be wrong, a fiasco.

It is the same thing in the Centre. The Master knows who deserves each post, so the Master gives out each post according to his inner knowledge. Some who do not hold the highest posts are, unfortunately, very sad. If an aspirant feels, that by holding a particular post, he will become very close to the Master or he will realise God sooner than the rest, then he is mistaken. In order to realise the Highest, one does not need posts; it is the aspiration of the seeker that counts most. When the Master gives the best or highest post to someone, it is because the Master has been commissioned by the Inner Pilot, the Supreme, to give it to that person. At that time, the Master knows that he is giving the post to this individual with God's sanction, so that both God and the Master can work in and through the seeker. If everybody wants to hold the highest post, if everybody wants to become the king, it is impossible. In the cosmic Game, *one* has to become the king and others have to become the ministers and subjects. Otherwise, we cannot have a cosmic Drama; there is no play. Only if the roles of the play are divided well is the drama perfect.

If the Supreme wants you to meditate at a particular time and at that moment your wife is doing selfless service, you can't say your meditation or her selfless service is by far the best. She is playing her part and you are playing your part. If you do her job, selfless service, when God wants you to do meditation, who is getting a good result? We shall help mankind because this is what God wants us to do. But our selfless service has to entirely depend on God's Will. If God at this moment wants us to meditate, we shall meditate. But if God wants us to do something else, we shall do that. This should be our attitude. But if we feel that we can just look at the world according to our capacity, see what is needed and then do the needful, we have to know that this will be just a self-imposed responsibility. Only one thing is needed: aspiration. If we aspire and do only what God wants us to do, we shall be serving mankind in God's own Way. Otherwise, if we do it in our own way, we only create problems.

SCS 113. *Maintaining a connection with one's parents*

Some parents are very nice, very sincere, very kind to their children. They themselves won't practise Yoga; either they are afraid of the path or they feel that it is too late for them. I don't blame them, although in the spiritual life, there is no such thing as too late. When you start soulfully, that is the hour for you. God's Hour for you is the day you wholeheartedly accept the spiritual life. But if the parents are good, if they are not accepting our path or any path but they are allowing their children to come, then certainly the children should maintain a connection with them. In Indian villages, the parents may be farmers who have no education, but they want their children to go to school and be cultured. These parents are so nice. They work very hard in the fields and make a little money so they can send their children to school. They could not study when they were children and now they feel they are too old, but they want their children to go to school. Here also, if the parents have never practised spirituality or Yoga and now they are forty or sixty years old and feel that it is too late for them, then I wish to say that you have to be very, very nice to them. They do appreciate the value of the spiritual life, inner life, inner joy and so forth, but they feel it is not for them.

But if the parents are *totally* against your spiritual path, no matter which one you follow, then you have to be brave. At that time you have to feel the necessity of your own spiritual life; that is to say, your spiritual life must come first and foremost in your life. But I am using the word "totally". If your parents want to make a compromise — that you follow the spiritual path and also keep a connection with them — then you should agree. You will say, "All right, you follow your own ideas, although I can't wholeheartedly appreciate your ideas. Now you also have to give me some freedom to follow my ideas." If you have some function at home or if somebody in the family is getting married or is sick, then naturally it is your bounden duty at that time to go and help. You should feel that there was a special reason why God brought you into that family. But if your parents are all the time against your spiritual life, if they do not understand anything or they do not want to understand, if they feel that you are wasting your time and that one day you will come to realise that you are making a Himalayan blunder, if they are preventing you in every possible way from pursuing this path, then you do not have to keep any connection with them. If they do not understand you and if they stand against you, they are in no way better than an enemy. But you should still offer your inner gratitude to them. For twenty-three or twenty-four years they have fed you, they have nourished you, they have brought you up. So you have to offer your gratitude to your parents, although they have not been totally divine. They have made mistakes and now they are making more mistakes in not allowing you to follow your own path, but still you have to show your inner gratitude. But to offer your inner gratitude is one thing and to mix with them, in spite of knowing that they are standing in your way, is something else.

So each one has to know how much opposition he is getting from his parents. There was a time, four or five years ago, when a few parents were dead against us. They felt that I had taken their children away from them. But the parents do not realise that I have not gone to anybody's house and pleaded with them to give me their children. The children came to me on their own. And then I tried my best to give them good ideas. I have not told any son or daughter, "Leave your parents." Oh, no, no! On the contrary, I always say, "Try to compromise." But if the parents are totally against us, then I feel miserable. I have come here to take the side of God and not the side of ignorance. If I see that somebody is getting tremendous opposition from his parents, and if he is very sincere, very dedicated, very devoted, how can I tell him to swim in the sea of ignorance along with the parents? That I cannot do. But my request to all of you is to try to keep as much as possible a good connection with your parents, a normal connection. But if you feel that it is your duty to mix with your parents, although they are very unspiritual and undivine, then I wish to say that you can do it, but your progress will be very, very limited. You have to make the proper balance.

scs 114. *Children and spirituality*

Children have no sense of judgement. They feel that whatever their parents do is always best. Children are often exact proto-types of their parents. It is true, to a certain extent, that if the parents don't tell lies, the children don't tell lies. The parents don't have to say, "Don't tell a lie," because the children don't know anything else but truthfulness. If the parents like some-thing, immediately the children like it. If the parents have some good friends, saintly friends, the children immediately become friends with them. Children always, in the beginning, try to imitate their parents. Imitation is really good, and the parents should always behave extremely well in front of their children. If the parents misbehave, the children will be totally ruined. If the parents tell a lie or do anything wrong, then the children will follow their parents' radiant example in their own life.

Early in the morning, if you get up and pray with folded hands, for a few days your child will remain fast asleep while you are meditating. But on the third day, a sweet sense of com-petition will come into him. If his father can meditate, what is wrong with his doing it? And then the child will sit beside you and meditate. The best example is the parents' own life. The parents' life is the child's ideal. When the child grows up, then he may have different goals. But in the beginning, the parents should always encourage their children to pray and med-itate if they have accepted a spiritual path. They should always encourage their children to be like them.

Anything you feel is nourishing, you give to the child. If the child does not want milk, you will say, "You must drink." But when it is a matter of spirituality, many parents think, "Who knows, one day the children may not like our path, so it is best not to make them pray and meditate. When they are fifteen, let them make their own choice and become Guru's disciple or someone else's disciple." This is no good. When the children are growing up, if you don't give them milk, they will die before they become old enough to make the selection themselves. In the spiritual life also, children will die spiritually if you don't give them inner nourishment. You are not injecting anything into them, only you are giving them food. They may not like that particular food, but they have to eat or they will die. In spirituality also, what you feel best for your child you should give him in the beginning. Then, when he grows up, that very thing he can continue if he likes. Otherwise, he may give it up and follow some other path or he may not follow spirituality at all.

SCS 115. *Imagination and creativity*

We get inspiration to create art or to offer art to the world at large only when we are in a position to become one with our imagination. Imagination is something totally different from reality, but imagination is not bad. Right now it is imagination, but when we consciously side with imagination, we feel we give birth to reality. Before something comes into existence in the outer world, it is already there in our inner life, in the form of imagination. If we feel this imagination with our love or enthusiasm or hope, immediately we see the dawn of inspiration. And inside inspiration is creation. Without imagination we cannot inspire others and we cannot be inspired ourselves. When I want to inspire you, it means that inside me there is someone who has already imagined the fact that you can be inspired and that I am the one who can inspire.

When imagination has played its role consciously or unconsciously, inspiration comes forward. Then, when imagination becomes completely and unreservedly one with inspiration, we see that inspiration has something to offer and that something is creativity. So imagination brings into existence inspiration and inspiration offers us its own wealth, which is creativity.

There is divine imagination and undivine imagination. War — this is also imagination. Here human imagination is being used in a different way. One kind of human imagination is used for a divine purpose, to build the Palace of Love, Light and Truth. The other kind of imagination wants to destroy the whole world. From imagination we are inspired to do something, either divine or undivine.

How do we get divine imagination? We get divine imagination by leading a divine life, a spiritual life; we get divine imagination by purifying our breath. Every second we are breathing in and out. While we are breathing, if we consciously repeat the word "purity" or think that purity is the only thing that we need in our life, automatically our breath becomes pure. Even by imagining that we need purity more than anything else, our breath becomes pure. And when our breath is pure, we have to feel that it is nothing but divine. So if we want to become a divine artist, then we have to feed the divine imagination within us. When the divine imagination offers its reality, it becomes inspiration. And when we consciously feel the divine inspiration, then we get divine art.

scs 116. *Thoughts and physical illness*

Very often physical illness will start in the mind. If you can stop it there, then it will not attack the physical. Now, how do you know if it has entered the mind? Easily you will know. Take the mind as a room in your house. If somebody has entered your room, naturally you will know. Before illness touches the physical, at least five or six times you will get some inkling in your mind. You are driving your car or talking or resting and all of a sudden you feel some uneasiness. It is not something serious at that time. It comes in a thought-form that is not wholesome or progressive. One thought that is not progressive can easily bring disease into the mind, into the vital, into the physical. If the thought is stagnant, like a stagnant pool, then problems arise; from there disease starts. Any thought that is not progressive is dangerous.

A seeker can easily trace a negative thought before it touches the physical. Take the mind as the third floor in your house. If there is water leaking up there, easily you can stop it before it flows down to the second and first floors. If you do the needful on the third floor, then you don't have to suffer on the other floors. When you notice something wrong in the mind, the best thing is to immediately invoke the Light and Peace of the Supreme. If you have Light and Peace, illumination and peace of mind, then the wrong force will be illumined. Either it will be frightened to death and leave you or it will be transformed by the Light and Peace that have entered the mind.

So all the time, while you are thinking or talking to friends, you have to know whether the thoughts you are using, or allowing to stay in your mind, are progressive or not. If you see a thought moving forward, then you should keep it. But if it is moving instead just like an insect, then it has to be thrown out. We have to be very careful of our thoughts, because we live in a mental world, a thought-world. One thought can take us to Heaven or to hell. Each thought is either nectar-like or poisonous. Each thought can be our saviour or it can be our destroyer.

scs 117. *What is the difference between human opinion and divine opinion?*

Sri Chinmoy: Human opinion is the play of imagination. Divine opinion is the expression of realisation. Opinion is power. Human opinion can harm you in your outer life. Divine opinion can fulfil your inner life. Human opinion is meaningless obeisance to what others have spoken. Divine opinion is energising and fulfilling surrender to the Inner Voice.

Opinion very often we get from the mind; conviction we get from the heart and realisation we get from the soul. The value of mental opinion is very small. The conviction of the heart, psychic conviction, is meaningful, but at times it is based on pure imagination. But when conviction is flooded with divine realisation, there is abundant reality in it. Realisation, which comes from the soul, is one's conscious oneness with the Ultimate, with the Supreme. In realisation, opinion and conviction are transformed into divine reality.

scs 118. *How can I become more aware?*

Sri Chinmoy: All the time you have to think of yourself in a positive way. You have to say, "What is wrong with me that I am sleeping all the time? I can run, I can write. Again, I can sleep. But I know that by sleeping for twenty hours, I won't get any joy." So you have to think of the result. If you think of the result, of awareness, then immediately you will be so happy. "That is the thing that I am going to get. If I become aware of God, the result I am getting is a peaceful life. I will have some joy, some sense of satisfaction." So think of the satisfaction you will get and that satisfaction will immediately compel you to be aware. Naturally everyone is running after satisfaction. God Himself is our satisfaction. Human satisfaction is to make more money, to become more prosperous, this and that. But spiritual satisfaction is to have an iota of Peace, an iota of Light, an iota of Bliss. Everybody needs satisfaction. So if you think of the satisfaction which you need most, automatically you will become aware. Give utmost importance to the satisfaction within you and then you are bound to become aware.

SCS 119. *How can I increase my surrender and purity?*

Sri Chinmoy: How can you increase your surrender and purity? If you can surrender your body, vital, mind, heart and soul, then you will feel purity. Again, if you can increase your purity, immediately your capacity to surrender increases. One depends on the other. If you are pure, your surrender increases; if you are surrendered, then your purity increases. How do you get purity and surrender from the spiritual life? You look at a flower and you know a flower is all purity. So you try to identify yourself with the consciousness of the flower or with the purity of the flower. Or you look at a little child, who is all surrender to his parents. Whatever his parents are doing for him, he is satisfied. So you can try to become like a child. If you can feel that you are a child in the Lap of God, then you can easily make surrender. Again, if you can feel that you are a flower, or that another flower is inside your heart and that this flower is blossoming petal by petal, then you will automatically become pure. So if you can imagine or feel a flower inside your heart, your purity will automatically increase. And if you can feel a divine child inside your heart, your surrender will automatically increase.

scs 120. *What is the relationship between aspiration and surrender?*

Sri Chinmoy: Aspiration houses everything in it, including surrender. Again, inside surrender we see our aspiration. Inside devotion and surrender exists everything: Peace, Light and Bliss. In the beginning, when we start our journey, we call it aspiration; when we complete our journey, we call it surrender. We start our journey with aspiration and when we reach our Goal, we have surrender. But this surrender embodies aspiration. Aspiration was necessary to climb up to the Highest and surrender is necessary to climb down to feed the hungry aspiring mankind.

scs 121. *How can one recognise a true living Master?*

Sri Chinmoy: One can recognise a true living Master if, when he approaches the Master, his inner being is inundated with delight and ecstasy. If you stand in front of a real spiritual Master who is meant to be your own Master, then even your outer being will be filled with immense joy and ecstasy. Now, he may be a real Master, but if he is not meant to be *your* Master, then you will not experience intense joy immediately. And, if he is not a true Master, and you are sincere, then you will not experience any joy at all. Of course, if you do not get anything from a Master, you cannot always say that he is not real; you may be in a very low consciousness and then you will not be able to feel that Master's Light. But if your heart is crying for a real spiritual Master, then you are bound to feel something in a true Master. And if he is your own Master, then you will find in him everything that you need in this life.

scs 122. *How can we proceed and make inner progress in the spiritual life if we get light and joy from more than one Master?*

Sri Chinmoy: Here you have to know that each Master is like a doctor. If you have a headache, you will go to a doctor, who will give you some medicine and cure you. Again, if you have some other ailment — say, foot pain — you will go to a foot specialist and he will cure you. But if you see that there is someone who has the power to cure you no matter what ailment you have, if there is someone who can enter into the root of all diseases, then naturally you will go to that person. If there is a doctor who will be able to give you so much Light that you will never suffer from any disease again, then you will go to him. So if you see a Master in whom you have implicit faith, and if you feel that he will be able to guide you until you have reached your destination, you will go to this Master and not go to any other Master.

It is like going to school. Some Masters will be able to teach only kindergarten, or only primary school, or only high school courses. Again, there are some Masters who will be able to teach you right from the beginning to the end — from the kindergarten level right up to the Ph.D. If you see a Master who can guide you right from the journey's start to the journey's destination, then you will go to that one. Otherwise, you will go to one who has the capacity to teach you at your level of spiritual development. Then, after a couple of years, perhaps you yourself will surpass him, and you will have to look for someone else to guide you for another couple of years. Then once again you will see that your inner progress has far surpassed your Master's realisation. This has happened in many, many cases. So again you have to look for a new Master.

Each time you go to a new Master, you waste time. Each one has a special way of teaching and you have to adapt yourself to the new way. One has taught you a particular truth and given you a specific way to reach it. The next one is giving you a higher truth, but he may not ask you to walk along the road where you have already made some progress. He may take you along a totally different road. He may take you to a farther destination, but he may also take you along a different road. So when you start along a different road, you may be bewildered or puzzled and it may create problems for you.

So if you get someone in whom you have implicit faith and confidence, and if you feel that he will be able to guide you, not only at your present level of consciousness but until you have reached your highest destination, then you should go to that person. He will show you how to walk along Eternity's road and also help you walk along the road. It is not his road but the road that he has discovered, that he is well acquainted with. In that case, it is advisable to walk along with that Master who, from the beginning to the end, can show you, teach you and guide you along one road to your highest Goal. Otherwise, you will just waste time going from one Master to another.

SCS 123. *I have read in the Bible that if one does not accept the teachings of Jesus Christ, his soul is damned forever to hell. Is this true?*

Sri Chinmoy: My simple answer to this question is that it is up to you whether you believe or do not believe. If you believe that you must have faith only in the Christ's teachings, then you must pray to the Christ-Consciousness to illumine you. However, if you do not believe this, then you have a perfect right to do what you feel is best. It is your inner being that will tell you whether to believe or not to believe. But if you accept the theory that you are damned to hell if you do not have absolute faith in Christ, then naturally you have to pray to the Christ-Consciousness to illumine and perfect you. I personally say that the Consciousness of the Christ, the Buddha, Sri Krishna, Sri Ramakrishna, Sri Aurobindo and other great Masters is all the same Consciousness known under different names. But it is up to you to decide what to believe.

Heaven and hell are inside our mind. They are a state of consciousness, not a country to which one goes. If you cherish a good thought, then inside that good thought is Heaven. If you treasure a bad thought, you live in hell. Heaven and hell are inside us; at every moment we experience either Heaven or hell. Heaven gives joy; hell gives a painful experience. We are responsible for every thought. If we cry to God for Light, that is a good thought, and we get illumining experiences from good thoughts. If we do not cry for Light, then we experience a painful reality, which we call hell.

SCS 124. *Was the battle of Kurukshetra a real battle, or was it the symbol of the battle of life on earth?*

Sri Chinmoy: The battle of Kurukshetra was a real battle. It did take place over four thousand years ago. Krishna was there in human form; Arjuna was there. It is absolutely true; Krishna did come into existence and it was a real battle.

But now we use it according to our own purpose. When we are in a position to use the message of the Gita in a practical way, we say, "Yes, Krishna did come." But the message of disinterested work — that we work for the sake of work, but offer the result at the Feet of the Lord — is very difficult for human beings. So we say it is all symbolic; it is all theory. It is not reality. But for spiritual people, everything is reality. For ordinary people, unaspiring people, everything will be imaginary or theoretical or just symbolic, with no reality in it. But for spiritual people, everything that the Gita says is reality.

The battle of Kurukshetra was real, and this battle is taking place every day deep within us between the divine forces and the undivine forces in us. Since we are seekers, ultimately the divine forces within us will gain victory. Also in the case of the Gita, the Pandavas did win the battle. If we are not seekers, the undivine forces will go on winning and keeping us under their control. But since we are seekers, we are bound to conquer our undivine, hostile, unaspiring forces. In the battlefield of life, we are bound to win because we are aspiring.

SCS 125. *If I devote myself to my family, is that contrary to the Will of God?*

Sri Chinmoy: If it is done devotedly and soulfully, then it is directly reaching the Heart of the Supreme. But it has to be soulful, and not something done out of compulsion; not outer compulsion, but inner necessity. Your family is part and parcel of your life, and to please them devotedly and soulfully is to please the divinity within them. But it has to be done with the feeling that they are your very own.

SCS 126. *When a realised soul leaves the physical body, can the soul still evolve?*

Sri Chinmoy: This planet Earth is the world of evolution. Whether we are realised or not, it is here that we evolve; it is here that we make progress. The other place, Heaven, is the resting place. Here we earn, as when we go to the office to make our salary. Then, when we go home, we do what we want. Heaven is rest, but not in the human sense. Far from it. Heaven is rest in the divine sense.

SCS 127. *What is the difference between heart, soul and spirit?*

Sri Chinmoy: There are two types of heart: the human heart and the universal heart. The human heart is a muscle. It functions while we are living, and when we die it stops functioning. The divine heart houses God the Universal Consciousness. The soul is the divine spark inside us. The soul is the link between God and us. There are two kinds of spirit. One spirit is part of the earthly existence; it is an unsatisfied soul. In the other sense, Spirit is transcendental Existence. The first kind of spirit wants to stay or remain on earth and bring messages from the vital world. This is all done in the vital world. The other Spirit is the transcendental Existence.

SCS 128. *If I want to find within my soul what the Supreme wants me to do, what should I do?*

Sri Chinmoy: Every day you have to pray most soulfully and try to go deep within and hear the message. The deeper you go, the more Light, the more sense of oneness and the more self-confidence you will achieve. Eventually you will feel that God needs you for manifestation as much as you need Him for realisation. So try to go deep within. The message is not something you get from the outside. Sow the seed of love within your heart and it will grow into a love-tree. Each time you meditate, dig deep within, as though you are sowing seeds. The seeds will germinate and then you will know and please the Supreme in His own Way. The answer is always within. There is only one question: "Who am I?" On the strength of my oneness with God, I am everything. Otherwise, I am nothing.

SCS 129. *What is the present role of humanity in the manifestation of God's Light?*

Sri Chinmoy: Humanity is composed of human beings. Here each individual has to feel the supreme necessity of the manifestation of divine Light. Once we become sincere seekers, we try consciously, devotedly and soulfully to become divine instruments of God. We become divine instruments through our constant inner cry. A child cries. He may be on the first floor while his mother is on the third floor, but she will come running to feed him. If I want to become a divine instrument, I must cry soulfully, devotedly and consciously. We cry to go up and then, when the Light descends, we smile. In order to ascend we cry soulfully; when the Light descends and divinity dawns on us, we smile soulfully.

A sincere seeker is he who has made friends with eternal time in the soul's world. If he refuses or wastes one second of God's time, manifestation is delayed. It is God's Will to manifest in and through him, and if the seeker is sincere, he will try to manifest God's Perfection. Again, we have to know there is something known as God's Hour. Before that Hour we shall do our best; we shall pray and meditate. Everything that is to be done we shall do. We shall make friends with wisdom-light, show our concern for mankind, make our life a sacrifice-flood. Everything we shall do to make ourselves ready. If we haven't yet reached the goal, we don't feel sad; we aspire. Then, when the Hour comes, we can run the fastest.

SCS 130. *What colour means "transcendence"?*

Sri Chinmoy: Usually blue has transcendence. Any colour can have transcendence, but not brown or black. Black has the inner tendency to fight, but by fighting, what is going to be transcended? Only things which want to expand have transcendence. Blue always wants to expand. From dark blue it goes to pale blue, sky blue. From a dark colour it gradually transcends, transcends until we get the feeling there is only Infinity.

SCS 131. *Sometimes when I write something or take a film, I get a certain sense of creative satisfaction. But I am not always sure whether it comes from the mental or the vital.*

Sri Chinmoy: You will be the best judge. But if you get satisfaction, that is more than enough. If you get real satisfaction, you don't have to worry about whether it is coming from the mind or the vital. Let us take the planes of consciousness as the floors of a building. Right now you do not have free access to the building. There are quite a few floors. But when you make considerable progress in the spiritual life, a day will come when you will be able to know which floor, which plane, these experiences are coming from. Whether it is the vital plane, the psychic plane, the mental plane, the over-mind, the higher mind, the intuitive mind — easily you will be able to know. But as long as you get joy, try to claim this joy. You don't have to know from which floor the experiences are coming. Continue creating. That is the right thing. As long as you claim divine satisfaction from the creation, that is sufficient. You don't have to know everything in minor detail. Just see the reality. If you want to become an expert, you have to realise God. When you are aiming at God-realisation, don't worry about the minor things that come along the way. As long as you are satisfied, it is more than enough.

scs 132. *Master, how may we increase our dedication?*

Sri Chinmoy: We can increase our own dedication by constant practice. If we dedicate ourselves to God, say, five minutes a day, then let us increase it to ten minutes, half an hour, two or three hours. But we have to do it soulfully. It is not enough just to increase the time; we have to know that soulful prayer should be our aim. Every day, when we dedicate our lives to the higher Goal, the higher cause or the divinity within us, we have to be extremely soulful. And if we are really soulful, then we increase the power of our receptivity and capacity in our life of dedication.

scs 133. *How can we increase our will-power?*

Sri Chinmoy: There are two types of will-power. One type of will-power we get from the third eye. Tremendous will-power we get if we concentrate here. The other type of will-power is from the heart. From here also we get intense will-power. Again, if we concentrate around our navel, there is a kind of will-power that we get, but that will-power is destructive; we cannot use it for a good purpose. This will-power comes from the vital world, and if we are not totally purified in our vital, especially in the lower vital, we may misuse this will-power. But if the navel centre is purified, then the will-power we get from there will be used for a divine purpose.

The will-power we have inside the heart is the soul's power. That power we can never use for a wrong purpose. The safest of the three is the will-power that comes from the heart. When you pray and meditate, try to feel that there is already some power inside, deep inside your heart, which has to be brought to the fore. Will-power from the navel centre we can use for good purposes and bad purposes, for constructive and destructive ends; but will-power from the heart can only be utilised for good. It is very fast, like a bullet. When we use the will-power from the navel centre, it will be very deep and electrifying, but in the heart's will-power there is motherly affection, concern. Tremendous will is there, but the mother's will is also full of love and compassion. Will-power from the third eye will be like the father's will-power. There will be concern, but wisdom will also be there.

The easiest way to use will-power is to take the positive approach. Use will-power to do something positive, not to keep yourself from doing something negative. If we say, "I shall not tell a lie," that is important. But if we say, "I shall tell the truth," that will-power is more effective. When we say, "I won't do it," already the negative thing has half its power just because we are thinking about it. If we repeat in our mind, "I won't be jealous," the word "jealous", the negative quality that it embodies, ruins our mind and then we do become jealous. If we say, "I won't be doubtful," the word "doubt" enters into our mind and automatically doubt comes. But if we say, "From now on, I shall be totally devoted to God. I shall be faithful. I shall be fully surrendered," these words are very good. Surrender and faith and devotion are very good. If we all the time have positive feeling, and make positive assertions, then automatically our will-power increases.

SCS 134. *I should like an elaboration on the link between music and spirituality as you see it.*

Sri Chinmoy: Music and spirituality go together. God Himself is the Supreme Musician and each human being is a note in His cosmic Game. God is playing His cosmic Role in mankind through music. Through His music, God is offering to His children the message of unity in multiplicity and also the message of multiplicity in unity. When we play soulful music, we elevate our consciousness most rapidly. Soulful music is a form of aspiration, a form of meditation. But if we play undivine music, then it destroys our aspiring consciousness. All those who are seekers of the infinite Truth will naturally play soulful music; and when they play soulful music, they have to know that they are consciously running towards their destined goal.

scs 135. *What is meditation?*

Sri Chinmoy: Meditation is the invocation of some higher force or higher reality into the lower part of our existence. The higher and lower parts are both ours, but the higher realities which we try to bring down during meditation are conscious of their oneness with God, whereas the lower realities in us are not aware of it. When we meditate, we invoke the higher realities to enter into the lower realities and make them feel that they also belong to God. So meditation is the invocation of our higher part into our lower part in order to illumine and convince the lower that it can also eventually be as good, as divine, as perfect as the higher in us, provided it receives the light that is descending from above. Then, when the lower realities are illumined properly, they will be able to claim God the same way the higher realities claim God.

scs 136. *You said we can increase our purity by repeating AUM five hundred times a day. But for me to repeat AUM five hundred times a day is very difficult. Can you advise me what to do?*

Sri Chinmoy: If it is difficult for you to do it at one stretch, then you can do it in pieces. You can do it ten times; each time you will repeat it only fifty times. You know that during the day you want to drink ten glasses of water. But if you drink all ten glasses of water at once, you are afraid it will upset your stomach; so you won't drink them all at once. But if you drink one glass now and then after an interval of an hour or two, another glass, easily you can drink ten glasses of water. So here also, instead of chanting AUM five hundred times all at once, early in the morning you can repeat it fifty times. Then, in an hour's time, you try another fifty. So each hour if you repeat AUM fifty times, each time it won't take you more than a minute or two. Since you can easily spend two minutes in an hour, you can do it. If you have a mantra or incantation of your own, you can easily do it fifty times an hour. It cannot take more than two or three minutes, and everyone can offer three minutes to God. It is not how many hours you can do it at a time that is important, but how soulfully you can do it.

When you chant AUM, please feel that life-energy, divine energy, is entering into you through your crown centre. The breath that you breathe in through the nose is very limited; but if you can imagine that there is a big hole in the top of your head and that life-energy, cosmic energy, is entering into your body through that big hole, then naturally you will be able to accelerate your purification and increase your aspiration and hunger for God, Truth, Light and Bliss.

SRI CHINMOY SPEAKS

BOOK 6

PART I

SCS 137. *New Year's Message*[§]

> The new year will be the year of destruction, frustration and satisfaction.
> The animal in us will unimaginably be destroyed.
> The human in us will unreservedly be frustrated.
> The divine in us will supremely be satisfied.
> The animal in us is self-doubt. The human in us is self-indulgence. The divine in us is self-offering.

SCS 138. *"Self-offering"*[§]

You all know what self-offering is. It is my fervent prayer to your souls that you increase your self-offering in the new year. Please try to increase the capacity of your self-offering to the Supreme. Self-offering is our constant remembrance of the Supreme. The best self-offering is to remember the Supreme all the time. Every day, early in the morning, please try to empty your inner vessel. Then I shall fill it with Light, Love and Concern.

Now I wish each of you to stand up for a second and tell what you would like to achieve next year individually or collectively for the Centre, the mission or yourself. Please tell one most significant thing that you will try to do next year — either individually or collectively. You can say that you are going to conquer a particular weakness. This is individual achievement, but your individual progress becomes the progress of the mission. If you become a better seeker, that becomes an achievement of the Centre. Or you can say you are going to do something significant for the mission. Again, if you do something for the mission, automatically it becomes your individual progress. This year you have suffered, everybody has suffered. Next year, if you can conquer your weaknesses or achieve something, then you are not going to suffer.

SCS 139. *Does this New Year's Message apply to the world at large, or primarily to your disciples?*

Sri Chinmoy: The message I gave applies to the world at large, but my disciples are affected more, whether divinely or undivinely, because they have more faith in me than the rest of the world has. Because you have faith in me, your progress can be rapid and boundless, whereas mankind's progress will be slow. Last year, I said, was the year of success and progress. Look at our achievements: more than 100,000 paintings, 16,000 paintings in one day, 843 poems in one day. These are your achievements, too — all the result of our joint aspiration. But in some of the disciples, all the success and progress was made by the undivine forces in them. These disciples are also part and parcel of my inner life. Good and bad forces all the time assail us. The bad forces we have to transform into good ones, and the good ones into better ones. This year, also, either the divine forces will win most powerfully — and they should win, must win one hundred per cent — or the undivine forces will destroy our life of aspiration.

Unfortunately, we do not pay enough attention to the new year which takes place every second in our lives. The new year is not just twelve months or 365 days. It is something that begins at every second in our life of aspiration. The new year means new hope, new promise to God and to mankind. This applies to all of mankind, but my disciples will be more inspired to do their best. If they are not inspired, then the wrong forces will plague them more and they will fall victim to doubt and self-indulgence, which are nothing short of self-destruction.

SCS 140. *Usually I think of self-doubt as the human quality and self-indulgence as the animal quality in us.*

Sri Chinmoy: You think of indulgence as an animal quality because it has to do with the physical, whereas doubt has to do with the mind. But I give more importance to the destructive capacity of the quality. If you are self-indulgent, eventually you will get tremendous pressure from your mind and body to alter your behaviour. Self-indulgence brings its own punishment, for it will tell upon your health. But when you doubt yourself, it is a slow poison. Gradually it destroys you totally. When an animal destroys, it destroys totally. It won't get satisfaction otherwise.

The animal in us is doubt because it is ready to devour us, the reality in us, at every moment. It is hiding inside the mind like a hungry wolf, and as soon as it sees something good, it tries to devour it. Anything that is good in us can be devoured by doubt. The human in us is indulgent because it has not received abundant light. The divine Light has not yet illumined the human in us fully. When it is indulgent, the after-effect of this pleasure-indulgence is immediate retribution. When the human in us goes to the wrong extreme, it suffers immediately. There is something called divine nectar, which is ecstatic Delight or Bliss, and when the human in us goes in the right direction, which means with the divine, then it will have all ecstasy and Delight.

So doubt is the animal in us because it is total destruction. If we doubt ourselves, doubt devours our divine possibility, potentiality and inevitability. It does nothing short of devour the reality in us. As long as we don't doubt the wisdom of our spiritual aspiration, no matter how many bad things we do, we will be able to leave them aside before long. But if we doubt, we will never be able to cast aside our undivine life. Once we start doubting, there is no end to it. No matter what we achieve and no matter what God gives us, we will say, "Perhaps somebody else has been given something sweeter." Then we will be disgusted and dissatisfied and we will totally give up our life of dedication.

SCS 141. *When I see myself cherishing indulgence and I start doubting my sincerity, what should I do?*

Sri Chinmoy: If you have real sincerity, sincerity will protect you. Sincerity itself has abundant power, but we underestimate the power of sincerity. If you think you are sincere to your goal when you make mistakes, at that time you are not being sincere. When sincerity is firm, you cannot make any mistake. Sincerity-power will negate temptation-power, and the result is that you will become more sincere. But when you do make a mistake, you should always try again. If you really have sincerity, your sincerity will appear a few minutes later to make you feel that the case is not totally lost. You have fallen; try to get up, walk, march, run again.

SCS 142. *What are the forms of self-indulgence that we must transform?*

Sri Chinmoy: Every form in your vital life, emotional life, mental life — everything that prevents you from going deeper and higher. Anything wrong that you do on the physical, vital or mental plane, anything that you cherish that lowers your consciousness and does not permit you to concentrate most powerfully on the Supreme is self-indulgence and must be transformed.

SCS 143. *"Fulfilling a New Year's resolution"*§

In some cases, fulfilling a New Year's resolution is a matter of an hour or three hours. If someone spends three hours doing it, then he feels that the rest of the year he can enjoy himself.

In some cases it is a matter of a second for me to grant their boon. If I say yes, then their resolution is all over; it is accomplished. It depends on the receptivity. If the person is receptive, immediately I can fulfil his wish. If he is not receptive, then I can't. The mother will run and catch the child and put food inside his mouth, but he will throw it out. Then the child will come again and say he is hungry, he is hungry. But when the mother comes with the food, he won't eat. If you have received everything that I brought down today, then I tell you, for six months you don't have to meditate.

During the New Year's meditation I really bring down. People used to meditate for years to get a little light. But my physical body brings down divine Peace, Light and Bliss. When I look at the seekers who are seated, I see literally that it is raining Light, Bliss. When the seekers feel gratitude, at that time they receive.

If we have any weakness in our life, if we feel that we have to conquer it, then we have started our journey. But if we don't take our weaknesses as something to be conquered, we will never conquer them. If we have self-doubt, we are one step ahead if we know that we have it. It is self-doubt that is not allowing my disciples to make very fast progress. Who doubts? People who remain in the mental world. Is there anybody who does not live in the mental world? If there is self-doubt, then there is self-indulgence, because self-doubt makes one feel, "I am not great, I cannot be good." And in that case, what else is there left for him but self-indulgence? If we can feel that we are good, if we can feel that we can be great, then let us feel this.

This year has been a year of achievement. At the same time, we have seen the so-called victory of the hostile forces in a few fields. But next year let us be wise; let us not make the same mistakes. Now that you know the New Year's Message, you can start right from today. You don't have to wait for the first of January.

SCS 144. *"Each year has a special message"*[§]

Let us try to satisfy the Supreme in us in His own Way cheerfully, soulfully and unconditionally. If we please Him in our own way even one time out of one hundred, we shall feel miserable because that one time we will be separated from our Source. For a sincere seeker, to remain separated from his Source even for a fleeting second is to suffer excruciating pangs. Therefore, let us try to satisfy the Supreme at every moment in His own Way.

It is a mistake to feel that each year has the same potentiality or opportunity. No, each year has a special message; although each day need not be God's choice Hour for realisation, perfection and satisfaction. If we don't do that, then this year will undoubtedly prove to be the year of destruction.

Last year was the year of success and progress. We made considerable progress in our inner and outer life. At the same time, the undivine forces also made considerable progress. If we properly cherish our sincere inner cry, this will be the year of inevitable satisfaction. If not, it will be the year of real destruction, disaster. If the divine forces within us win, then our self-doubt and self-indulgence will be destroyed, which means transformed. Self-indulgence and self-doubt will not be there; alertness and self-offering will replace them. But the divine forces will win only if we consciously and constantly side with the divine forces. Otherwise, there is every possibility that the undivine forces will destroy us. This does not mean that we will die this year, but our inner life may die. Then we will feel that we are dead souls.

So let us be very divine and careful. We have not yet been assailed by the destructive forces. If we can continue with purest aspiration in the months that are ahead of us, we shall really and truly please our Inner Pilot.

scs 145. *Receptivity and assimilation*

When you meditate, receptivity is of paramount importance. Spiritual wealth is like the sun. The sunlight is for everyone, but if you close all the windows and doors to your house, then how can the sunlight enter? When the Master meditates, he brings down from above Peace, Light and Bliss. But if you keep your heart's door closed, then what he brings down won't be able to enter.

I always tell my disciples to keep their eyes open when they meditate. Otherwise, I will be in my highest and you will be in your own world. Sometimes I am bringing down infinite Peace, Light and Bliss, but you are in the world of sleep. If your eyes are open you will see the source, where it is all coming from, in my eyes. My eyes are just pulling down Peace, Light and Bliss from above.

Also, it is good if you can fold your hands when you are in a very high state of consciousness. When you pray and meditate with folded hands, at that time your attention, concentration and everything in you become one-pointed. Your physical mind, your physical being become more devoted. Some of you are folding your hands very devotedly and soulfully all the time while you meditate. Some of you are folding your hands only some of the time, for a few minutes. I don't blame you, because your hands become tired after a while. If it is physically tiring and you are in pain, you have to know that this pain is not going to bring you satisfaction. You can pray and meditate and still go into a very high state of consciousness without folding your hands. But there are some who fold their hands soulfully almost from the beginning to the end and it does help their aspiration.

Again, many times when you fold your hands, there is no sincerity or depth in it. If you can keep your hands folded with utmost sincerity, I will be very pleased.

If you are sincere, others will be inspired when they see you with folded hands; they will see or feel something in you. But sincerity has to be the safeguard. Just because so-and-so folds his hands, or because you are worried about what he or she thinks of you, that is no reason to fold your hands. If you don't feel the necessity from within, there is no obligation. Just because you feel the Master will know if you don't fold your hands, there is no need to do so. Only if you feel your aspiration is increasing, that you are receiving more devotedly, should you fold your hands. But if you feel you are not getting anything more by folding your hands, then don't do it. But again, not out of insincerity or because others are doing it, but if you feel Guru will be very pleased if you do it, then you should fold your hands. So there is no hard and fast rule. Again, towards the end, when I am looking at each of you individually, please keep your hands folded. When you keep your hands folded with utmost sincerity, at that time, like a magnet you pull from me. Also, when you sing the Invocation, all of you without fail should fold your hands.

When I tell you to fold your hands, I am not the one who gets your devotion. Never, never! If you fold your hands, I don't get a cent of devotion. But your physical mind is convinced. The reluctant, unwilling, stubborn physical mind becomes devoted. At that time, the whole being, the entire physical being becomes devoted. Devotion is like a magnet; it pulls Light from me. If you want to increase your devotion, then always you should try to do something on the physical plane. Indians are wise. When they see a Master, they immediately touch his feet. If you touch the feet, the entire being surrenders — at least for a second. But even if you can offer surrender for a second, you can achieve something which otherwise might have taken months.

The best way to receive during meditation is through gratitude. You are offering gratitude to the Supreme because He has chosen you to be in His Boat. Because your consciousness is elevated, you are seeking what I am bringing down. Some don't even see it. Others see it, but they feel they don't need it. But you see it and you are hungry for it. Others are not hungry in spite of seeing the food; or they are hungry, but they don't want to eat the food which the Master wants to supply. In your case, you are hungry and you have recognised the fact that there is someone with food. And who created your hunger? It is not you who created it. The person with the food has created it in you. So you are grateful to the person once more. And your gratitude goes directly to the Supreme. It doesn't go to me, I am just the messenger-boy. It goes to the Source, the Supreme.

Gratitude is always more intense if it goes to the personal God, rather than to the impersonal God. When it is the impersonal form, for a fleeting second you get joy. You feel your oneness with the Vast, but the sweetness is not there. Vastness, immensity, is indispensable; but if the seeker wants to grow into sweetness and feel a sense of delight in his being, then the personal aspect is indispensable.

If you have a high meditation, you should not talk immediately afterwards. You should first try to assimilate what you have received. Once assimilation takes place, it becomes your property. Before that it may disappear. If someone says, "How are you?" he may take it away. But once you assimilate it into your system, it has become yours. Again, it may happen in meditation that while you are receiving, you are also assimilating. So when it is time to stop meditating, it is all assimilated.

In the past, when we used to hold meditations in Manhattan, right after meditation the disciples would go to a restaurant and eat. Everything they had received they gave to the restaurant. Here, at least, the disciples cook and the disciples serve, so we are able to maintain some of the spiritual light and power that we have received. We feel that the soul has received spiritual food during the meditation and now after meditation, we want to offer something to the vital and physical. That is why we have food and mix together. If you leave the Centre and immediately go to a cafeteria, it will be a different consciousness. You have to feel that here at the Centre you have real spiritual brothers and sisters with whom you can mix and exchange sweet words. You speak about innocent things concerning your daily lives or spiritual life. Just looking at one another's faces, you get joy. This very joy perhaps you may not get from your physical brothers and sisters if they don't follow the same spiritual path. So when you mix together, you get a little vital joy. This vital joy has nothing to do with the lower vital. Far from it! This joy strengthens and energises your dynamic vital quality. And in mixing together you can all feel true oneness.

scs 146. *Meditation experiences*

When you meditate, it is good to keep your eyes open. I know that when I bring down Light, it radiates in my face, and if your eyes are open, then you are bound to see something. You don't have to look at me. If you keep your eyes open, that is more than enough. What I bring down you can see not only in my face, but all around me. It is like a glow that radiates around my body. So you don't have to look at my eyes or nose to appreciate the Light. It spreads as soon as I bring it down. And that is the time for you to receive. But if you keep your eyes closed, it is very difficult for you to receive because your consciousness, instead of going up — God knows where it goes. When your eyes are open, you don't feel you are having any hallucinations.

When your eyes are closed, you may feel a certain experience was a hallucination and naturally you will reject it.

When your eyes spontaneously roll up, you are flowing in the experience itself. Once you know it is an experience, once you feel and touch the fragrance of the experience, the flower of the experience, you can continue. But in order to enter into a garden, you need some preparation. You have to know it is a garden and not a forest. Otherwise you will become afraid and reject the experience.

In the U.N. Church Centre, most of the time the meditation is most sublime, but the disciples don't receive. The people who are supposed to receive everything are fast asleep. I am concentrating on everybody in the whole world. I may look at you, but by looking at you as an individual, I see you as a representative of the Universal. So if I look at an individual, from the individual I go to the Universal, which includes everybody. Again, from the Universal, I come to an individual. When somebody is holding the Universal Consciousness, he is also holding each individual. So, from the individual we go to the Universal and vice versa. Both these things we do most of the time together.

If a particular person doesn't receive, the highest consciousness that has been brought down goes to the Universal Consciousness and it stays there if it is not utilised. The Universal Consciousness is the storehouse, but usually the customer does not want to go to the warehouse, the storehouse. Usually there is a store where many things are available. On rare occasions you go to the storehouse if what you want is not in the store. It is always advisable to get the thing in the store itself. The individual is the store. The storehouse, unfortunately, is not like an ordinary storehouse. It has all kinds of things. When you come there you get puzzled, confused. Everything is extremely beautiful to such an extent that you want to buy everything, but you don't have enough money to buy everything. Whereas when you receive something during meditation, you receive a specific thing that you like; so you take your money, which is aspiration, and you buy it. But your aspiration is right now limited. When you go to the storehouse, you see millions of things that are beautiful and you are sad. You have a very limited amount of money. You can't buy this and that because you don't have enough aspiration. When you go to the store, when you like something, immediately you buy it. You don't think about what is available at another store. Once you are satisfied, you don't go to another place. But in the storehouse of the Universal Consciousness, millions and billions of things are so beautiful that you feel sad since you have not been able to buy everything with your aspiration-power.

PART III

SCS 147. *How do you meditate?*

Sri Chinmoy: Each Master has his own way of teaching his students how to meditate. But no matter which path you follow, the first and foremost thing is to make the mind calm and quiet. If the mind is constantly roaming, if it is a victim of merciless thoughts, then the seeker will make no progress whatsoever. The mind has to be calm and quiet so that when the light descends from above, the seeker can be fully conscious of it. In his conscious observation and conscious acceptance of light, the seeker enters into profound meditation. And in his profound meditation he sees the purification, transformation and illumination of his life.

So I tell my disciples outwardly that they should offer their thoughts and ideas and the incidents of the day to the Supreme, the Inner Pilot. Then inwardly I try to bring to the fore their soul's light. When I accept a disciple, I have a free access to that individual's soul. I try to bring the soul to the fore and then the soul convinces the heart and mind to do the right thing. So it is the soul's light that actually meditates in and through the seeker. But each spiritual Master has his own way of teaching meditation.

SCS 148. *Can we feel the experience that you have offered our souls?*

Sri Chinmoy: When you enjoy experiences, it is like seeing my paintings. Four thousand I have done and they are all in my house, let us say. If you can go to my house, it is a question of whether I am willing to show you all the paintings. Then you can take your own time, a few hours, to see them. The paintings are there in my house and you can see them. But you have to know that I as an individual am the possessor. It is up to me whether I shall show you. So also in the soul's world, the soul is the possessor of all your inner experiences. It has everything recorded. If you can enter into the soul, the soul's reality, the soul can show you these experiences as I can show you the paintings in my house.

SCS 149. *If I want to do* japa, *should I chant your name, or AUM or* Supreme?

Sri Chinmoy: The best way to do *japa* is to chant the Supreme's name. But if you do not get joy from chanting *Supreme*, then chant AUM: God the Creator, God the Preserver, God the Transformer. Either use this term or *Supreme*. The seers of the holy past chanted AUM. When you chant *Supreme*, it embodies everything. Sometimes the mind operates when you chant *Supreme*, but with AUM it is a different approach. Because *Supreme* is an English word, you may not get joy from it, whereas AUM is new to you. When we do something new, we get joy.

SCS 150. *You said the Invocation is our mantra and our realisation. If I want to do* japa *by singing the Invocation, how many repetitions should I do?*

Sri Chinmoy: If you want to do it seven times, that is more than enough. But it need not be seven. If you can do it soulfully, once is more than enough. When it comes to, "I am Thy glowing Grace," if you can feel this, then all your problems will be solved. That particular line is your salvation: "I am Thy glowing Grace." If you can sing that line soulfully and feel actually that you are the Supreme's glowing Grace, then all your problems can be solved.

scs 151. *Guru, I sometimes say the* Gayatri Mantra *even though I am your disciple. Am I doing the right thing?*

Sri Chinmoy: If you are doing the *Gayatri Mantra,* it will be most effective. But if you use another mantra, which another spiritual Master gave you, and if you are following my path, then it will be a problem. The Gayatri Mantra is above all gurus. The Gayatri Mantra will not be able to create any problem, because just by repeating this mantra people have realised God. In India there are people who have realised God only by repeating the Gayatri Mantra most soulfully by the Ganges. If you repeat the Gayatri Mantra most soulfully in front of my picture, it will add to your aspiration. But if it is some other mantra, you have no idea what it will do. It may be a spiritual word, true, but your nature may not correspond to that particular aspect of God.

Each mantra represents an aspect of God. If right now you need God's Love-power more than any other power, and if you are not paying any attention to Love-power, then your progress will be very slow. But once you realise God, all the aspects of God enter into you. Very often I tell disciples who have accepted our path not to practise their old mantras, which they have gotten from other Masters or from books. It becomes a hindrance on the path. They want to be totally devoted to our path; but the forces and the energy they create by repeating those particular divine words may interfere with their spiritual progress. It is like walking along two roads at the same time; it is very dangerous. But the Gayatri Mantra is above all this. The Gayatri is the mother of all mantras. So if you practise the Gayatri, it will really add to your progress on our path; and when you follow our path, it will intensify for you the meditative power of the Gayatri Mantra.

I would be very happy if you could learn the tune that I have set to the Gayatri Mantra. If you can sing it most soulfully, it will be as good as repeating the mantra one hundred times. This is the difference between reciting and singing. While we are singing, our entire being is elevated and transported into the highest plane of consciousness. When we recite something soulfully, sometimes we may get dynamic power; sometimes we may get vital power, uncontrolled vital power. But if we sing a song soulfully, immediately psychic power comes. Psychic power comes to the fore and makes us swim in the sea of Light and Delight. If we are singing soulfully, this is more important than to be technically correct. When I sing, many times I make mistakes. But God does not care about my technique. He cares for my soulful qualities. So when you learn the Gayatri Mantra, please do not worry that you cannot sing it like a professional singer. As long as it comes from your heart, God will be really pleased.

scs 152. *When I am trying to offer gratitude while I am meditating and I am not feeling sincere, should I keep trying or should I stop?*

Sri Chinmoy: If you feel insincere, the best thing is to continue, not to give up. It is like hunger. Every day you don't feel hungry, but you do eat. If you are not properly hungry, the food may not taste good. You may not feel great joy in eating, but you do eat because it is the necessity of the body. Similarly, even if you are not feeling sincere gratitude, it is better to continue because in this way you maintain the habit. If you stop eating today and you don't feel like eating tomorrow, then you become weak. Here also, if you don't continue your offering you become weak. If you don't try to offer the little gratitude you feel today, tomorrow it will be worse, and the day after it will all go away. So the best thing is to continue. It need not be your best meditation, but continue; do not stop.

SCS 153. *To attain joy, should we always meditate the same way as we do in the Centre?*

Sri Chinmoy: The highest type of meditation is done in silence, with one objective in mind: to please God in His own Way. When you meditate, if you can feel that you are pleasing God in God's own Way, then that is the best type of meditation. Otherwise, if you start meditating in order to get joy, you will get joy; you are *bound* to get joy if that is your intention. But you may not get boundless joy, precisely because you have not pleased your Eternal Beloved, your Father and Friend, God, in His own Way. During your meditation, if God finds it is necessary to give you an experience of suffering, world-suffering, if He wants to enlarge your heart for a few seconds and offer you the world of suffering, if that is His intention but you want to have only joy from your meditation, He will grant you joy. But just because you have separated your existence from the experience He wanted to give you, you will not get the highest joy. "Let Thy Will be done." What the Saviour Christ said is absolutely the highest truth. This is the supreme message humanity can receive from the absolute Highest. Before you meditate, if you can offer the result of your meditation to the Source and say, "I wish to become Your perfect instrument so You can fulfil Yourself in and through me in Your own Way," this is the highest, absolutely the highest, type of meditation.

scs 154. *How can I become your disciple?*

Sri Chinmoy: Please come to this Centre regularly. Please feel this is your spiritual home. You have an earthly home and this is your spiritual home. Here you will get love, concern and the feeling of divine oneness. Only my request to you is to come here regularly and throw your heart and soul into our path. The Supreme in me will do the needful. I accept you wholeheartedly. You kindly come and pay your fee, which is aspiration and regularity. If you come regularly and devotedly and offer your aspiration to the Supreme, you are giving me my salary and fee.

scs 155. *If someone wants to become your disciple, is it necessary for you to see the person's picture or actually see the person in the physical?*

Sri Chinmoy: No, it is not at all necessary. When a person wants to become my disciple, it means a portion of his soul is hovering around me. When it is time for me to decide on the physical plane about this particular person, immediately his soul will appear before me. That is why when I go through the seekers' pictures, sometimes I flip through very quickly without even pausing. It is because the soul appears before me and it is not necessary for me to concentrate on the picture. Sometimes, though, it is not the soul but the mind or the vital or the heart that wants to become my disciple. Then I have to concentrate for a second or two to bring the soul forward so I can see if the person is meant to follow my path or not.

The reason I ask seekers to send in a picture is for the human aspect. If they think that I want to see their picture, then they feel that I care about them. It helps to convince their mind and makes them feel more familiar with me. But to be frank, it is not at all necessary.

scs 156. *If somebody were to be awakened in the middle of the night and hear a clear voice say, "Come to me. I am your Teacher," how would he interpret it? Is this a kind of initiation?*

Sri Chinmoy: You have to know that initiation can be accomplished in various ways. Sometimes you get a Teacher on the physical plane. Sometimes after you study books written by a spiritual figure, the inspiration you get leads you to a kind of inner initiation by a particular spiritual Teacher.

Again, God may come to you Himself to initiate you. At that time, this inner voice is the Voice of God telling you something. God may show you Light. This Light can take the form of a particular Teacher. Or through this Light God will take you to a particular Teacher.

But when someone says, "Come to me; I am your Teacher," the word "I" is very complicated at that point. If you have a spiritual Teacher who has left the body and if the Teacher feels that you need more spiritual help and guidance, he may appear to you in a vision and say, "I have come back." This "I" doesn't mean that he has physically returned to earth. It means that he sees that somebody else is capable of helping you; and he will say that he, in some other form, is ready to guide you more.

I have three or four disciples whose Guru passed away three or four years ago. Their Guru came to them during a dream or meditation and said, "I have come in another form." By "I" he meant myself. He used the term "I", but it did not mean that he had entered into me. No! The other Master realised his oneness with me and used the term "I". So we have to know what that particular "I" is and what it stands for.

SCS 157. *What is the essential quality which a seeker needs in order to enter into your path?*

Sri Chinmoy: The essential quality that a seeker needs, not only to enter into my path, but to enter into any path, is sincerity. The seeker has to ask himself whether he really needs someone to fill his life. Right now he does need someone, because he has not yet established a free access to his inner life, where he is absolutely and inseparably one with God. A day will come when the seeker will realise that his own highest, transcendental height is God Himself. But he cannot claim the Highest as his very own right now because most of the time he is swimming and drowning in a sea of ignorance. Therefore, he has to feel that there is someone who is trying to illumine him. How can he search for that someone? First of all, he has to look inside his own heart, and he has to look with sincerity. If he can feel that his whole life — body, mind, vital, heart and soul — is composed of sincerity, then he is not only meant for this path, but for all paths, and he will make the fastest progress.

There are many paths and many Masters, but each path has a special quality of its own. All paths and all Masters lead the seeker to the destined Goal, but each path has something different and original to offer. In our path, we have divine love, devotion and surrender. To acquire these divine qualities of love, devotion and surrender, we must give of ourselves; and while giving, we shall feel our oneness with the Supreme. So, if someone wants to try our path, he has to feel the necessity of realising the highest truth through divine love, devotion and surrender. If he has divine love, devotion and surrender along with the true sincerity, then he is more than qualified to follow our path.

scs 158. *I find it very difficult to be a student and your disciple at the same time. Sometimes I become very tense over my studies.*

Sri Chinmoy: Kindly feel that you are only studying to please the Supreme in you. Whatever the result, don't take it as success or failure; take it as progress. Otherwise there will always be a competitive spirit and you will be tense. But if you feel that you are studying to please God, then you won't separate your outer life from your inner life and there will be no tension. Keep in mind that you are not doing these things for name and fame. If you are doing something just to please God, then you are not responsible for the result. At that time you live in the soul; and when you are in the soul, there is no tension.

scs 159. *My friend is not a disciple. She has begun to meditate on your picture and she feels great fear.*

Sri Chinmoy: There is no fear. It is only a matter of whether she is ready to give up certain things. Fear is not of the Real, but of giving up something. Very often people say they are frightened to death of my picture. But it is not my picture; only inwardly they are unwilling to give up their old habits, their old life. They look at my picture and see an ocean of uncertainty. But it is not actually an ocean of uncertainty. They are only holding onto old habits that they are unwilling to give up. "What will happen if we give them up? Right now we know what we are and what we are doing." Her experience has to be interpreted in this way.

If one can obliterate the past and be ready to enter into the new, the ever-new, consciously and soulfully, one will see that the new also has its reality, a more fulfilling reality than the past. Then there can be no fear, never. Fear comes only when either we are unwilling to give up our old life or we are not certain of the new life. But mostly people are unconscious of the fact that they don't want to give up their old life. Because they want to become spiritual, they feel embarrassed that they are still cherishing mundane things and they don't want to admit it. Some are sincere; they say they are not going to give up drinking or drugs. They want the spiritual life, but they don't want to give up their old life. Let us only encourage them and say that the new life will definitely give them a sense of satisfaction. It may be my path or somebody else's path, but so long as spirituality is practised, they will get some satisfaction. And if it is followed sincerely and devotedly, the satisfaction will be abiding.

SCS 160. *You use the word "seeker". When does the seeker cease seeking and become a disciple?*

Sri Chinmoy: We are all seekers. Even though I have reached the height, my highest height, I am also a seeker. There is no end to our inner discovery, there is no end to our realisation. Even if you have realised the Truth, I wish to say that today's realisation is just the starting point for tomorrow's discovery.

When we want to make a distinction between seeker and disciple, we feel that a disciple is under an inner obligation to follow a specific Master, to walk along a specific path, whereas a seeker is at liberty to go to all the Masters and get a little knowledge from each. Sometimes a seeker becomes unnecessarily greedy. He feels that if he goes to ten Masters, then he will be immediately satisfied. But it is not like that. The one Master that is meant for him has the most nourishing food. A seeker becomes a disciple when he comes to realise that Yoga is only one subject and that only one teacher is necessary.

Each teacher has a specific way of bringing the disciple's soul to the fore. Each teacher has a specific way of offering meditation to the disciple's outer being. If one keeps switching from one teacher to the next, he wastes a lot of time. Also, he finds that his aspiration may decrease. When a seeker becomes a disciple, at that time he claims to have a house of his own. "This is my father, this is my mother, this is my brother, this is my sister." A disciple who follows a specific path, will say, "These are my spiritual brothers and sisters; this is our spiritual family."

scs 161. *I showed my grandmother your picture, but she is getting very old and senile, and I don't know if she received anything.*

Sri Chinmoy: Definitely she will get some benefit in the inner world if she is aware of us, of what we are doing on earth. And you can help her more by helping her remember sweet experiences that you had with her during her lifetime. If you can recollect some sweet experiences that she shared with you or that you shared with her, and while you are experiencing them again, if you can remember us and bring us into the experience itself, then her soul will receive additional joy, love and oneness that will help the soul fly into the higher worlds. It can be done in that way, by remembering a few experiences.

scs 162. *I believe very much in the emancipation of religion, but I am Roman Catholic and I just wonder about serving two Masters. Can I also become your disciple?*

Sri Chinmoy: Certainly. There is nothing wrong in your realisation, but you have to know that Christianity is a religion, whereas what we are following is not a religion. We are following a path.

There is only one Master and that Master is God, the Absolute Supreme. A spiritual Master is only an elder brother in your family. The younger brothers do not know where the Father is or they do not know all about the Father's capacities. The elder brother teaches them about the Father's capacities or he takes them to the Father. Then his role is over. So there will be no conflict if you follow my path because I am not the destination. I am just a messenger; I take you or your message to the Supreme.

If I say my Hinduism is by far the best religion and if you say your Christianity is by far the best, then we shall only quarrel and fight. But we say, "No, you stay in your religion and let me stay in mine, and let us meet together to do something great for God and for humanity." We will meet together and do the needful. Then we will go back to our respective homes, our religions, to take rest.

When we follow a path, we do not encourage any seeker to look down on religion. On the contrary, we feel that our love for religion is strengthened because we follow Yoga. Yoga means oneness with God. If we can establish our oneness with God, or if we can have a free access to God's Heart, then we can add our strength, our light, to our own religion. Right now, like a divine beggar, we are trying to grab everything from our religion. But a day will come when we get light from within, when our being is surcharged with light. At that time we will be able to offer light to religion.

SCS 163. *Before I was a disciple I was studying Tarot and the Kabbalah. Does it conflict with our path if I continue to do so?*

Sri Chinmoy: The best thing is not to do these things. You are in a different boat, one that will only encourage you to love God and devote your existence to serving God. The best thing is to try our path wholeheartedly. I don't want to say the others are wrong, but you will have more success on this path if you try it wholeheartedly.

SCS 164. *If someone is always away from the spiritual Centre, what is the best way to keep up with the other disciples?*

Sri Chinmoy: You will try to read my books and concentrate on my photograph and keep in close touch with someone in the Centre. If you can read my writings, they are like friends, like your brothers and sisters. Also, try to get some of our records and listen to our music. It is not always possible to meditate, but you can read and listen to music. In this way you will make progress. Distance cannot take away our inner connection.

SCS 165. *Since entering the spiritual life, I feel I don't want to spend time with my old friends. But I feel sad about not seeing them so often.*

Sri Chinmoy: If you have undivine friends, then right now do not mix with them. According to your standard they are undivine, but according to others' standards they are not undivine. You have entered into the spiritual life, so you know that these people are undivine. Once upon a time you were also, let us say, undivine. That is why they were your friends; that is why you mixed together. Now you have become spiritual, but they are still in that other world.

Those people have many friends of their own standard, so do not feel sorry; do not feel that just because you are giving them up, they are totally lost. No, they are perfectly happy. Perhaps they are also equally sad because they think that you are totally lost. They feel some crazy ideas have entered into your mind and they have lost you. In this world it is like that. You will unnecessarily feel sorry for them. They will unnecessarily feel sorry for you. But the world is very vast. They have their own friends. You are not indispensable in their life and they are not indispensable in your life. Only God is indispensable. So when we know where we stand and where others stand, then we do not feel at all sorry. Sometimes you have false attachment, let us say. Attachment is very bad, but sometimes it is false. You say, "What about me? I have so much to offer them." But you have nothing to offer to them. Only you have to offer whatever you have to God. During your prayer and meditation, if you can give your aspiration, love and devotion to God, then everything will be done for you. Every moment, every day, there will be many to give them joy. Do not feel you are the one person who can be of any use to them. With your own modesty and humility you will see that you will make the fastest progress; and they will also make the fastest progress if each of you follows his own path.

scs 166. *The Master's fragrance*

When a saint or a holy man meditates at the foot of a tree for a few minutes, if later you sit under the same tree and your consciousness is good, then you are bound to feel tremendous purity and joy. There is a funny Indian story. A slave wanted to sit on the king's throne. He felt that the king was enjoying everything so much and everybody was listening to him. So he went and sat on the throne. Immediately all the world's worries, anxieties, curses and other problems attacked him, because the king was a victim to all the undivine forces. But if you sit on the throne or chair of a spiritual Master, you are bound to feel something. Naturally you won't sit on his chair without taking his permission.

The spiritual Masters all the time embody Peace, Light and Bliss. If your consciousness is high, you are bound to feel these qualities. There need not be any flower inside the meditation room: If the spiritual Master meditates well, then you don't need flowers, you don't need incense, you don't need candles; but all the qualities of flowers, incense and candles you are bound to feel. When your consciousness is high, you even can smell a kind of fragrance around a spiritual Master. Consciously he may not offer this fragrance, but it is your own aspiration-power, that, like a magnet, has pulled it from him. But if your consciousness is not high, you won't feel anything.

I am a spiritual Master. When I go to a bookstore, if the owner of the bookstore is in a high consciousness, I tell you he will look at me. Even if there are forty or fifty people in the store, he will look at me. It is not because he has my books or has heard something about me. It is because of my spiritual consciousness. When I go into bookstores, immediately there is something that I offer. And some of the owners feel it.

So when our consciousness is a little high, we receive when the spiritual Masters move around. Here I am speaking and some of the seekers are receiving more than others. Why? Everybody is hearing the same thing, but receptivity is not the same for all the seekers here. The expressions, thoughts, ideas and light are distributed equally here. But according to their receptivity, some are receiving more than the rest.

SCS 167. *The power of thought*

Someone has written me a note: "Sometimes I feel that you are my enemy. Sometimes I feel that you are my friend." He speaks on behalf of all of you. When you think I don't fulfil your desires, naturally I am your enemy. He told me that sometimes he feels like leaving the Centre. I scolded him like anything. That is a thought, a very powerful thought. When you think you are going to leave me, rest assured that one step you have already taken. You take a few more and you are gone. People who have left always started with one step. When you think you have already taken one, then it is easier to take a few more. Then it becomes a one-way street and you can't come back.

So if you have the feeling, even in the mind, that you are going to leave, I wish to tell you that one thought is enough. You can create a thought-world that is so powerful that you are finished. Thought itself, I tell you, you have to take as poison. If you drink poison, you die; one part of your consciousness is affected. Spiritual Masters say one bad thought is like a whole world. One bad thought, a lower vital thought, is enough to destroy a whole day. You have to know whether you have allowed it to enter your mind or gone further and actually cherished it.

And again, one divine thought is enough to keep the whole day cheerful.

All spiritual seekers and Masters have come to the conclusion that one impure thought is enough to destroy the consciousness and one pure thought is enough to illumine the consciousness. The impure thought can be doubt, suspicion, meanness, lower vital desire, insecurity. In my eyes, doubt and suspicion are worse than insecurity. Whatever defect you have, that is your worst enemy. If one has insecurity, then that is his worst enemy. Doubt is the worst enemy of all, that is true. But if somebody does not have doubt, but he does have jealousy or insecurity, then that is enough for him: that is the worst enemy for him. And when one keeps getting the same disease over and over, it becomes very powerful.

When someone's enemies are already inside him, he has to fight very hard. If the thought is already inside, it is difficult. But it is not impossible. No, never! Throw it out. Once you throw it out, remain always alert so it doesn't enter into you again. It usually strikes the forehead; the thought-world comes just here and strikes the forehead. Feel that you are a fort and somebody is coming and striking you. Just don't allow the wrong thought to enter. But you not only allow it to enter, you usually go further: you cherish it.

SCS 168. *Sincerity and obedience*

Sincerity is of paramount importance in the spiritual life. But sincerity has no value unless it is lasting. Suppose you have done something wrong and you tell me. Your sincerity I appreciate. But then you have to take the next step, and that is called obedience: You will not do it a second time. Otherwise, if you keep doing the same thing wrong over and over again, and each time you say, "I have done it," then your sincerity becomes a mockery. You blow your own horn, "I am sincere," but what kind of sincerity is it?

If you do something wrong, you should tell. But then you have to listen to me and not do it again. Insincere people I can do nothing with. I am helpless. Sincere people give me the opportunity to take them one step forward. But then obedience is necessary. If obedience is there, each second you can jump, jump. Hundreds and hundreds of things you will do to make the fastest progress.

If you are a little afraid of me, then tomorrow you will have a little obedience. Until you have established your total identification with me, a little fear is good — not destructive fear, but constructive fear: "I will see Guru's sad face if I disobey him." This kind of fear is good. If you feel you are all love and concern for my mission, then my sad face will be much more powerful than my angry face.

scs 169. *Cherishing something unconsciously*

Many times I see that the disciples are cherishing something unconsciously. If you are cherishing something unconsciously, your mind is not aware of it. But there comes a time when you get the results of what you are cherishing in the form of pleasure. At that time you are not disgusted; you like it. You are getting a kind of joy or pleasure or comfort, but you do not know why you are getting it. It is not that consciously you have done something. But still you are getting the after-effect. The consciousness of the action you are getting. The fruit is at your disposal, and you are eating the fruit voraciously, like a greedy person. When you get the result, you could say, "This very thing I did not want. Although it looks delicious, I know the after-effect is poisonous." But what do you do? You become clever. You eat it consciously, and then you simply say you are not to blame. You say you didn't do it; you didn't want the fruit but somebody brought it. "It came to me. I am not responsible." But you are eating it consciously.

The first time that you eat, immediately you say, "I am not the culprit. Somebody has stolen something and left it in my room." Nobody says that you stole it, but the very fact that you are eating it or you are using it, is enough for you to be the culprit in the inner world. Consciously you have not gone to anybody's house to steal. But when you enjoy it, you open up the door. And the next time somebody throws this thing in front of you, you are again ready to utilise it. It is something alluring, something tempting. Unconsciously you are cherishing the thing when it is placed before you.

Somebody places doubt inside your mind. You cherish it, and doubt itself becomes wisdom for you. When you have doubt, immediately you feel it is not doubt; it is a proud wisdom. Everywhere in the world, when people doubt, they feel they are very wise. They feel that other people are credulous. They say, "Look at their stupidity!" Just because they themselves don't believe in something, they feel they are wise. This is their self-imposed wisdom, that they are cherishing. But if we live the spiritual life, we go deep within and we try to believe. God is for believers. When we believe in something twenty times, if we are deceived, God will forgive us. If I believe you, and again and again you deceive me, God will forgive me. But if I doubt and you doubt and the world doubts without rhyme or reason, then no progress will ever be made. If you doubt, you have to feel that you are not entering into the game. If you believe, you *are* entering into the game, although you may lose if somebody has deceived you. But if you doubt, you don't even enter into the game. And then what can you do?

Enter into the game and see; maybe somebody will teach you how to play. Enter into the game and see your fate. If it is good, naturally you will win in the battlefield of life. If it is bad, then feel that you have Eternity at your disposal. But if you don't play at all, if you stay off on the sidelines, thinking all the time that the game is too dangerous, then how are you going to win in the battlefield of life? At that time there is no game, no fun. "If I play football, something will happen to my foot. If I throw shotput once, my fingers may be ruined." There is no end to fear. Life is always illumination. It comes only to those who are brave, who face life, not to those who are afraid of life.

SCS 170. *Telling secrets to the Master*

It is the worst possible crime to keep secrets from the Master. If someone keeps a secret from me, he is digging his own grave. I am not happy to know about your secrets. Knowing your secrets means only knowing your weaknesses. If I become happy to know your weaknesses, then I am the worst possible fool. But if you tell me outwardly, I get the opportunity to work on you before the situation becomes too powerful, before the weakness becomes an incurable disease. When you tell me a secret, it means you are unburdening your life.

Especially if you are having vital or emotional problems, you should tell the Master. If you do, a big heavy load, a dead load, you throw off from your shoulders. And now you can breathe in properly. You should have implicit faith in the Master. If you feel the Master will expose you, tell twenty individuals, then the best thing is to keep it a secret and suffer to the end. But you have to know that a secret is weakness. Keep a secret and you are only cherishing a weakness of life. And if you try to hide your personal and emotional problems, you have to know that these things are absolutely weaknesses, nothing else.

Even if the Master tells others about your weaknesses, he is not doing it out of malicious pleasure. He is doing it because he feels that they can learn from your mistakes. Whatever weaknesses you have, they also have. You have entered into the spiritual life to transform your weaknesses into strength and perfect your life. So please don't cherish these things. Just throw them into the Master. Then, what he does with them is his business. You have to have that kind of faith in the Master.

SCS 137–144. *(p. 195)* On the New Year's Message for 1976 — commentaries, questions and answers.

SCS 137. *(p. 195)* At his annual public meditation for the New Year in December 1975, Sri Chinmoy offered the following message about the upcoming year of 1976.

SCS 138. *(p. 195)* After reading out the New Year's Message at a meeting of his New York Centre on 18 December 1975, Sri Chinmoy made these remarks.

SCS 143. *(p. 199)* After holding his Public Meditation for the New Year on 19 December 1975, Sri Chinmoy offered these remarks during an informal gathering with some of his disciples.

SCS 144. *(p. 200)* After holding a New Year's Eve Meditation in Puerto Rico, Sri Chinmoy commented further on his previously offered New Year's Message.

SRI CHINMOY SPEAKS

BOOK 7

PART I

SCS 171. *Hope human and faith divine*

Human hope has no strength in it. It is only wishful thinking. But faith, divine faith, is the result or fruit of the inner message that we are getting constantly from within. When we have faith in ourselves or faith in God, immediately we get a message and that message has life in it. With human hope, a messenger brings a message but there is no life in it. Or the messenger may bring all kinds of destructive news, disheartening news. But when faith becomes the messenger, at that time we see life in the message. Faith, inner faith, is always fruitful, for it carries the message of light, and light is the life of the inner world. So the best thing is to remain in the domain of faith, to make yourself feel that you are nothing but constant faith in God. In that way you are bound to have divine hope. In faith, divine hope looms large. Divine hope is like a dream which comes at the end of the night, bearing the promise that soon the day will dawn. From dream, reality comes into existence. But when it is human hope, ninety-nine times out of a hundred the dream will not materialise, because there is no life in it.

When we have human hope, the thing we are hoping for may or may not materialise. But if it is divine hope, then we feel that somebody is telling us to sow the seed and promising us that tomorrow the seed will germinate, the day after tomorrow it will grow into a plant, and a few months or a few years later it will give us a bumper crop. When we have divine hope, there is a kind of inner feeling that something will come out of something, and we are inspired to work for the result. If we do this today, tomorrow we will get something, and the day after tomorrow something else will happen, it is like climbing up a ladder a few rungs at a time. We are going step by step. We are creating something and because of our creation we will get a certain result. If we are not satisfied, we will create more and more and then finally we will be really satisfied. This is divine hope.

Let us say that today I have the hope that tomorrow I will become a very sincere seeker. If it is human hope, it is just wishful thinking. When tomorrow dawns, I will be fast asleep, and I will hope that the following day I will be a very sincere seeker. But if it is divine hope, then immediately there will be action. I will do something. I will feel that just thinking or hoping that I will become something is not enough. I will enter into the field of activity. So, in this case, hope is the mother of merit. If we enter into activity, then we get the fulfilment of our hope or the transformation of our hope into reality.

Human hope is like human desire. When today's hope is fulfilled, tomorrow there will be something else we are hoping for. There is no end to it. But when divine hope is fulfilled, we do not ask for something else, for a higher reality. Inside the hope itself, reality expands itself and becomes large, larger and largest.

SCS 172. *Fatigue and meditation*

When it is time for meditation, you may say you went to bed at three o'clock, so you are not able to get up. But who asked you to go to bed at three o'clock? You will say it was unavoidable; you had to do something most important. While you are up late doing that important thing, you can make yourself feel that at five o'clock there will also be something unavoidable to do, that at five o'clock you will have to get up to meditate. If the ordinary thing that you did late at night was so important that you could not avoid it, then I wish to say your meditation is infinitely more important; nothing can be more important than meditation.

Sometimes our fatigue is real; sometimes it is all mental. Even if we sleep for ten hours, sometimes we feel extremely tired. There are many young boys and girls, as well as adults, who sleep much more than they actually need to. It is their mind that makes them feel they are very tired and exhausted, that they have not eaten or slept enough. The mind is so clever. It will make us feel that if we can sleep for only five minutes more, then we will have the whole world. If we are supposed to get up at five o'clock, the mind will tell us that if we can have one minute more, then we will be all right. Then, if we give that one minute to the body, immediately the body will say it is not enough.

So sometimes we are really fatigued, and sometimes it is only the mind that is making us feel that we are tired. We may not be tired at all, but the mind does not want us to meditate. Sometimes, even if we take only two or three hours' rest, the mind is kind enough to allow us to meditate, for the monkey in the mind is taking rest and is not going to bother us. Although our physical body has taken only two hours' rest, at that time we are very, very refreshed. So I wish to tell you that sometimes the body does not need six hours or seven hours of sleep; sometimes it needs only five hours, or less.

While you are driving to meditation, if you are tired and exhausted or you don't feel alert, then you should not drive. At that time your wife or husband or your friend has to drive. Or you can try to invoke divine Power. When you come to the Centre, if you feel you are not doing good meditation but are falling asleep, then try to invoke the Power aspect of the Supreme. At that time, do not invoke Peace or Light. Try to bring forward divine Power from within or bring down the Power from above. Immediately, in five minutes' time, you will feel energised. If you invoke dynamic power within yourself, you will see that your whole body will become energised with divine

Power. This divine Power will make you feel that your body is burning with fever, although you are not actually running a temperature.

Also, please make your car more divine, more spiritual, with flowers and pictures and so forth. That is to say, make it like a shrine so that while you are driving, you feel that you are in my presence, in God's Presence. When you leave your home, start your meditation right inside your car. And if you can make your car spiritual, then the drive will be the continuation of your meditation. But you have to know what kind of meditation you should have. Please do not go into a high, deep meditation. No, the best thing is at that time to do *japa* or to sing spiritual songs. If you do *japa*, then automatically you will see a kind of energy inside yourself. But if you want to invoke sublime peace, then it will create problems.

SCS 173. *Overcoming anger and hatred*

If you are a victim of anger and hatred, try to feel sincerely that these forces are your enemies. This is not imagination; it is reality. They *are* your enemies. Think of anger as a thief. When you are angry with someone, feel that your anger is a human being who has come to steal your inner wealth, your peace and poise. If you are wise, you will never allow a thief to enter into you. Think of hatred, too, as a human being who has come to rob you of your love, which is also your inner wealth.

When you know that somebody is a thief, immediately you take precautions against him. So you have to feel that your anger is a veritable thief, your hatred is a veritable thief. If you regard your anger and hatred in this way, then naturally you will always stand at the door to your existence and keep your door properly guarded. If you see a thief there, you won't allow him to enter.

You have to feel and realise that there is no peace, no joy, no satisfaction in the anger or hatred that you are offering and becoming. When you offer anger, you have to feel that you have become anger. When you offer hatred, feel that you yourself have become hatred. The moment you want to give something to someone, feel that you yourself are that thing, and that is why you are in a position to give it. When you offer something to someone, you expect to get some inner satisfaction. But if you give anger to someone, he does not appreciate it and you also do not get any satisfaction from it. Now, when you give something to someone and he does not appreciate it, then you feel miserable. If your gift is not going to be well appreciated, then you don't give it. You try to give something else, which will please the person.

Do the same with hatred. Feel that it is something you are offering to someone which he does not care for. Since he does not care for it, you will have to offer him other wealth. What he will care for is your love and your peace of mind. If you offer these qualities or some other divine qualities, naturally they will be appreciated. Let us think of a customer and a shopkeeper. If the customer does not want to buy what we are offering him, then we offer him some other thing which will please him.

scs 174. *What is your path all about?*

Sri Chinmoy: We aspire to become good, to do good and to serve mankind. Inside each individual there is the living presence of God. Our path is the path of love, devotion and surrender. We love God in a divine way, and we pray to God to guide us so that we can please Him in His own Way. We serve God so that we can become a good instrument, a perfect instrument of His. And we surrender to His Will, soulfully and devotedly, out of a genuine feeling of oneness with Him. So divine love, divine devotion, which is in the form of service, and divine surrender are the cornerstones of my philosophy.

scs 175. *How can I tell if you are meant to be my Guru?*

Sri Chinmoy: When a seeker feels that he is ready to go to a spiritual Master, he wants to notice a few things inside the Master: Peace, Light and Bliss. When he sees these qualities inside the Master and feels joy when he is with the Master and confidence that the Master can take him to the Golden Shore, then he tells the Master that he is ready and anxious to be his disciple. The Master will either accept him or he will say that he is sorry, but he cannot accept the seeker as a disciple. If he cannot accept the seeker, it is because he feels the seeker will make better progress, faster progress, if he belongs to somebody else. When the Master does not accept someone, it doesn't mean that the seeker is useless. No, he has aspiration, but the Master feels that if he studies under the guidance of some other spiritual Master, he will make much better progress.

I accept most of the seekers who come to me and want to accept me as their Master. Only on rare occasions do I not accept someone. But again, some people come to me and do not see anything in me, so they go away. They are doing absolutely the right thing. But in your case, if you feel confidence in me, if you feel inner joy and peace when you look at me, if you feel that this is your spiritual home, if you feel that these are your spiritual brothers and sisters and you are a member of this family, then you should accept our path as your own.

SCS 176. *Sometimes you speak of the human and the divine or the Supreme in yourself and distinguish between these two aspects. Should a disciple try to distinguish the two or regard them as one and feel that everything is divine?*

Sri Chinmoy: The disciples will never be able to know whether I am acting like a human being or a more divine being. Even when I am angry, when I am shouting and screaming and insulting, it is only the human in me expressing my divine Authority on the strength of my oneness with the Supreme. When I am furious, you may think it is absolutely the animal consciousness that you are seeing. But, it is not the animal. Believe me, it is the divine Authority in me that is trying to perfect you in that particular way. If you do something wrong, sometimes it is useless for me to smile and ask you not to do it again. I see the destructive force dancing inside you. If I see something destructive inside you, I have to come with a hydrogen bomb. If you do not see superior power there, you will not try to surrender to that power.

scs 177. *Is it possible for a disciple to learn from a more advanced seeker?*

Sri Chinmoy: It is not at all necessary for the seeker to go through all the mistakes in order to arrive at truth. If a disciple is a beginner and he happens to meet an advanced seeker — a really advanced seeker, and not just one who has been a disciple for many years — then the advanced seeker will be able to advise him from his own experience. It is like a mother and child. The mother tells the child not to touch fire because she knows from her own experience that touching fire causes pain. The mother had previously touched fire and burned her finger; so she is speaking from experience. If the child thinks that the mother is lying, then he doesn't profit from his mother's experiences and he will touch the fire with his own finger. So, just as the child comes to the mother and asks what happened when she touched fire, so a beginner in the spiritual life seeks advice from an advanced seeker. The beginner recognises the advanced seeker because he sees that the advanced seeker is leading a divine, disciplined life; the advanced seeker is an example for him.

If a beginner takes the advice of an advanced seeker, it will take him less time to reach the goal, just as the good advice a parent gives his children, to speak the truth and to meditate, will help them grow up to be better adults. An advanced seeker is like the father or elder brother of those who have just entered into the spiritual life. If the beginner has to do everything on his own and go through all the sad experiences, then he will waste a lot of time and reach the goal much later.

SCS 178. *In your life do you show negativity?*

Sri Chinmoy: I try to offer the positive side of life — no negativity. From Light we move to more Light, abundant Light, then infinite Light. We try to walk along the sunlit path. Reality is both positive and negative, but we do not take both sides of reality. We feel that from lesser Light we go to higher, more abundant Light, infinite Light. So we always approach the Truth with a positive inner conviction.

SCS 179. *When I am not meditating and when I have no work to do, there are vacant spaces which I can no longer fill with things I used to do before I became a disciple. I don't know what to do with this spare time.*

Sri Chinmoy: You feel that you don't want to kill time. So instead, in your spare time try to create. Try to be creative in any field. Each one has some capacity. You can draw or you can sing spiritual songs. You can write a poem or an article or compose a song. Or you can call a friend and speak of spiritual things. When you speak of spiritual things, it is also a form of creation. There are many ways to create. Creation does not necessarily mean to write a poem; it can also mean to talk to someone. If you talk to a spiritual friend, if that person needs inspiration, your talk itself is creating something deep inside that person and that person is creating something deep inside you.

scs 180. *What is the best way to think of you and the Supreme during the day?*

Sri Chinmoy: The best way is through gratitude, soulful gratitude. Offer gratitude: that is the best way, the only way. The second you offer gratitude in your thoughts and in your feelings, your oneness will be perfect. If you offer gratitude, you will understand more; your mental vision, psychic vision, everything will become perfect. Gratitude, gratitude, gratitude is the only answer. Try to grow the gratitude-flower inside your heart and watch it blossom petal by petal. As it blossoms it is spreading its beauty and fragrance.

scs 181. *The love that we have for you, Master, is it the same love that we should have for Mother Kali?*

Sri Chinmoy: The love that you have for me will be the same love that you have for Mother Kali and also for the Supreme, because we are all one. In the highest world I am totally one with Mother Kali; I am totally one with the Supreme. Here also in the field of manifestation, the Supreme is consciously operating in me and through me. I am His conscious representative for my disciples, for those who have accepted me as their Guru — but not for others. For you I am certainly His conscious representative. I am your Master, so you will have the same deep love for me that you have for Mother Kali. The Divine Mother represents infinite Power and infinite Compassion together. I am most fond of Her and She is most fond of me. If you show Her the deepest love, I will feel it. If you show the Supreme the deepest love, I will feel it. Similarly, when you show your deepest love to me, the Supreme automatically gets it. So there is no difference between your Guru and Mother Kali and the Supreme in your life of aspiration and realisation. A dearest disciple should feel that in his Guru lies the real divinity, realisation and manifestation of the Supreme. You cannot separate the Guru from Mother Kali or from the Supreme. In the inner world, we three are one, absolutely one. This is the thing that each disciple has to feel and realise.

scs 182. *Why is it that whenever you ask for questions my mind suddenly goes blank?*

Sri Chinmoy: When we meditate, we bring down Peace, Light and Bliss from above. At that time, the questioning mind is illumined. In illumination there are no questions. A question comes from darkness, when the mind is not illumined. This room has light. Everything is right in front of our noses. So, you don't have to ask me every ten minutes where this flower is. Similarly, when we pray and meditate, we receive Light and everything is clear to us.

scs 183. *What is the significance of children in the fulfilment of your mission?*

Sri Chinmoy: Children have more love for me. They listen to me. If I ask a child to do something for me, he just runs. If I ask a grown-up person, he will take ten hours. A child means obedience. If obedience is there, then God-realisation is not a far cry. Children run the fastest, unless they are spoilt by their parents. Children don't have the doubting mind. They don't use the mind; they use the heart. If I ask them to do something, immediately they will do it and they will get tremendous joy from doing it. But if I ask a grown-up, sometimes he will listen with reluctance. After waiting to prove his independence, then he will do it. But children don't do that. They won't say, "Why has he asked me? I will not really get any benefit."

A child means God's Dream, God's Vision. That is why I ask everybody to act like a four-year-old child. If everybody can become a four-year-old child, then all problems will be solved. But we act like we are fifty or sixty years old. That is why we are suffering so much. It is the child-quality in us that will fulfil our mission. We have a mission that will be fulfilled only by the child in us, the divine child. The child is all eagerness; he always wants something new, new, new. The importance of the child in our life, in our mission, is incalculable.

SCS 184. *Sometimes we want to do something for the mission which requires money, but we have difficulty getting it. Is it the Will of the Supreme or the hostile forces?*

Sri Chinmoy: The Will of the Supreme already has been given us. Where there is a will, there is a way. When the Supreme has given us a good idea, a good thought, rest assured that He has also given us the capacity to discover money-power. The only thing is that we do not work hard. We work hard in some aspects, in some fields, and in others we don't work hard. In order to get money it is necessary to make an effort, to work soulfully and devotedly. We don't do it. When we have an idea that requires money, if money does not come automatically, then we are apt to feel it is not the Will of the Supreme. No! If we have the aspiration to do something for the Supreme, do you think He has not given us the capacity to get the money? We have to pay some attention to getting money-power. But for that we don't spend the time.

SCS 185. *How can we maintain our inner cry and intensity when we are not around you?*

Sri Chinmoy: It entirely depends on your inner connection. In your office, you may speak to your colleagues for hours, but your heart is not in them. And needless to say, their heart is not inside you. But your heart is inside your Guru, inside God. Your heart lies inside your Guru, but your outer being is with your colleagues, doing office work and other things. You have already established a very, very close, intimate connection with my soul and the Heart of the Supreme. All my good disciples have done it. You also have done it. The mistake that you make and that others make is that you have a fixed goal. During your meditation, if you come to a certain standard, you feel that you have reached your goal. Or in the inner life, if you get a little joy, immediately you get a complacent feeling. You always want to remain with yesterday's laurels. Yesterday you got a little joy and now you are crying to get that same little joy. But how do you know that the Supreme wants you to have that little joy? Perhaps He wants you to go farther, higher and deeper.

On the physical plane, our goals are very limited. When I started to lose weight, my goal was 165 pounds. Then came 160. And then it went on to 156 and 154 and 146. Now I can come back to 140 or say 130, maximum. But then I can go no further. The physical goal is always limited. But in the spiritual world, the goal is not fixed; there is no end in the inner world. Here we are dealing with Infinity, Eternity and Immortality.

Where is Infinity, where is Eternity, where is Immortality on the physical plane? Immortality is in consciousness. If you have developed an immortal consciousness, then you are serving the Supreme all over the world. Physically, all spiritual Masters leave the body. But the consciousness that they have brought down to the world is immortal. The Christ brought down the immortal Consciousness; Sri Krishna did it; all the spiritual Masters did it. It is the Consciousness that they offered that remains immortal.

Every day you have to feel that you have a higher goal. Do not think that yesterday's goal is the final goal in your life. In your case, you always try to reach a particular goal. If you can run fifty metres, you feel that your part is over. If you cannot run fifty metres one day because of a stomach upset, you feel miserable. But God does not want you to be satisfied with fifty metres. He wants you to make your goal fifty-one, fifty-two, fifty-three, fifty-four metres. When you have a higher goal, automatically your aspiration increases. Otherwise, if you are using the same capacity to aim at the same goal, you are not going very far. Then your inner life becomes monotonous. But if you feel that your goal is always transcending itself, then you have constant joy in your achievement and progress.

Do not think about success. Success ends your journey, but progress never ends. When you have a fixed goal and you reach it, this is your success. Then you are finished; after that you are not doing anything. But if you don't have a fixed goal, you are going on constantly. Then you are making progress, and in continuous progress your goal is constantly going beyond, beyond, beyond. At that time, you get the greatest satisfaction. So do not be satisfied with success; success ends the journey. Progress continues. And each time you make progress, it is a real form of success. Every day when you meditate, feel you will dive still deeper, fly still higher. Then you will be able to maintain a conscious feeling for the Supreme, for your Guru, because you are marching towards an eternal goal.

scs 186. *When we feel joy in working for you, can we take this as pleasing you in your own way?*

Sri Chinmoy: If you get joy from doing something, that doesn't mean you are pleasing me in my own way. Suppose I have not asked you outwardly to bring me a flower, but you try to please me by bringing me one. If I have asked you inwardly to bring me a flower and you have brought me the flower and are now getting joy, then you have the right to say that you are pleasing me in my own way. But very often you do a thing in your own way and at the same time you do it soulfully. At that time you deserve joy and you do get joy from within. That joy is really quite good, but it cannot be as divine or as fulfilling as the joy you would get from pleasing me in my own way.

Very often you may not or cannot know what my wish is. Then what can you do? Remain silent? No. You try to do the right thing, whatever comes from your heart and soul. This may not be what I wanted, but as long as it comes from the heart and the soul, your devotion will come to me. From your good action you will definitely get joy. I cannot say it is not divine joy, but there are degrees of divine joy, let us say. When we speak of conditional and unconditional surrender, we say it is better to make conditional surrender than not to make surrender at all. In the beginning, let us try to do something conditionally. Then gradually, gradually we make progress and do the thing unconditionally.

scs 187. *Could you talk about the meaning of the line in the Invocation, "My breath, Thy Vision's kite"?*

Sri Chinmoy: Breath is the eternal life. So "my breath" means eternal life. God's ultimate, ever-transcending Dream or Vision is the eternal life. Kite symbolises divine glory. The kite is flying, which represents the revelation or manifestation of the divine glory.

God existed as the Absolute unmanifested. He wanted to manifest Himself constantly on earth so He brought down the eternal life. We see only the earthly life, which lasts sixty, seventy or eighty years; but here on earth there is also the message of eternal life. That eternal life we can find inside the heart, for that is where the soul is. The Supreme's highest Wisdom can be seen and felt only here. The physical heart is one thing; the spiritual heart is something else. The physical heart is a tiny muscle, but the spiritual heart embodies God's entire universe. When we think of our spiritual heart, we feel it is something very tiny in comparison to the universe. But this is wrong. When we concentrate on the divine heart and feel the real divine heart, we will see that inside it the entire universe exists, that the heart is vaster than the universe itself. Although the spiritual heart is eternal, at times it does not feel that it is; so the Supreme first enters into the heart and makes the heart feel that it is eternal, that it has eternal life. Then the Supreme starts His journey. He is going to transcend at every moment His own transcendental Reality; and while He is transcending, He is proclaiming or revealing or manifesting His divine Glory in the form of a kite.

SCS 188. *Sometimes I am very happy and joyous, like at circus practice when I am having fun with my brothers and sisters, but I don't feel that I am soulfully happy because I am not consciously thinking of you.*

Sri Chinmoy: If you are happy but you are not thinking of me, that doesn't mean your happiness is not soulful. Not at all! You don't have to think of your Guru or of God for twenty-four hours a day. If you get spontaneous joy from within, feel that your soul has come to the fore and that the joy is coming from your soul. At that time you do not need to think of the Supreme in His personal aspect. If you don't think of me while you are getting joy, that does not mean that this joy is coming from the lower vital or emotional vital. No, your joy can be very sweet, very pure and very divine provided that your soul is giving you the joy. While you are walking along the street or while you are singing, at that time you may not even think of the Supreme. But if you are singing soulfully, where do you think this soulful song comes from? It comes from the soul. Wherever the soul is, rest assured that your divine existence is there also. So you don't have to bring forward the form in order to convince your mind that you are thinking of me or God. It is not necessary at all. If you feel a kind of joy in which there is no demand, a joy that is not going to grab or possess anything, a joy that gives you a sense of self-offering, then that is divine joy, which is very good.

SCS 189. *It seems in my office that the people most receptive to you are the people I have the most conflicts with.*

Sri Chinmoy: If they are receptive, you will have no conflict. Receptivity comes just because the vessel is empty inside and the door of the heart is wide open. If the heart-door is wide open, how can there be confusion? Only if the door is blocked from inside will there be a conflict. If the door is wide open and the vessel is empty and waiting for the divine light to fill it, then how can that person have confusion? It is self-contradictory.

Ten people from your office have come to our meditation. Some received most powerfully; I felt real spirituality was there. When you bring a new disciple, you should be so happy. If a new disciple comes, it means he will come and pull on your side. Against you is ignorance. If you are really clever, if you want to win against ignorance, then you will bring some strong people to fight on your side in the battlefield of life. On one side is light; on one side is ignorance. Still you have much weakness and imperfection; you can't conquer it. But if somebody who is very strong takes your side, then easily you can win. When you bring someone, you have to know that he also needs you. His strength is not enough. Your strength is not enough. But his strength and your strength combined then become so powerful. Each time you bring a solid disciple, feel that that person is going to help you in your own life and you are going to help him. You don't lose anything. When you bring a new seeker, don't feel that your glory will go away and that the new disciple will be better than you in every way. Far from it. When a new disciple comes, it is to your advantage.

PART III

SCS 190. *How can I know if I am executing God's Will or I am fulfilling my own ego?*

Sri Chinmoy: When you fulfil the demands of the ego, immediately you will feel that you are the lord of the world or that you are going to become the lord of the world. You are bloated with pride, and you feel that the rest of the world is at your feet. Once a desire of yours is fulfilled, immediately you feel, "Oh, my desire is fulfilled; I have become something, and the rest of the world will not achieve what I have." Always there will be a feeling of superiority when the ego is fulfilled.

But when you execute the Will of God, the question of superiority or inferiority does not arise. At that time you feel only your oneness. You feel that God has appointed you or that God has accepted you as His chosen instrument, and that He is acting in and through you. No matter what you achieve — even if it is something very grand, extraordinary, unusual — you will not have any sense of personal pride. On the contrary, you will feel extremely grateful to God that He has chosen you to fulfil Himself in and through you. There is no pride; there is only a feeling of expansion. To execute God's Will means to achieve something. When you achieve something, you feel an expansion of your consciousness. But when you fulfil the demands of your ego, at that time you feel totally separated from the rest of the world. You are the lord and the rest of creation is at your feet. So, in this way you can know the difference between the two.

SCS 191. *What is the difference between desire and aspiration?*

Sri Chinmoy: There are two significant polarities in our human life: one is desire, the other is aspiration. Desire is something that brings us the message of the unfulfilling and unfulfilled finite, and aspiration is something that brings us the message of the fulfilling and eternally fulfilled Infinite. Desire always binds. But unfortunately, before we can bind someone, we find that we ourselves are already bound. Before we can possess something, we are already possessed by that very thing. Before we succeed in possessing someone as our slave, we discover that we have become a perfect slave to that particular person. But the nature of aspiration is to expand and to offer oneness at every moment. When we use our aspiration, from a river we become a sea, and from a sea we become an ocean. We are constantly expanding our consciousness with aspiration, but with desire constantly we are binding ourselves.

When we aspire, we feel that there is something called Infinity, Eternity and Immortality. These are not mental hallucinations but something very real. The seekers who soulfully pray and meditate feel in the inmost recesses of their hearts the presence of Infinity, Eternity and Immortality. Of course, these must be highly developed seekers, seekers who have sincerely practised spiritual life and have meditated for a number of years.

What today we call desire, tomorrow that very thing we will call frustration. And the day after tomorrow we will call that thing destruction. From the divine point of view, anything that does not help us in our spiritual progress is nothing short of destruction.

We have to know that there is no end to our desires. Before we fulfil today's desire, we have ten new desires. It is endless. No matter how many desires we fulfil, we will never be able to put an end to our desires. We will feel that the one desire we have fulfilled has not given us enough satisfaction. Perhaps if we fulfil another desire, then we will get real satisfaction. So we try. But each time we fulfil a desire, we discover that we have become worse beggars. Before we fulfilled our desire, we were beggars because we wanted something which we did not have. Now, after we have fulfilled our desire, we feel that our sense of insufficiency has increased rather than decreased. But when we fulfil our aspiration even to a small extent, we feel a sense of completeness.

SCS 192. *What is the significance of marriage, and can a married couple follow spirituality together?*

Sri Chinmoy: If it is God's Will, then in this oneness of two souls you double your capacity. If you feel that God wants you to get married, then feel you can have four arms, four eyes, four legs, two hearts, double speed, double strength, everything double. If it is not the Will of God, but only your vital that is demanding marriage, then it will only be a burden for you on your spiritual journey. So I tell people that if it is not the Will of God, they should go alone. That is the best thing. But if it is the Will of God, then try marriage and continue on the spiritual path together. A good marriage sanctioned by God is God's veritable Smile; a bad marriage instigated by the vital is a veritable curse.

Two married people can work together in the spiritual life provided they have the same goal. If both of them have sincerely accepted the spiritual life, then their common Goal is God. But if the husband follows one spiritual Master and the wife follows the path of another spiritual Master, a problem is likely to arise. The husband will say that his Master is by far the best, and the wife will immediately say, "No, my Master is by far the best." But if both of them are wise enough, then each will say,

"You follow your path and let me follow my path. After all, the Ultimate Goal is the same. Although there are two different inner roads for us, the destination will always remain the same." If the seekers are really sincere, if they are really dedicated to their Masters, both Masters can widen the husband's and wife's mental vista and heart's capacity so that each can follow his own path without any conflict.

But it becomes infinitely easier if both husband and wife follow the same path. Then there is no competition, there is no subtle rivalry. Then the two are really together. Both of them are climbing together, walking together, running together. But in case it is not possible, if the wife has a special preference for one spiritual Master and the husband has a special preference for another spiritual Master, then let them follow their respective spiritual paths, while they always bear in mind that each one is doing the right thing. In that way there cannot be any conflict between the two.

SCS 193. *Why has God made women so insecure that it is hard for them to become detached?*

Sri Chinmoy: First of all, God has not made women insecure. God has not made men impure. God has given men and women freedom. Let us call it limited freedom, since they have not re-alised the Ultimate Truth. When God gives us limited freedom, we have to try to use it for a divine purpose. We have to use this freedom so it will increase its own capacity and grow in us on a larger scale. Suppose somebody has given you a dollar and told you to use it in your own way. Now, you can use it to make two dollars, three dollars and so on, or you can just go and squander it. Our inner wealth is our inner freedom. We can either try to increase it, or we can misuse it.

Insecurity has grown in women because women have used their limited freedom to feel that there is no one to care for them. If women can use their freedom to nourish and cherish the feeling that there is Someone who calls them His own, and that is God, the Inner Pilot, then their insecurity will vanish. Even in the ordinary world when you know that a few friends or even one individual thinks of you and cares for you, you don't feel insecure. But now that you have entered into the spiritual life, you know that there is Someone who has infinite Power, who has infinite Patience, infinite Light, who cares for you and is more than eager to call you His very own. So where is insecurity?

How can we know that a particular thing or person cares for us? We can know only through our self-surrender. As long as the tiny drop retains its individuality and personality, it will remain insecure; the waves and surges of the mighty ocean will scare it to death. But when the tiny drop consciously enters into the ocean, it becomes the ocean. Then it is not afraid of anything.

You are the finite. If you want to become one with the Infinite, you have to surrender your existence to the Infinite. Offer your human life to the spiritual life, which is the Breath of the Divine. Always try to be aware of your Source, which is eternal Peace, Light and Bliss. If your Source is something divine, eternal and infinite, then how can you feel insecure? If you feel that your human parents are your only parents, you will feel helpless. If you feel that your source is darkness, ignorance, bondage, limitation and imperfection, then you will always feel insecure. But if you can become consciously and constantly aware that you are of the Source and from the Source, if you can convince your mind that you came from Light and Delight and your ultimate Goal is to go back to Light and Delight, then you will have no sense of insecurity.

A person is insecure when he feels that darkness is all around him, not when he sees that there is light. At night you are frightened because there is no light. If there is light all around you, you are not afraid. So in the spiritual life we must always be aware of the fact that the Being who is inside us and around us is all Light. And this Being is immortal. Whatever is real, divinely real, is immortal. My hand is real, but my hand is not divinely real. It will die when I die. But my soul is divinely real, so it will remain eternally. The Reality inside us is divine and eternal. If we have something eternal within us to think of us and care for us, how can we feel insecure?

So in the spiritual life we always have to be aware of the Reality. This Reality exists for you, for me, for everybody. If we want to utilise the Reality, first we have to be conscious of the Reality and then we have to grow into the Reality. Right now, millions and billions of people all over the world have only a vague idea of God. For them God is not a living reality; God is just an idea. They are not atheists; they feel that God exists. But they have nothing to do with Him. For them, God is like the Empire State Building. It is there, but they don't have anything to do with it, they don't need it. Every day the sun is there, but if you want to keep your window shades shut, or if you don't want to watch the sun, you have that much freedom.

SCS194. *What is the best way to deal with dry periods in one's sadhana? That is, how does one maintain aspiration and good feelings while one experiences a dryness in his meditation?*

Sri Chinmoy: When you feel dryness in your meditation, you can easily mix with a friend who is not going through that experience. Take dryness as darkness. When you think of dryness, think of going through the Queens Midtown Tunnel. You know that there will be some light at the end because you have been through the Midtown Tunnel many, many times before. After you enter, for some time you know that there may be no light; but if you have patience you know that you will see light.

In the spiritual life no one is experiencing dryness for the first time. This dryness is fairly common. There are very few seekers who have not gone through it. Some spiritual Masters of the highest order went through dry periods for six or eight months, and sometimes for as long as two years. During a four-year period some of them went through dry periods five or six times.

This dryness can be avoided by doing only one thing: shedding tears of gratitude. You may say that you are not getting any joy, any satisfaction, anything, from your meditation, so why should you offer gratitude? But you have to offer gratitude just because you are trying to meditate. Who is asking or compelling you to try? Somebody deep within you. The Supreme is asking you to meditate despite the fact that you are going through a dry period. So if you can offer your gratitude, soulful gratitude, tearful gratitude, to the Supreme, the dry period will pass very quickly. Think of the Midtown Tunnel. You can easily cover the distance when the time comes. You know it is only a matter of time. For a short time you will remain in darkness, and then it is bound to end. But if you want to run the fastest, then gratitude is the only answer.

SCS 195. *What is the quickest way to silence the doubting mind?*

Sri Chinmoy: One of the quickest ways to silence the doubting mind is to feel that the mind itself is just a full wastepaper basket, something that you have to empty. Another way to silence the mind is to consciously say, "I have no mind, I have no mind, I have no mind. I have only the heart, I have only the heart." That way also you can silence the mind.

But in your case, it is not the mind that is the problem. Your vital does not aspire; that is where the problem starts. Your difficulty is that your vital is tamasic, lethargic, and so your brilliant mind is very restless, doubtful and destructive. In your case, your doubt comes from the unaspiring vital. The vital means determination, or will-power, let us say. You are lacking in will-power in your dynamic vital. If you or anybody else is wanting in will-power in the vital, automatically you will suffer from the doubting mind. If the vital is strong, dynamic, then the heart is able to give peace, love, light and bliss from the soul. Then the heart and the vital can and will go together, and with the soul's help, automatically they can silence the mind. In your case especially, make the vital very dynamic, progressive, and do not allow it to remain lethargic.

SCS 196. *Right now I am under psychoanalysis, but it seems that the more I become involved in spirituality, the harder it is for me to talk about it with my analyst. I feel that the things offered by analysis are not really what I want. And yet my analyst, who seems to be a very strong person, is reluctant to let me go free. And I don't know if there is any reconciliation between myself and him.*

Sri Chinmoy: If a friend of yours comes and gives you a most delicious mango, will you immediately eat the mango, or will you ask him a million questions: where he got it and how much it cost and whether it was imported from somewhere or grown in the States? In the spiritual life there are two types of seekers. One type will just see the reality and immediately try to become the reality. The other type will immediately begin to question the reality, examine the reality and doubt the reality. Suppose both of these seekers are hungry and you take them into a mango garden where there are many mangoes and many flowers. The first kind of seeker will say, "All right, since there are many mangoes, I will now be able to eat." But the second type of seeker will say, "I wonder how many mangoes are here," and he will start counting the mangoes. Then he will want to know which one is the best, so he will start examining all the mangoes to decide which one he should take. While he is wasting his time, the first seeker will take a mango and just eat it, and he will be satisfied. If we use the mind, we will always try to analyse everything and we will never experience the reality. But if we use the heart, we will immediately take the thing we want. And at that time, even if we eat only one mango, we will get the delight of eating all the mangoes, because the heart means oneness. From hundreds of mangoes we take out one individual mango, but when we eat it with our psychic consciousness, we get the delight, or the wealth, let us say, of all the mangoes. But if we start counting all the mangoes, perhaps we will never begin eating. Or after a while, we may get disgusted and say, "Who wants to know?" But during the time we spend in counting, we lose our spontaneous inner joy.

In the spiritual life we always have to go from the heart to the mind, not from the mind to the heart. If you really want to follow the spiritual life, if you use the heart as your instrument, then nothing can be more simple. But if you use the mind, you will feel that nothing is as difficult and complicated as spirituality. In the spiritual life there should be no hesitation, no calculation. In the spiritual life we only give and become, see and become, offer ourselves and become. It is so easy if we use the heart. But if we use the mind, there will always be calculation and hesitation.

So if you really want to follow the spiritual life, you have to remain in the heart. Then this mental psychoanalysis will be of no avail. Already you are feeling that it does not offer what you want. If you have a sincere question, there is only one place to get the best possible answer and that is from the soul. The soul will answer you through the heart. Otherwise, no matter what kind of answer you get, either from your own mind or from your psychoanalyst, your mind will doubt and contradict it. It will contradict all suggestions and all advice, and then a few seconds later, your mind will doubt its own discovery. But when the heart gives you an answer, it is a permanent reality.

SCS 197. *Does one use a mantra during meditation?*

Sri Chinmoy: If you have received a mantra from a spiritual Master, then that particular Master is in a position to tell you how to practise it. Usually the mantra is practised when the mind is calm, quiet, vacant, tranquil. If the mind is agitated or disturbed or restless, at that time it is not advisable to practise your mantra. And if you are in a position to dive deep within, or enter into the highest meditation, then there is no necessity for practising a mantra during the time of your meditation. But if you cannot enter into your deep meditation, then it is advisable to practise the mantra. Here the mantra is the path-finder. The mantra paves the way for a better and deeper meditation. But again, at times it is possible for someone to practise his own mantra to heighten and deepen his meditation, his meditative power.

SCS 198. *In the last couple of days, when I have been meditating I have been getting a desire not to breathe. Can you tell me what this is?*

Sri Chinmoy: It is not a desire in your case. It is a most soulful, most powerful, most devoted experience. Breathing in and out in the normal way is not necessary when you concentrate on your heart. It is most pure and divine. This is a very good experience.

SCS 199. *Sometimes when I am meditating I see different visual perceptions, shaking and concentric circles that seem to rise up. What are they?*

Sri Chinmoy: In these visions you are entering into different worlds. These worlds are real; they are not mental hallucinations. What you need most in your life is purification of the body, mind and vital. These visions will not go away. Out of His infinite Bounty, God has shown you these worlds. But if you want real access to these worlds, you have to become pure. Especially in your outer life you have to become purity incarnate if you want to receive these visions.

SCS 200. *How many incarnations do souls usually have to go through before they realise God?*

Sri Chinmoy: Each time the soul comes into the physical, into the earth-consciousness, it is an incarnation. Now, the soul has to go through the mineral life, plant life, animal life, human life. It takes many thousands of years to reach the human stage. Then, once the soul enters human incarnation, it takes many thousands of years before it realises God. But again, some are tired soldiers. They want to take rest for a long time between incarnations, so they make slow progress. Others come back again and again, but make no progress at all. Like bad students, they keep repeating the same course.

scs 201. *Why is it that limited light has to expand into the unlimited Light?*

Sri Chinmoy: It is our human nature to expand, to have more and more. This is one reason. But there is another reason. The infinite Light which created the world is a real magnet. It gives us limited, very limited, freedom in the beginning and then it pulls and pulls our limited light. It pulls this light for its own divine satisfaction. The infinite Light is not satisfied unless and until this little streak of light enters into the infinite Light and becomes part and parcel of that Light. The Infinite will continue to pull the finite until finally the finite will be merged into the Infinite. Then the Infinite will experience itself through the finite and the finite will experience itself through the Infinite.

scs 202. *What is the relationship between morality and the spiritual life?*

Sri Chinmoy: In order to realise the Highest, if the Highest demands that your moral attitudes change, that they be transformed, then naturally you have to surrender to the Highest. You have to know where you stand. If the Master tells you to do something that you think concerns your morality, you have to feel that he would never ask you to go back to your animal life just to please him. He is asking you to do something which has been commanded by the Highest Supreme and the Supreme knows His cosmic Play better than anybody else. If the Supreme wants you to do something, then if you are sincere you have to do it. Your life has to be totally dedicated and surrendered to only one person — and that is the Inner Pilot, the Supreme.

Morality is extremely necessary when we are transcending our animal life. But once we are trying to divinise our nature, we try to make our conscious surrender to God's Will. If we want to swim in the sea of God's Light, then morality and immorality have to be surrendered to God's higher Truth, which is beyond both morality and immorality.

SCS 203. *Why do so many Americans, especially young men and women, seem to be turning to Indian spiritual leaders when there are so many churches and religions in the West?*

Sri Chinmoy: The answer is very simple. Americans find in the Indian spiritual Masters what they actually want and need. What is it that they do not get from the churches that they do get from Indian spiritual Masters? They get joy, they get love and they get something else: inner purpose. They learn the importance they should give to inner divinity. The spiritual Masters make them feel that they also can be perfect channels of spiritual light and truth.

Spiritual Masters are offering Yoga to Americans, but Yoga is not a new religion. Yoga is only a path. If one follows the path of a spiritual Master, he does not have to leave his own religion. The young men and women of America are not making a mistake by following Indian spiritual Masters. It is just that they have discovered a path and they feel that by following this path they will get what they want sooner.

SCS 204. *Guru, what is the difference between a soul leaving the body when someone dies and our souls coming to you to give you a message?*

Sri Chinmoy: When your soul comes to me, it only takes a minute to communicate a message to me and receive a reply. In one second in soul's time one can accomplish what would take two or three hours in earth time. When your soul comes to me, there is no question but that it will go back. But in the case when someone has practically died, the soul is only watching;

it is deciding. Like a bird it has left the cage, and it is thinking, "Shall I go back?" Sometimes the bird comes out of the cage and is reluctant to return. However, some birds are determined to come back. It is a matter of aspiration and manifestation.

SCS 205. *Can a soul transmit messages without leaving the body?*

Sri Chinmoy: Yes, certainly. Just as you send messages by telephone, the soul also is able to transmit messages without actually leaving your body.

SCS 206. *Is it better to go deep within or to go high during meditation?*

Sri Chinmoy: Both are effective. If you are going deep within, that is a good experience; and if you feel that something is going high, higher, highest and expanding at the same time, then I wish to say that this experience is also sublime. You do not have to give all importance to one and pay no attention to the other. Let your inner being take care of it. If it happens for five minutes that you feel you are going deep within and the next five minutes you feel that you are going up and expanding, let it be like that. It can even happen simultaneously, for, as a matter of fact, both experiences are the same thing. It is like a springboard. The higher you jump, the deeper you go. They happen simultaneously, only our conscious mind takes them separately.

How does one best move the consciousness from the mind to the heart?

Sri Chinmoy: The best way to move one's consciousness from the head to the heart is to think most of the time, all the time, of the heart. If you think of the living room, then your consciousness is in the living room and not in the kitchen. The consciousness that is in the heart has to be brought to the fore, where it illumines and expands. The consciousness that is in the mind we shall not negate. We shall only illumine it. The friend that we most need to help us is the heart. If we stay with the mind, we only hesitate; the mind stands in our way. The mind is unconsciousness. If we can bring our friend, the heart, always with us, it becomes easy to illumine the mind. The presence of the soul is living in the heart, so the consciousness that we need is in the heart. We must put all our attention on the heart and not on the mind in order to make the fastest progress.

SCS 208. *Is it difficult for intellectual people to have faith?*

Sri Chinmoy: Some people spontaneously have faith, even if their minds are not intellectually developed. When the mind is predominant, it becomes very difficult to have faith in God. That is because the mind has thousands of doors to enter into God's Palace, whereas the heart has only one door, and that door is faith; so it just goes right in. But the mind tries to find out which of its doors is best. It goes to one door and then it thinks that the next door might be better. In this way the mind is constantly hesitating and going from here to there. So it takes some time before it actually enters into God's Palace.

Again, if a person has tremendous aspiration, even if he is intellectually developed, his heart may also be developed and he may have faith. Sometimes the conviction or perception of the heart will enter into the mind and be reflected in the mind. Then the mind will have faith along with the heart.

Why does our evolution go so slowly that it takes us many hundreds of incarnations to realise God? Why do we have to go through so much struggle?

Sri Chinmoy: God can give you realisation overnight, but if you have worked for something consciously, you will be more satisfied when you get it. Then you will appreciate it. There is a poem about how the farmer ploughs the field, then sows the seed. Then he puts on manure as fertiliser and he waters the field. Everything he does. Afterwards the farmer asks, "Mother Earth, how is it that it takes so many months to get the bumper crop? How is it that everything did not germinate in one day from all that I did?" The poet answers for Mother Earth, "If I do everything for you, then your joy will be next to nothing."

Again, thousands of years is nothing when compared with God's eternal Time. When you live in the soul, a few incarnations is next to nothing and you will not feel that your evolution is going slowly. But if you live in the body, even one minute will torture you.

scs 210. *I have been getting sensations in the middle of my forehead and I wanted to know if this indicates that my third eye is opening?*

Sri Chinmoy: Right now it does not indicate that the third eye is opening. It is an opening of the inner sight. In your case, it is an indication that you are simplifying your life. In the beginning there is a necessary rejection of things in life which are not necessary to make progress. There will come a time when your third eye will open, as it did in my case and in the case of other

Masters. But right now what you are experiencing means that you are removing unnecessary things in your life.

SCS 211. *While I am working, is it possible to meditate?*

Sri Chinmoy: If you feel that your work is meditation itself, there is nothing wrong with this. Meditation does not mean that you have to be closeted away from the world. Meditation means conscious oneness with the Inner Pilot. If you can meditate while you are serving your customers, and if you can feel your own oneness with the Supreme inside your customers, that is true meditation. If you feel that your consciousness is high and you are able to maintain a kind of peace of mind while working, then I assure you that this is a true form of meditation. Meditation is not only sitting for half an hour before a shrine. But if you feel that it is not possible for you to enter into your highest and deepest consciousness while you are working with people, then it is necessary for you also to meditate in private.

SCS 212. *Should I meditate on my navel to purify the vital?*

Sri Chinmoy: The navel is the centre of the vital. Anything that is near the navel we can purify only through the soul's light. The soul's light is inside the heart. So when you meditate, do not meditate on the navel itself. Meditate on the heart first, the heart chakra, and bring the light forward. Light is everywhere, God is everywhere; but when we think of God inside the heart, we are more convinced. God is inside my thumb, inside my nose, everywhere. My body is full of God. But I know that there is a special place where I can feel His Presence most powerfully, and that is inside my heart. So first you have to meditate on the heart, on light. God means light. From here you can descend to the navel. And try always to meditate consciously. If you see that your consciousness has fallen while you are meditating and it is not on the heart chakra but on the navel chakra, then you have to bring it up. Always lift the consciousness up, lift it up.

SRI CHINMOY SPEAKS

BOOK 8

SCS 213. *Where is the best place to meditate for purity?*

Sri Chinmoy: The best place is the heart. Meditate on the heart, and the moment you feel the presence of light there, bring it into your navel. Then try to imagine that the navel centre, the vital, is constantly circling or that there is a disk that is rotating all around it. It is going on, going on. And while it is turning, you just repeat, "Supreme, Purity, Supreme, Purity." Or you can say, "Purity is the Supreme, the Supreme is Purity." That is even easier.

SCS 214. *Is there a different technique for women and men when it comes to meditating on purity?*

Sri Chinmoy: When the girls meditate for purity, they should try for a few seconds to breathe through the left nostril. If you are breathing through the left nostril, it will be easier for you to bring purity into the system. And if the boys can try to breathe in through the right nostril, then it becomes easier for them to develop purity. The left nostril is for softness, for the soft and sweet inner flow; the right nostril is for power and dynamism. So, in this way the girls can establish purity and the boys can establish purity. But the exercise that I just mentioned applies both to men and women.

SCS 215. *How can we keep our mind pure?*

Sri Chinmoy: You can keep your mind pure by feeling constantly that you do not have a mind at all; you have only the flower-heart of a child. If somebody asks you, "What is in your mind?" you will say simply, "I don't have the mind. I have only the heart of a child." You don't have to keep your mind pure if you don't have a mind. In that way you can solve your problem immediately.

SCS 216. *How can we constantly be aware of the fact that we have no mind?*

Sri Chinmoy: Ask yourself what the mind has done to you. It has brought you only impurity, insecurity, limitation and so forth. If you feel that your mind has something nice to give you, then you will find it difficult to give up your identification with the mind. But if you feel that the mind has only given you suffering, suffering in every form, then it is easy not to care for the mind. This is the physical mind that I am referring to, the mind that is inside the physical and subjected to the physical. There is also something called the illumined mind. This you will get only when the heart is fully awakened and transformed by the light of the soul.

If somebody has given you a tremendous, sharp slap, then you will have nothing to do with that person. When you can consciously and continuously refuse to have anything to do with someone, that person does not exist for you. If somebody constantly bothers you, and if you can constantly say that you have nothing to do with him, nothing to do with him, nothing to do with him, then automatically that person drops out of your life. So when you say, "I have nothing to do with the mind, nothing to do with the mind," then the mind will say, "All right, if you will have nothing to do with me, then I also won't care for you."

SCS 217. *If there is much impurity in your environment at work or school, how can you best keep it out of you?*

Sri Chinmoy: If you feel there is much impurity where you work, if your colleagues are full of impurity, then you have to be more careful, more conscious. You have to concentrate more on purity in your life. There is no other way.

If it is easy, then you don't have to concentrate much on purity. But if you find your relatives, neighbours and colleagues are all full of impurity, then you have to pray more and meditate more. At every moment you have to feel that there is a battle going on between your aspiration and the pull of the material world. So you have to be more careful, more vigilant, more spiritual.

But you have to do it with utmost sincerity and humility. If you have the feeling that you are far more spiritual or more pure than others around you, then it will be all self-deception. You may think that you have more spirituality, more purity, but who knows? Someone else may have more spirituality and humility and other divine qualities. Just because you follow a spiritual path doesn't mean that you are more pure. There are many people who are not conscious of spirituality, but they are more pure than you are. Unfortunately, many people who enter into the spiritual life look down on others, thinking, "They don't go to any spiritual centre, they don't go to church, they don't pray, they don't have purity." That is a wrong idea that most of you cherish. It is a false aggrandisement of the ego. Undoubtedly there are many people who are far, far inferior to you in terms of purity; but again, I see all around many people who have more purity than most of you have. So just because you follow the spiritual life, it does not mean that you have more purity.

If we are really pure, then we don't see impurity in others. If we are not pure, then we see mud in everybody. A child is pure, so he does not see mud in anybody. Only when he becomes fourteen or fifteen or so does he see mud everywhere, because at that time he has his own mind. If his mind is all impure, naturally he sees impurity everywhere. Real spiritual people are not at all disturbed by impurity, because they have tremendous inner light and that light saves them. So in your case, I wish to say, do not seek impurity in others; only think of your own inner light. The more you can bring to the fore your inner light, either the impurity you see will be illumined or you will not see impurity at all.

SCS 218. *When we are attacked by impure thoughts and feelings, or when they arise in us, how can we invoke purity?*

Sri Chinmoy: When you are assailed by impure, undivine thoughts, just think of somebody who is infinitely more powerful than these thoughts, and that is the Supreme. The Supreme is omniscient and omnipotent. It is His world. So you have to feel that He is infinitely more powerful than the invasion, than the attack you have just received from the hostile forces.

Unfortunately, when a seeker is attacked by an undivine force, immediately he feels that this undivine force is omnipotent. He does not think at that time that the Supreme is the only omnipotent Power on earth. You have to have more faith in God's Reality, God's Concern, God's Compassion for you.

If you have real faith in God's Concern and Compassion, then the attack of the hostile forces will lose all its strength. So think in a positive way that there is someone who is infinitely more powerful than the force of undivine thoughts, and that His infinite Power will immediately come to your rescue, provided you are sincere and soulful at the time of your desperate need.

scs 219. *Guru, it seems that purity in the waking state is under our control, while purity in the sleeping or dreaming state is out of our control.*

Sri Chinmoy: It is absolutely true. In the waking state you have more control over purity, whereas when you are sleeping, you have practically no control. But here it is a matter of practice. When you want to become a good singer, you practise, practise, practise. Then you can carry all the tunes perfectly, right from the beginning to the end. But if you don't practise, you are bound to make mistakes. If you want to become a good dancer, you have to practise all the steps day in and day out; otherwise, you can't be perfect.

So here also, during the waking state if you can meditate on purity most soulfully and if you can be perfect in your inner life during the day, then I assure you that you will also be perfect even while you are fast asleep. Even in a dream, if you have purity you will be most satisfied, because dream represents reality and reality represents dream. What is dreamed is a reality in some other world, a higher world or a lower world. But since you are in the physical world, if you can have some mastery over the subject that you are dealing with, then I assure you that in the dream world also you will have mastery over your impurity.

In the morning when we meditate and become established in purity, what is the best way to keep it for the rest of the day?

Sri Chinmoy: If you can establish some purity on the strength of your very best meditation, then the best way to preserve it is to feel that you have a most fragrant rose inside your heart. From time to time, try to feel its presence and smell its fragrance and see its beauty. If you have a flower right in front of you, sometimes with your eye you appreciate the beauty, sometimes inwardly with your heart you feel your oneness with its beauty. So if you can see, smell and feel the flower, then you are bound to feel throughout the day the purity that you achieved during your best meditation early in the morning.

SCS 221. *How can you cultivate purity with your family and the people you love and make sure it is not attachment to something else?*

Sri Chinmoy: You have to know that one thing is detachment and another thing is devotedness. If you want to offer your devoted qualities to God, to the Supreme, inside your wife and children, then you can never, never be attached to anybody. You are loving your wife not because she is your wife, not because she is beautiful, not because she is full of love and affection for you or because she does everything for you. No, these are only the outer manifestations of somebody within her. God is inside her; that is why she has all these good qualities. From now on, if you show your devoted gratitude to God, then you will never be attached to your wife or to your children. If you are devoted to God within your wife and children, then automatically you will establish purity with them.

But if you only appreciate the good qualities that you are seeing in your wife and in your children, then you will be tempted. The good qualities will only make you forget your own reality and their reality. If you want to go to God through the good qualities of your family, it will not be possible. You have to know that it is from the root that you get the plant and the tree. The root is God. There will be no flower, no leaf, no plant, nothing if there is no root inside. The root comes first; then only will you have the plant and leaves and tree. So if you go to the root of the good qualities, then you will never be lost, because the root is absolutely divine. But when beautiful leaves and flowers appear, then the evil forces of the eyes may enter into the picture. When somebody looks at beauty, he can destroy it with his impurity. Nobody is able to look at the root, but with your eyes you will be able to see the flowers, the leaves, the branches. At that time it is up to you whether you will love them with joy and divine feelings or curse them with ego and jealousy and pride. But the best thing is to try always to go only to the root inside your nearest and dearest ones. Then there can be no attachment, because the root is all love. Impurity is attachment, but devotedness is all-love, and all-love is all-purity.

SCS 222. *How can we obtain purity?*

Sri Chinmoy: You can obtain purity by constantly feeling that you are a three-year-old child, or you can feel that you are a flower, a beautiful flower with fragrance, and nothing else. In this way you can obtain purity.

SCS 223. *Once we achieve purity, how may we maintain it?*

Sri Chinmoy: Once you achieve purity, you can maintain it only through constant remembrance of God's Compassion and through constant offering of gratitude to the Supreme. Only then will your purity stay with you permanently.

SCS 224. *Is purity different for a married person?*

Sri Chinmoy: When it comes to purity, there is no difference between a married person, a spinster and a bachelor. The only thing is, one has to know what real purity is. Real purity is detachment from the things we consider undivine and devotedness to the things we call divine. It is attachment and detachment that determine purity. If you are totally attached to the gross physical, then you can have no purity whether you are married or unmarried. And again, a married man can be totally detached from the gross physical, the lower vital, just as a bachelor can be. So there is no hard and fast rule that purity will be greater or less for a married or an unmarried person. It is a matter of how soulfully each individual deals with his own life, whether he is devoted to God's Will or attached to his own desires.

SCS 225. *Guru, at this time of our development, should purity be in our mind most of the time?*

Sri Chinmoy: Purity and impurity are not only in the physical; they can be in the mind, in the vital, anywhere. So purity has to be established in the heart, in the mind, in the vital, in the physical. When an undivine thought comes, first it comes to the mind and then it goes to the vital. If you can establish purity in the mind, then impurity will not come down to the vital through the mind. Similarly, if you start cherishing a good thought in the mind, then naturally the vital will have purity, because what the mind has it will bring to the vital. Again, what the vital has will come to the physical. If you have divine thoughts in the mind, automatically impurity diminishes in the vital and physical. One moment we think, the next moment we act. It is not that we act first and then think. First we think, then we act. So if the thinking process is divine, then naturally there cannot be undivine action.

SCS 226. *What is the role of purity?*

Sri Chinmoy: The role of purity is to make us feel that we are totally one, inseparably one, with God as Consciousness and God as Light. What is Consciousness? Consciousness is the expansion of Light. What is Light? Light is the solidity of the Breath of Consciousness. If we ever want to establish God-

Consciousness and God-Light, then we need no other thing save and except purity. Purity is as important as breathing in our spiritual life. Without inhaling and exhaling we cannot live on earth. Purity is like that. It is as important as our living breath.

scs 227. *Can a person who is pure spread his purity to someone who is less pure?*

Sri Chinmoy: Certainly he can. Even if he does not consciously spread it, his very presence will spread it. It is like this. The very nature of a flower is to spread fragrance. The flower may not talk to you or tell you, "Look, I have purity! I am now giving it to you; so take it, take it!" No. But the very fact that you are near a flower will immediately bring you purity. If you have something, if you have a dollar, you can give it to me. Again, if you don't give it to me, then I don't get it. It is up to you. But when it is a matter of purity, even if you don't want to give it, already it is spreading, because purity is something divine. Anything that is undivine will bind you and try to bind others. But anything that is divine you cannot bind; you cannot hold it back. It is free, absolutely free; it is immortal, eternal. When you have purity, automatically it will flow. If you stand in front of a saint, your whole being becomes purified. His very presence makes you pure. A spiritual Master, by his very presence, spreads Peace, Light and Bliss. When he comes in front of you, he spreads it. He can't hold it. Always it is going out.

scs 228. *Can we purify our daily actions?*

Sri Chinmoy: Certainly, that is what we are aiming at. If we cannot purify our daily actions, then how are we going to make progress? Again, if we make progress, then only can we purify our life. These things go together. If I become good, only then will I become a good instrument of God. And if I become a chosen instrument of God, then only will I become really divine. They go together. It is like meditation in action. If I meditate well, then only can I think of loving God and serving God. Again, if I serve God devotedly and unconditionally, then only can I think of meditating at my highest. As action and meditation go together, so purity in our day-to-day life and spiritual progress must go together; they are complementary. If we don't have purity, we cannot make very fast progress. And any progress that we do make does not remain permanently if we do not have purity. So, purity is of paramount importance in the spiritual life.

scs 229. *A child has no idea of impurity or purity. How do you achieve that kind of purity?*

Sri Chinmoy: Two months ago you accepted our spiritual path. So feel that you are two months old. The day that you accepted the spiritual life was the real birth for you, and not twenty-four or twenty-five years ago when you came into the world. The moment you accept the spiritual life becomes your spiritual birth, a new birth for you, a new incarnation. So if you are only two months old, how can impurity enter into you? It is impossible. Always think how many years you have been with us and how many years you will be with us. Today you are two months old. Now you have to feel that you are an eternal child of God; but consciously you have to feel that you are an eternal child of God. As a child you will always remain pure. So if you say, "I will remain an eternal child of the Supreme," then naturally you will maintain all purity.

SCS 230. *How can I purify my mind of its pride and its unwillingness to bow to my soul?*

Sri Chinmoy: Your mind has pride because you feel you have achieved something that others have not achieved. Suppose you think that you are more beautiful than your sister and your mind is giving you pride. Immediately be sincere to yourself. You will say, "True, I may be more beautiful than my sister, but there are thousands of other people on earth who are more beautiful than I." So your mind will get a slap. Or suppose your mind tells you, "I have much more knowledge than my sister; my sister is an idiot and I know so much." At that time just think of how many people there are on earth who have more wisdom than you. Just think of some of the professors at Yale or Harvard and make a comparison. Immediately your sincerity will make you feel that those professors are like intellectual giants. You can be proud only when you keep everyone under your feet. You can be proud just because you know a little more than your sister or you are a little more beautiful than your sister. But you must compare yourself with someone who is infinitely superior to you. Then pride will go. Pride will see that it is nowhere. Since it is comparison that is creating pride in you, you have to make comparisons with somebody that will make you humble. So when comparison makes you proud, haughty, at that time, make a comparison with somebody else who will immediately make you humble.

SCS 231. *Can the ego ever have purity?*

Sri Chinmoy: Human ego can never have purity. Human ego wants only to bind: "I, my, mine — *my* brother, *my* father, *my* friend." I am limited as an individual and I think of my mother and my father as limited. So when I am limited, and the world that I am claiming as my own is limited, how can there be purity? Purity is something vast, infinite, whereas ego makes us think that we are meant only for one or two or three. First ego says that we are meant only for ourselves; there is no world around us. We are our only world. Then ego says, "My mother, my father, my brother." This is our only world. But this is all impurity. When we are binding someone or bound by someone, it is all ignorance. It is ignorance that makes us feel that only our immediate family is ours and that the rest of the world has nothing to do with us and we have nothing to do with them. Ignorance and impurity go together, whereas wisdom and purity go together. So this ego can never be pure.

But there is also another type of ego. We call it ego, but it is not actually ego. It is our identification, our feeling of oneness, with God. "I am God's chosen daughter, so how can I do this? How can I tell a lie! How can I deceive someone! How can I waste my time! It is beneath my dignity. God-realisation is my birthright." That kind of feeling is called total identification with God, but the mind may tell us that it is a form of ego. If we had to make a choice between calling ourselves God's son and Satan's son, would we not say that we are God's son? Here also we have to make a choice between our little ego that says we belong to mother, father, brother, sister, and the big ego that says we belong to the Infinite, the Eternal, the Immortal. So that type of ego, which is actually our sense of identification with the Absolute, is most welcome. When we talk about ego, it is the little one, the little "I". But when we think of God, immediately

"I" goes away and becomes "we". I represent "I", you represent "I", he represents "I", everybody represents himself or herself. But God does not represent Himself, because God has created everyone; so God has to become "we".

We always have to feel that the human ego is all impure. But the divine feeling of oneness — "I am God's child, God-realisation is my birthright, God-manifestation is my birthright" — is divine ego, and that is extremely good.

SCS 232. *I find it difficult to distinguish between the small "I" and the divine self. Are there any meditations or practices I can use?*

Sri Chinmoy: The small "I" will always make you feel that you are most important — not the Centre, not the Mission, not your spiritual brothers and sisters, but you. If something is to be done, the little "I" says, "I will do it and take all the credit." But the big "I" will say, "No, let us do it together." The little ego is thinking only of your own progress; it cares only for your realisation, for your illumination. But the big "I" will say, "If it is God's Will, I will remain absolutely useless. But I want God to be fully manifested on earth." If God-manifestation comes first, that is the big "I", the big heart. "I will remain obscure, but God should be fully manifested. Our Mission should be fully manifested. Our Centres should be well-known so that we spread Light. Our brothers and sisters should be together so that we can have a very strong family." These are all big "I"s. The little "I" will say, "Let me remain in a Himalayan cave and realise God. Why should I be bothered?" That is the little "I". When you care only for your own self-perfection, your own liberation, and you ignore the rest of the world, then you are gone. You have to take the entire body as a whole. If you pay attention only to your eye or nose, then you are lost. If you make your nose totally perfect while your arms and ears are imperfect, then what will people think? Do you think people will appreciate you? No, they will see your arms are defective, your forehead is defective, everything is defective; only your nose is perfect. But if it is the big "I" that is operating, then you will care for full perfection: "We shall be perfect together. Eye, ear, nose, leg, knee — everything will be perfect." The big "I" will tell you, "Go together," and the small "I" will tell you, "Go alone." So during your prayer, always first think of the Supreme, then think of the Mission, then think of the Centre, then think of the disciples, then think of yourself. If you do that, immediately you will be able to separate your little "I" from the big "I".

SCS 233. *How can you embody purity?*

Sri Chinmoy: You can embody purity through your constant aspiration for purity. You achieve something when you feel the need for it. Just say, "I need purity, I need purity, I need purity!" Your eternal Father Supreme will give you purity. When the child cries for something, the mother gives. But sometimes she waits to see if the child really wants it, or whether he will stop crying and no longer care for the thing. Sometimes when a child cries for something, before the mother gives it the child goes away and plays somewhere else. You cry for two minutes, "Purity, purity," and God is bringing down purity. But when you don't feel purity in your whole being, immediately you become impatient. You think that God will not bring you purity so you change your mind and you do something else. But if you really want and need something, you will keep on crying for it. If a child really needs something, he continuously cries unless and until he has got the thing he needs. In the spiritual life also, if you cry for purity until you have achieved purity, God is bound to bring purity into your life.

SCS 234. *Since I think of you as my Master and the highest truth, what for me now is purity?*

Sri Chinmoy: For the disciple, the Master is the highest purity, and the highest purity is the Master. During the day when you breathe in and out, you have to feel my presence in your heart. When you breathe in you have to feel that you are breathing in the highest purity from me, and when you breathe out you have to feel that I am bringing out all the impurities you have inside your system and throwing them into the Universal Consciousness.

If you can constantly feel in your mind, in your heart, in your soul, in every incident in your day-to-day outer life that I am the highest, then you get the best purity. It cannot be a vague idea, but a constant living feeling that I am the highest. Otherwise, at this moment you will feel that I am very high, even the highest, but the next moment, when your desires are not fulfilled, you will feel that I am not only low, but the lowest. If I do not fulfil your inner desires, you will feel, "Either he turned a deaf ear or he has no ear, he has no capacity." This kind of tribute I get from the disciples.

If I don't fulfil your desires, if you can feel it is for your own good, absolutely for your good, and if you can consider me always the highest in spite of so-called defeat, failure and frustration, then the problem of impurity is solved. In everything if you can feel that I am the highest and the best, then you are bound to get the best and the highest from me. Then, if you have everything that is best, you will see that purity will come first and foremost. Everything that your soul needs, everything that your life of aspiration, your life of realisation, your life of manifestation needs, is bound to come if you are placing me first and foremost in your life. This is what a real disciple does.

scs 235. *How far are we from purity?*

Sri Chinmoy: You cannot ask a collective question because you may have achieved one state of consciousness and somebody else may be one inch higher or one inch lower. Somebody may be ten miles ahead of you and someone may be ten miles behind. So I cannot make a general statement, because everyone has established purity according to his spiritual development.

If you want to know how far you yourself are from purity, then you have to ask the question, "How intimately do I feel God in my day-to-day life, in every moment of my life?" If you feel the living Presence of God every moment of your life, that means you are extremely pure. The moment you feel consciously the Presence of God, at that time you are one hundred per cent pure. If inside your heart you feel God's living Presence, and not just a vague idea that God exists, at that time your whole body is pure. Again, when you don't feel God's Presence, no matter how many times you wash your hands or how many flowers you keep in front of your nose, you will not have purity. You are a perfect stranger to purity at that time.

scs 236. *How can we purify the kind of love and devotion that we are trying to offer to you?*

Sri Chinmoy: The easiest way to do this is to say to yourself early in the morning, "Guru thinks of me infinitely more than I think of myself. Guru loves me infinitely more than I love myself." Say it only once, most soulfully. In the beginning you will do this like a parrot, since I am requesting you to do it. But the day will come when you will see that there is no parrot there; you will see with your soul that this is absolutely true.

When you say that I think of you more than you think of yourself, you have to know that "thinking" is not the proper word. "Thinking" here is the soul's feeling of oneness. In the outer life, in the ordinary life, we say, "I am thinking of you." But it is only to convince the mind that we even mention the thinking process. In the soul's world it is not thinking; it is all identification, or let us use the term "oneness". Your mind may tell you, "Right now Guru is talking to my brother; he is doing this and that, so how can he say he is thinking of me?" But if you know the real meaning of the word "oneness", then you will be able to convince your mind that I really think of you much more than you think of yourself. Otherwise, your mind will say, "He is always thinking of his success, his progress, his deeds. He does not use my name even once a day." But you have to feel that my oneness with you is infinitely more secure and well-established than your oneness with me. You have to feel that I have done my part and I will all the time do my part. Now it is up to you to do your share. If you can feel that way, then anything you have to offer me will be divine.

Then again, you have to feel that the thing which you want to give me I have already given to you. If you feel that I gave you divine love and devotion first, that it is not your own and that you are just returning it to me, it is easy. But if you feel that you are giving me, whereas I am not giving you anything, then there will be some difficulty. Again, if you feel that you are giving me love and devotion for the first time, then naturally you will give me earth-bound love and devotion. But if you feel that you are giving me something that I have already given to you, then it comes to me as something divine, because what I gave you was divine.

scs 237. *Is there a way to get purity through action?*

Sri Chinmoy: Certainly. You can get purity through action, but you have to know what kind of action it is. The action that demands constant satisfactory results will not be able to give you purity. You do something; you throw the shot. You have practised very hard and now you will wait for the result. You say, "I want to place first." Your mind will say that you deserve it. From the mind's point of view, you deserve it. From the vital's point of view, you deserve it. From the physical's point of view, you deserve it. But from the soul's point of view, perhaps you don't deserve it, because the soul will say, "It is not what you do, but how you do it." Did you do it devotedly, did you do it soulfully? If there is a competitive spirit inside, if there is any jealousy inside, if there is a kind of pride or vanity inside, the soul will observe.

Then God will come and see; He will be the judge. He will see whether you are doing it with the idea or the feeling that you are just the instrument. If you have the feeling that you are the shot and God is the thrower, then automatically you become the instrument. If you are just the instrument, you are bound to get one hundred per cent in purity. You are doing nothing; God just picked you up from the ground and He is doing the throwing. So how can you not be pure, since God is all Purity? If you do it with the idea that you have become one with the soul, if it is immaterial to you whether you stand first or last, if the result you will offer to God, then you may get 75 out of 100. If you are throwing it most devotedly, without any jealousy, without any feeling of competition, but only with selfless detachment, you are bound to get 70 or 75 out of 100. Again, if you do it with an aggressive feeling, just to feed your pride and vanity, at that time you will get probably zero or five or ten. Five you may get because you have worked very hard, but when it is time for the real judgement, you may get zero. But if you do it devotedly and soulfully, 75 you will get. And if you can feel that you are not the doer, but that you are the shot itself and God has thrown you, if you can feel you are not responsible at all, then you will get 100 out of 100.

Again, when you do something, you have to use your heart and soul. Otherwise you will strike your younger sister and say, "No, it was not I. It was God who slapped my sister." God is not there. But if you become absolutely one with your younger sister with your love, affection, concern and compassion, then if she has done something really wrong and your love-power does not work, then perhaps your threatening-power is needed. If you feel this from the very depth of your heart at the time you give her a slap, then you will feel that it is not you who have given her a slap, but God who has done it. You are just an instrument; God has utilised you. If you feel this, then you are getting again 100 out of 100.

But just because you are older than your sister, if you feel, "She is an idiot. I know so much about spiritual life and about earthly life, so I have every right to slap her," you are wrong. You will do the action, but who is inspiring you, who is guiding you? It is your undivine vital that is instigating you. If your vital makes you feel that by striking her you are bringing her to some understanding or divine wisdom, then you are getting zero, absolutely zero.

So when you do something, you have to know whether you are being instigated by your vital or inspired by your soul, or illumined by the Supreme. If the Supreme is illumining you, if the Supreme is using you as an instrument to perfect your sister, then you are purity itself; your action is all purity. And if your soul, which sees the light, is inspiring you to do the right thing, then there is 50 per cent purity. But if you are being instigated, then there is 99 per cent impurity.

scs 238. *How can we purify our feeling of gratitude towards God?*

Sri Chinmoy: You have to know if it is real gratitude. Gratitude itself is pure. If it is real gratitude, it is all purity; but if it is false gratitude, then it is impurity. How do you know if it is false gratitude or genuine gratitude? It is very easy. If God has given you a dollar, and you offer your gratitude to God with the idea that He will be so pleased that He will give you ten dollars, then your gratitude is impure. You will offer your gratitude, but inside your gratitude hope will loom large. You are offering gratitude, but you are consciously or unconsciously cherishing the hope that He will give you much more.

But divine gratitude is different. When you offer divine gratitude, you are offering it because God has done something for you. You know that there are millions of people on earth to whom God has not given a dollar, but to you He has given it, even though you don't deserve it or you feel that you don't deserve it. God is doing everything unconditionally. If you feel that He is doing everything unconditionally, then automatically you feel pure gratitude. If you feel that what you have is coming unconditionally from God whether or not you deserve it, then your gratitude is bound to become pure.

scs239. *What does God's Compassion do when we resist God's Grace?*

Sri Chinmoy: Compassion and Grace are the same thing, but Compassion is much more intense. The same Grace, when it has tremendous intensity, is called Compassion. Water is everywhere, but when there is a torrential rain, you can say Compassion is descending. It is like a heavy downpour from above, with tremendous force. Grace is also water, but water is here, there, everywhere. This is the difference between Compassion and Grace.

When an individual resists God's Compassion, God either waits indefinitely and uses His Patience-Power, or He uses more Compassion. In His case He deals with infinite Compassion. He does not accept any defeat. If we resist His Compassion, He may use more of His Compassion-Power to conquer us, or He may allow us to stay for ten, twenty, fifty, sixty or a hundred years more in ignorance. He is dealing with eternal Time. It is up to Him whether to force us to accept His Light in a different way. But this forcing does not occur in a human way. His forcing means that He will use more of the Compassion-Power which He has and which He is. From His infinite Compassion-Power He will use more Compassion-Power in order to conquer our ignorance. But if He meets with tremendous resistance, then He may change His mind. He may say "No, he wants to sleep; let him sleep for another hundred years. There is no hurry in it." But God will never withdraw His Compassion for good, no matter how we resist His Compassion. Only we delay our progress, our onward, upward, inward progress, by resisting God's Compassion-Power. For God's Compassion-Power is His magnet-power, His magnetic power that draws us to His very Heart, which is all Light and Delight.

scs 240. *How can we show the Supreme gratitude for His Compassion?*

Sri Chinmoy: We do not actually show gratitude; we *become* gratitude. Gratitude is not a matter of showing. Here I have a finger and I can show it. No, it is not like that. The moment we want to show gratitude, we take away the sweetness, the real wealth, the real secret or real power, the very *raison d'être* of gratitude. So gratitude we don't show; we don't even express it. Gratitude is something that we grow into, we become. It is not a matter of offering gratitude when God shows us infinite Compassion. We have to just become gratitude itself.

Suppose I do something for you. Let us say I give you a smile or I help you in your meditation. Immediately become a garland of gratitude, but not with the idea of expressing it. The moment you express, the reality goes away from its Divinity's height. During your meditation, if you feel that the Supreme, our eternal Guru, has given you a good meditation, then without using the human tongue, you can say, "O Supreme, I am so grateful to You. You have granted me today a very high meditation. It is all due to Your Compassion." Instead of uttering this, instead of using the human tongue, just feel inside that your heart is all gratitude. If your heart is all gratitude it means your real existence has become all gratitude.

scs 241. *When you show someone compassion, can this other person see light or anything in your compassion?*

Sri Chinmoy: If you show sincere compassion to someone, then you are bound to receive Light from God. As a matter of fact, the moment you show compassion to someone, you have to feel that it is God's Light in the form of compassion which is flowing through you. When you show compassion it means that Light has already descended into your inner being, into your system, and you are just a perfect channel. The Light is flowing in and through you to the person who is in need. So you have to know that you have already received Light; otherwise, you would not have cared to show compassion to anybody.

SCS 242. *Guru, how can I feel more compassion from the picture of the Divine Mother Kali?*

Sri Chinmoy: You are identifying yourself with the Mother Kali that you are seeing on the gross vital plane. Here she is killing the asuras, the undivine forces that are standing against the divine manifestation. Within and without it is all destruction. She is destroying the unlit, impure human, or let us say animal emotions and propensities.

But you have to know that this Mother Kali has her Source. Her Source is *sat-chit-ananda*: Existence-Consciousness-Bliss. There she is all golden. If we identify our inner or spiritual existence, our inner cry with her reality, then we shall see that she is all compassion. She is taking our side against those who are obstructing our progress. She is fighting for the divine soldiers who would like to become totally dedicated, totally surrendered to God's Will.

When a human being conquers someone, he conquers only to show his supremacy. But when the divine forces conquer the undivine forces, they do so with the view of transforming the undivine qualities of those asuric forces. When Julius Caesar conquered, he immediately said, "Veni, vidi, vici," "I came, I saw, I conquered." But when a spiritual Master conquers someone, he says, "I love you. I have become what you are. Now let me use you the way I want to use you so that you can make the fastest progress." This is the difference between Julius Caesar and a spiritual Master.

In your case you have to know that you are having difficulty finding Compassion in Mother Kali because you are seeing her outer face, outer arms, outer movement. There you see her destructive or, you may even go to the length of saying, ferocious capacity. But just go deep within and you will see that she is the Mother of Compassion. In a fleeting moment she can take us to the highest plane of consciousness. She is the Mother of Power and she is Mother of Compassion both. Mahakali is the Mother of height and speed, tremendous speed. If other cosmic gods grant you something, it may take ten years for you to get it. But if you can satisfy Mother Kali, you can get it in a day. She has that capacity. She is the fastest in giving. But in return, naturally she will demand from us more purity, a more consecrated life. If she is granting us a boon in such a fast way, she has every right to expect this from us.

So in order to see Mother Kali's compassion-aspect, you have to identify yourself with her inner existence, not with her outer existence which is depicted by the imagination of some artist. When the soldier is on the battlefield, you see in him a kind of quality or capacity which is not noticeable when he is with the sweet members of his family. When he is in the battlefield, he is a totally different person. There he has to be very brave, very powerful; otherwise ignorance will devour him. So here the Mother Kali is fighting against the ignorance-forces in order to conquer them and transform them eventually. It is for their good, plus it is for the manifestation of God.

scs 243. *Guru, how can I be more compassionate to others, especially those not on the spiritual path?*

Sri Chinmoy: Think of yourself as a member of a family. When you were seven or eight years old, you made many mistakes. You committed even Himalayan blunders, let us say. But your elder brother forgave you, your father or your mother forgave you, because you were a child. Your elder brother was older than you in terms of years and your parents were older than you, so they forgave you. Automatically compassion descends when you feel that somebody is a child and does not know better.

People who have not consciously launched into the spiritual life deserve your special compassion because they are like little brothers. An unconscious, unaspiring person — a little brother — is someone who does not know how to walk along the path. He just stumbles. So the elder brothers in the family just go and pick him up.

Unaspiring people deserve our compassion. But this compassion is not pity. There is a great difference between compassion and pity. When we show compassion, at that time our whole heart becomes one with the suffering of others. If somebody is poverty-stricken and we offer our compassion, we become one with his poverty itself. But when we show pity to someone, we feel he is inferior to us and we maintain our own height. We remain on the Himalayan height and the person to whom we are showing pity is at the bottom of a chasm. We stand millions of miles away or thousands of miles higher than the reality of the other person. But in compassion we just come to him and become one. When God shows us His Compassion, He just becomes one with our deplorable reality.

So you can show compassion to these people only by becoming one with them. Feel that they are your little brothers. Today they do not know, but tomorrow they are going to learn. Once upon a time you were a little child; now you are in a position to run, not to speak of walking or marching. Similarly, these children will also start walking, then marching, then running, running the fastest towards their goal.

scs 244. *When we suffer unpleasant experiences and make mistakes, does that mean that the Supreme has withdrawn His Grace?*

Sri Chinmoy: No, no, that is not true. It is just that ignorance-forces are there. A child goes and puts his finger in the fire. That doesn't mean that the mother has less concern for the child. The mother has tremendous concern. But the mother is upstairs and the child has gone into the kitchen and placed his finger in the fire. Does that mean that the mother has no concern for the child? No. But the child is still ignorant. He does not know the power of fire.

When we do something wrong, at times it is because we do not know, and at times it is because we are tempted to do the thing. Sometimes the child knows that the fire will burn his finger, but he gets a kind of malicious pleasure in touching fire. With us also, in spite of knowing better, sometimes we enter into ignorance. It is like eating food. We know there is something called a sufficient quantity, but we overeat. We eat voraciously, and then we pay the penalty. But when we become, consciously or unconsciously, a victim to temptation, we can't say that God's Grace has withdrawn from our lives. Far from it! The only thing is that we are deliberately entering into ignorance. The mother can prevent the child from touching fire. She can say, "Don't do it, don't do it." But the difficulty is that if the determination does not come from within, no matter how many times the divine forces try to prevent us from doing the wrong thing, we will feel a sense of loss. We will feel that we have missed something.

From within we have to feel that we are not losing anything by not entering into ignorance; or we have to feel that it is only a temporary necessity for us to make mistakes, because of our ignorance. If we live in light, there is no necessity to make mistakes. It is not because the divine Grace has been withdrawn that we become victims to ignorance. Far from it. But what can the divine Grace do? Limited freedom God has given us. To everybody He has given it. This limited freedom is like a knife. Somebody will use the knife to cut a mango and share it with others, and somebody else will use the knife to stab another person. We are suffering not because God has withdrawn. God has given us the capacity; so now let us use it wisely with our discretion and wisdom.

SCS 245. *How can I bring down the Supreme's Compassion to make my spiritual life evolve faster?*

Sri Chinmoy: You can bring down the Compassion of the Supreme into your being so that you can make faster progress just by crying like a child. When a child cries helplessly, he feels that his mother is in a position to fulfil his need. He cries most helplessly just because he knows and feels that his mother is there to fulfil his need. As a seeker you will cry soulfully, not helplessly. If you cry helplessly, you may at times fall victim to despondency; whereas if you cry soulfully, from deep within, then your cry is bound to be heard by the Supreme Mother, the Supreme within you. And then you will make the fastest progress in your spiritual life. The moment your cry is heard, rest assured that your progress becomes infinitely faster.

SCS 246. *What does God's Justice do when jealousy and impurity are brought before the Supreme's Court?*

Sri Chinmoy: God's Justice is not human justice; it is not punishment. God only says, "I have given you chances time and again, but you have not properly used the golden Hour. Again, I am ready to give chances endlessly." God at that time deals with His infinite Patience. First He deals with Light, He tries to illumine our jealousy and impurity and transform them into a feeling of oneness and purity. But if the seeker does not want that, if he does not want his jealousy or impurity to be illumined, then God uses another weapon: His Patience-weapon. The first weapon he uses is His Wisdom-weapon. Patience also is a form of wisdom, and wisdom is patience, but we separate them.

Suppose you are a selfish person. God says, "The moment you forget about your personal, selfish, self-seeking life and care only for self-giving, then your jealousy will go away. The moment you pay attention only to purity, then impurity will leave you." First this wisdom God will try to shower on you. But if you do not avail yourself of this opportunity to receive God's Grace or Wisdom, then God will use another weapon which is called patience. He will wait until you feel the necessity of purification and transformation of your nature. Then, after ten years or twenty years or fifty years, again He will try to inspire you. At that time, if He succeeds, well and good. Otherwise, there will be another time. In this way continuously He will go on, go on, go on. In the course of time, the seeker will fulfil the demands of his inner being and God's Promise to His own Reality.

scs 247. *Is force excluded in Justice?*

Sri Chinmoy: The Supreme uses force, but it is not human force. Beating or striking someone, showing supremacy or authority: this is the human force. But the Supreme's Force operates in a different way. His Force is the intensity of necessity. Suppose the seeker is not intense in his aspiration. The Supreme will make him intense. This intensity you can call a force, but it is not thrust upon him. Somebody is lethargic. He wants to go slowly, at the speed of an Indian bullock cart. But God says, "Now I have invented the jet plane. Why have you to use an Indian bullock cart?" So God will use His intensity-power. This intensity we may misunderstand. We may think that God is forcing us, that He is compelling us to go. No, He is just awakening us. He just says, "Look, open your eyes. Here is the fastest speed." When He awakens our consciousness, we feel that it has been done by pressure. But if we are sincere and devoted and surrendered, we don't feel any kind of pressure; only we feel that the time has come. God has selected a choice Hour and He has awakened us.

Human force is a vital force. In vital force there is a compulsion. The force is coming to frighten us, to threaten us. But when there is force in divine Justice, it does not frighten or threaten us. Only it increases the immensity or the intensity of our aspiration so that, like a bullet, we run towards the goal. When God uses force, God will ask us to run towards the goal at the pace that He has set, not at our pace. If we don't identify ourselves with God's Will, then it really becomes a kind of pressure, a force. But if we become one with Him, then it is not a pressure, it is not a force.

We are right now in the body, let us say. Our superior, most illumined part, the head, has discovered some truth, but the feet have not yet discovered the truth. The head is telling the feet, "Look, this is the reality." If the feet do not identify themselves with the head, then they say, "Don't bother us. We don't need you. We don't need your realisation." But if the feet also feel the necessity of wisdom, then they will be so grateful that the head has helped them to know the reality.

I am now talking here, offering light. I am trying to convince you of something. To convince someone is a way of exercising one's authoritative force. But when it is a divine way of operation, we don't convince; we just illumine. The part that is still unillumined, we try to illumine. Then there is no force at all. The illumined part is just making the unillumined part aware of our own higher existence. If the lower existence feels that there is a higher existence which is part and parcel of its own reality, then naturally the lower will fly into the higher and become one with the higher.

SCS 248. *What is your view of the part of the Bible that says we should fear God's Justice?*

Sri Chinmoy: You have to forgive me, but I cannot subscribe to that view. We must not fear God's Justice and we must not fear God. If we fear God, we will never be able to reach God, we will never be able to get anything from God. If a child is afraid of his father, he will not be able to receive anything from his father. He will not even go to his father. If he sees that his father is so tall and robust and powerful, then he will not go to him. But if the child loves the father, even though the father has power and strength, the child feels that the father is not going to use it to strike him. On the contrary, the child feels that the father will use that power to protect him if he is in danger. The child feels that his father's power is all for him. And he will be able to brag that he is so great, so powerful, because of his father's strength. A child does not have even a dollar, but if he knows that his father has thousands of dollars, he goes and tells his friends, "Look, I am so rich; my father has so much money." How he identifies with his father's wealth!

Only through love do we become one. The moment we are afraid of someone, his reality and our reality become separate. I am your spiritual leader, but how am I going to give anything to you if you are afraid that it will just burn you? Reverential awe is one thing; fear is something else. In reverential awe you feel that someone is a little higher than you, so you have to behave well. God is infinitely better than you in every way, so you feel that you must have that kind of reverence. But deeper than reverence is love, true love. A child does not need reverence; he does not have to show reverence because he knows he has love, which is infinitely more effective. A child does not have to go and touch his father's feet every second. No. The moment he shows his father his love, his heart, that is enough.

To approach God with fear or through fear is very unhealthy. We only love God. We feel that what our Father has, we also have. Unfortunately, we are still children; that is why our Father is unable to give it to us. The father does not give his vast wealth to a child. But when the child grows up, he gets what his father has and what his father is. If we can love God soulfully, then God will give us everything.

When a child is playing in the mud and then all of a sudden he is called, he is not afraid that his mother will beat him because he is dirty. He will go running to his mother and his mother will immediately take his dirt, his filth, as her very own. She will wash him in order to show others that her son is also very clean. We have to take God like that. No matter how many undivine things we do, we run towards Him and feel that with His Compassion He will just clean us immediately.

SCS 249. *How do you forgive injustice?*

Sri Chinmoy: When we think of injustice in human terms, we have to go to the very depth of our realisation. When we came into the world we made a solemn promise to God that we would realise God, manifest God and fulfil God here on earth. This was our most sincere, most soulful promise to God. When we made that promise we were in the soul's world. We didn't have the physical body; our real existence was the soul. At that time the soul said, "I am descending into the world only to please You, to fulfil You, to manifest You unconditionally." But now, the word "unconditionally" immediately frightens us. It is a poisonous word; we can't use it. All is conditional, conditional.

These people whom you feel are very unjust have done something undivine, true. But look at your own promise. You expect from these people perfection; you feel they have to do everything in a perfect way. But perfection comes only when we fulfil our promise. Our first and foremost promise was to God, to please Him and fulfil Him on earth. We have not fulfilled *our* promise; yet we expect others to fulfil *their* promise. As spiritual people, we should always see what we have done wrong. Millions of things we have done wrong. If we do millions of things wrong, then naturally God is forgiving us. Otherwise, we would not be able to exist on earth. If He is ready to forgive us in spite of our countless defects and mistakes, how is it that we cannot forgive someone else?

A spiritual seeker immediately claims himself to be a chosen child of God. An unaspiring person, a person who is wallowing in the pleasures of ignorance, would never dare to claim this. He does not dare to claim God as his very own. But you do dare to claim that you are God's chosen child, just because you have got an iota of God's good qualities. God is good, God is divine, God is perfect, and all His divine qualities you have to some extent. So if one of God's qualities is forgiveness, and if God forgives you twenty-four hours a day, can't you forgive a person for one second? If your source has the capacity to do something in infinite measure, naturally you also should have the capacity to forgive or illumine others who have done something wrong, according to your standard.

scs 250. *When somebody performs an act of injustice, does the soul of the victim always learn something from the experience?*

Sri Chinmoy: In this case you have to know that the real soul is not getting any kind of experience. If someone gives you a slap unnecessarily, your soul is not getting an experience. The outer being is getting an experience. The soul is dealing with your whole realisation, outer revelation and divine manifestation. The soul has all experiences that are encouraging, inspiring, illumining and fulfilling. But sometimes the outer being also needs experience. When your outer being gets an unpleasant experience, then it will be more cautious. "Why did somebody give me a slap? What have I done?" If you have done nothing then immediately you will feel, "I have to be more cautious. It was not because I did something that I am being struck. No, it is because of the ignorance of the world. Whether I have done something wrong is immaterial. Just because the world is full of ignorance, the world's ignorance may enter into me. So I have to be more careful."

Sometimes when we do something wrong, we are afraid that somebody will come and take us to task and we will have to pay the penalty. But there are many, many wrong forces around us that attack us even if we do nothing wrong. These hostile forces, undivine forces, are moving around. But the real experience belongs to our outer being, which is trying to perfect itself. The soul gets the experience to some extent, but the real experience belongs to the outer being. The soul is dealing with Infinity, Eternity and Immortality; it has a very big task to do. It is not that the soul is ignoring the outer being. The only thing is that the outer being also has to undergo some changes through these experiences.

SRI CHINMOY SPEAKS

BOOK 9

PART I

SCS 251. *Sleep and aspiration*

To maintain your aspiration during sleep, first of all you have to meditate quite a few hours during the day. Now, that meditation need not be in a secluded area or in front of a shrine. While working, if your mood is very high, if what you are doing is pure, devoted service, then it is a real form of meditation. When you go to sleep, you must feel that it is an extension of your conscious meditation. Do not think that you are jumping or entering from one room into another — that is to say, during the day you were in one room and at night you are going into another room. No. Only feel that right now is the time for you to stretch your legs and arms, but that what you are doing is only another type of work.

If you take sleep as a brother to death, then you cannot make any progress. But if you take sleep as an extension of your meditative consciousness, then automatically the power of meditation, like a river, flows into your sleep. During the day, when you pray and meditate, you have aspiration. During sleep, you don't have aspiration because there is a conscious break. You feel that the day has ended and now you are entering into a totally different enterprise. But if you feel that in sleep you are extending the power of your meditation, the wealth of your meditation, then it is a continuous movement. Like a train it goes on. So when you meditate during the day, please feel that it is not the real end. There is no end. While you are sleeping, feel that the train is still going on. You are the passenger. If you feel that you are inside the train, you may sleep, but the pilot is still there. He is continuing to pilot the train. The boatman is still piloting the boat. If you fall asleep, no harm, for you have faith in the boatman. If you have conscious communication with the boatman, an exchange of sweet thoughts, ideals, ideas, then it becomes very easy, for you have already established your friendship with the boatman during the day, while you were meditating. Now, do you think that while you are sleeping, the boatman will deceive you? No. The boatman will go on, go on sailing the boat. As you make inner progress, even during your sleep, you will be able to meditate. You may be fast asleep, snoring, but conscious meditation, absolutely conscious meditation, is going on.

And then, if you can gradually minimise the number of hours you sleep each night, that will be very good. If you are sleeping eight hours, you can try seven and a half hours and then seven hours, six hours, five hours, four hours, three hours, two hours, and then become a Guru like me. It is quite possible. If I did it from the age of thirteen or fourteen, why is it not possible for you? More than two or two and a half hours of sleep a night is not necessary. If you can get up at four o'clock instead of seven o'clock, three hours are at your disposal. If you take time as money or wealth, then naturally the time from four to seven is like additional money you are getting. During the day, when you are doing something, you are sharing it with others. But if you get up in the small hours of the morning, you are getting the full wealth. You don't have to share anything that you are getting. If you want to pray, you can pray. If you want to meditate, you can meditate. If you want to write something, you can write.

Let me give you an example. By God's Grace I can do many things at a time in the inner world. Just because I get up early in the morning I can meditate on the consciousness, on the souls of my disciples. Then, during the day, I can devote myself to the disciples' outer problems. But if I had to start concentrating on the disciples at, say, six o'clock or seven o'clock, then I wouldn't have time to solve any problems. Then, you know, by God's Grace, I am a prolific writer. God knows how many things I have written by now. Here is an example. Yesterday *[16 November 1973]* I wrote 150 poems in one day. I am not boasting; it is all recorded. At 3:30 a.m. I started. From 2:00 to 3:30 I was doing my spiritual work, meditating on the disciples. So at 3:30 I started. Now 3:30, 4:30, 5:30, 6:30, 7:30; it goes on, goes on, goes on. Then I had to go to the U.N. for one hour. Then there were a few problems. By two minutes to eleven at night, I had completed 150 poems, and in between there were quite a few obstacles, oppositions, telephone calls and some serious problems that arose. And sometimes the physical revolts. My elbow was failing because I was not dictating these poems to anybody; I was writing myself. So you see — 3:30 to 11:00. In this way I achieved it. But if I had not begun at 3:30, I would have been nowhere. Perhaps one poem I could have written.

If you can minimise the hours of sleep, it is very good. Too much sleep means you are making friendship with death, nothing else. If you cannot make conscious progress, it is as good as death. I have a disciple who sleeps eleven and a half hours every day. I will bless her. She says that if she does not sleep eleven and a half hours, she gets an immediate headache. She is not here, so I can say it: if any disciple sleeps for twelve or thirteen hours a day, then it is my headache. It is my headache because it will be so difficult for me to take that person to God. If one has to sleep for thirteen hours, then what is one going to accomplish in life?

scs 252. *The inspiration-bird*

In our Indian philosophy, we have a particular goddess named Saraswati. Saraswati is the goddess of learning, the goddess of art and the goddess of inspiration. In the West you use the term "muse". As we have a human world, where we get all earthly things, even so there is a world of inspiration. If we go deep within, we can enter into that world and find that the poems are already written. If you want to write an article, you can enter into the world of inspiration and actually see the article written. Then all you have to do is copy it down in your notebook. When I was sixteen or seventeen years old, I wrote quite a few poems this way. Of course, it was with my third eye that I looked. The lines are written there on the wall, you can say — on the inspiration-wall — and you just copy them down and they become your possession. Our greatest poet, Tagore, did it. He entered into the world of inspiration and from there he got many poems. There is a world of poetry, a world of prose, a world for all literature that exists.

What do we do? We go deep within and jump, as though we were on a springboard. But often we are not aware of what plane we have reached. We get only a vague inner feeling of the reality of that world. So when that reality enters into us, it is like a thief entering into us. And then we become the channel of expression for that reality, according to the power of our receptivity, according to how we have reached the inspiration that has dawned in us.

Right now you are at the mercy of inspiration. If you don't have any inspiration you cannot write anything. It is like this. The inspiration-bird is flying in the sky and all of a sudden it passes by you. You see the bird of inspiration and you get a few opening lines, but before you complete these lines, the bird flies away. But when you have become a very great spiritual seeker, you have the capacity to encage the bird. The bird is flying past, but with your will-power, with your own aspiration-power or spiritual power or occult power, you can stop the bird's flight. What happens? You compel the bird to stay inside you until you have completed your poem or your article. Before we have this capacity, we are at the bird's mercy. It can come right in front of us and stand for a few minutes or a few seconds, and then it will fly away. But if we have become very highly developed seekers, then we acquire the capacity to compel the bird of inspiration to stay with us for as long as we want. Anyone can develop that capacity, provided he prays to God, meditates on God and devotes himself to the inner life.

I started writing poems at the age of twelve. At that time I was at the mercy of the inspiration-bird. If I had no inspiration, I could not write. If I had forced myself to write, it would have been all useless words. But gradually, gradually, on the strength of my aspiration, I developed the capacity to grab the bird of inspiration at will.

scs 253. *Cleanliness and purity*

When I see sincere, devoted disciples in front of me during meditation, it gives me tremendous inspiration. It is like this. Before we invoke the Supreme or a cosmic god, the power that they have remains dormant; it does not increase or expand. But when it gets inspiration, it can roar like a lion. Sri Ramachandra, our first Indian Avatar, inspired Mother Durga to bring forward her own qualities and then she conquered all the undivine forces. Similarly, the members of an orchestra can come and inspire their conductor. It is like a father with his children. When the children play, the father can come and inspire them and, similarly, when the children are playing, they can give tremendous joy and inspiration to their father and mother. So it is absolutely true that when you people come with aspiration, it helps me a lot and makes it easier for me to give. Otherwise, it is like trying to give to a solid wall.

But when I see that disciples have not taken a proper shower, I forget all about their inspiration and aspiration. A few days ago I blessed the mothers in one of our Centres for Mother's Day, and how they cursed me! I had to ask the Centre leader to bring me hot water and a towel to wash my hands. I said to these disciples, "I bless you and you simply give me all your impurity and physical dirt." If they had come to me with purity, they would definitely have inspired me.

Some of my spiritual children are very bad in this respect. The Centre leader can scold them, but even then they will come back the next week, like naughty children, without having taken a shower. On the one hand, these disciples are really devoted and dedicated. How they give when it is a matter of selfless service or love-offering! But on the other hand they do something that creates a most deplorable problem for me. And this has been going on for a long time. It is a real shame.

God-realisation will not come from taking a shower ten times a day. No! There are fishermen who spend all day in the water, but will their God-realisation come before ours? I don't think so. But again, if we keep our body very clean, the soul gets more of an opportunity to come forward. A shower cannot take more than ten minutes. It is simply a matter of wanting to please me.

On rare occasions, when I bless people on their birthdays, for example, as I gaze at them their impurity enters into me like an arrow. If a person is impure, I feel as though somebody is attacking me with an arrow. I don't even have to look at the person. I may be looking this side or that side, but I keep myself absolutely open on all levels so that everyone and everything can come to me, to attack me or receive from me.

Now, on weekdays if you cannot take a shower before coming to the Centre because of your office work or your other activities, I won't blame you. But please at least wash your face and hands and sprinkle water on your arms; you can easily do this. It would be good if the young men would buy one extra white outfit which they will keep only for meditation. Then it will keep a purer vibration. It will be like a costume. You should not wear to meditation the same old clothes that you wear every day. This place is like a temple. When you come here, your body and your clothing should be fresh and clean.

In our consciousness, our spiritual consciousness, there is always purity, but when we are dealing with the physical it is a different matter. It can happen that somebody may be inwardly spiritual but physically dirty. Tradition says that Ganges water is the purest, but now you cannot even go near it, although higher — near Rishikesh — it is a little cleaner. When the physical is dirty, it is like offering poison to the Master. Instead of that poison, people can offer something really divine. Again, sometimes a disciple's consciousness may be bad but physically he is clean. Perhaps in the inner world he is cherishing jealousy or other undivine thoughts.

When my disciples give me food or water, I don't use my occult power to protect myself as I do when I eat in a restaurant, because I expect that my disciples will give me the purest food and water. But one or two times when I was giving lectures at universities, you can't imagine the kind of water my disciples gave me! My expectation is my mistake. Many times I have suffered in this way. Sometimes at the Centre, when people give me the food that they have prepared, it is beyond my capacity to eat it. I may take one spoonful, but many times it happens that I can't even touch the food I am given, although I may be really hungry. If they were cherishing undivine thoughts when they were cooking, all these forces will be in the food and their food will be like poison to me. If they haven't cooked with love, devotion and surrender, their whole day of cooking is wasted.

When I go to disciples' houses, forgive me, there are a few places where I really suffer. I have two disciples — a husband and wife — of whom I am most fond, but once when I visited their home, how difficult it was for me! It was not the poverty of the place, but the uncleanness. If I hadn't accepted their food, they would have been really sad, so I said, "All right, although it is unclean, I will eat it to give them joy!" I ate it; then I suffered like anything. In India also I used to suffer. It is not always true that birds of a feather flock together. Very unspiritual boys used to eat beside me in the dining hall and give me their impurity. It would all enter into me; then I would smile at them and throw it into my Universal Consciousness. And if I didn't sit beside them, they would feel I was indifferent. You can't imagine how spiritual Masters can suffer in this way.

Usually when I travel or go to new places, I have several close disciples with me. One of them always goes to see if the place is clean. While I was travelling by car to Canada recently, there were two or three places on the way where I literally could not enter because of the uncleanliness. Believe me, disciples have to protect me; I need protection. And since I need protection on the physical plane, disciples should be more pure when they give me anything.

scs 254. *Mental receptivity*

Spiritual answers cannot satisfy a purely intellectual person, unless this person also uses the heart. When he opens his heart to a spiritual Master, immediately he is fulfilled, he is satisfied. Although intellectually he is trying to grasp what the Master is saying, his heart is functioning at the same time.

The heart is like a door wide open. The mind is like a tiny window which is not fully open. In your house, you have kept the door wide open, and the window you have kept just a little open. So when your divine friend, the spiritual teacher, has to enter into you, he can easily enter into you through your heart-door. If your divine friend wants to come in, you will let him in through the door if you really care for him. Then when you feel his presence within you, inside your heart, you are bound to get satisfaction. But if you say, "No, he has to come only through this window, the mind, which I am keeping half open; otherwise I will not accept him," it will be a mistake on your part, because he will not be able to enter properly with his divine blessings and light.

You have both the heart and the mind. It is up to you to open your heart and get total satisfaction. Then gradually, gradually, you can open up and expand the capacity of your mind. The mind has great capacity, but this capacity has to be released by the light of the soul. On the one hand the mind feels that it knows everything; on the other hand it feels that it knows nothing. When it is a matter of inseparable oneness with the infinite Vast, the mind does not dare even to think of it. The mind thinks that it will lose its very existence. But the heart is not afraid of oneness. The heart is like a child who is two years old. His father is very tall and stout, but the child is not afraid. He has established his oneness with his father, so he will go and play with his father. But somebody who is not a friend or relative will be afraid to approach the father. Like this, the heart immediately identifies itself with the infinite Vast, whereas the mind does not.

If one utilises only the mind while receiving the answers of a spiritual Master, one gains very little. But if the same person has even unconsciously opened up his heart, naturally the message, the light that the spiritual Master is offering, enters into the seeker's heart. He may not immediately get the full wealth of the Master's message-light, but it will grow inside him because he has kept his heart's door wide open. And as the light grows inside the heart, it will go up and illumine the mind.

When the mind is illumined by the soul's light, there will be no difference between the mind and the heart. They will both become most devoted instruments of God. Right now the most devoted instrument of God is the soul, and the heart sometimes consciously, sometimes unconsciously is trying to be equally good. When we pray and meditate most soulfully, the heart becomes one with the soul. Then, like the soul, it becomes the most effective instrument of God. Similarly, the mind also can be as effective as the heart and the soul, provided the mind consciously wants to become one with the heart and soul.

Mind, heart and soul are like three brothers in a family. The soul is the eldest brother, the heart is the middle brother and the mind is the youngest. It will be more accurate to say that the body is the youngest, then the vital, then the mind, then the heart and then the soul. Right now the body is absolutely the baby in the family. It is out of the question right now for the body to think of God. But if the mind can consciously offer the responsibility for its illumination to the heart, as the heart has offered the same responsibility to the soul, then the problems of receptivity can easily be solved.

scs 255. *Fear*

Why are you afraid of someone? Because you feel that that person is different from yourself. You do not claim him as your very own and he does not claim you. He is not yours and you are not his. But fear is not the right reaction. Through your inner light, through your prayer, through your meditation, you have to try to grow love and oneness inside you. Again, that does not mean that you will go and embrace all and sundry on the street. It does not mean that you have to go and mix with the whole world. Not at all. If you don't like a person or a thing, just offer your goodwill from a distance. You do not have to like everyone and everything. But you will have nothing to say against them and you will not hate them. You will offer your goodwill, but you will not try to become intimate with those persons or things.

Right now you are afraid of a snake. But if you can conquer your fear, still you will keep your distance. If you go and stand in front of a snake, the snake will play its role and bite you. You may say, "Inside the snake there is God," but inside you there should be some wisdom. God in the form of a snake is not to be approached. When there is a tiger in front of you, you are afraid that the tiger will devour you. In the inner world you should try to conquer your fear. But, at the same time, if you act like a fool and say, "God is everywhere, so let me go and embrace the tiger!" then you will be devoured. Some human beings also have a very ferocious consciousness. When you think of those human beings, you don't have to have fear; but at the same time you are under no obligation to embrace them.

There are many, many people on earth. They may be your friends, they may be your neighbours, they may be your relatives or your associates. Many times they may throw their personal grievances on you, or you may feel that you are under obligation to please them. There are a million reasons why you may feel an obligation to them. If you don't fulfil this obligation, you feel that they will be displeased with you; therefore, you are afraid of them. But if you are a spiritual person, you will realise that the only one you have to please is God. If you can please God inside yourself, inside your friends and neighbours, then how can you have any fear?

There is no limit to our fear. From any place it can enter into our existence. The important thing is to conquer the inner fear. Inner fear is fear of the vast, fear of the unknown. In the spiritual life we want God, but as soon as we see a little of His infinite Light, we are scared to death. We feel that all our imperfections will be exposed. Instead, always we have to feel that God's Light is there only to illumine us. There is no limit to our achievement, no limit to our realisation, no limit to our God-manifestation, because the Light within us will constantly be guiding us. So we do not have to be afraid of anything. A child is not afraid of anything when his mother or father is holding him. He moves around and knows that if anything happens, his mother will protect him, his father will take care of him. In the spiritual life also, we must feel that we are all children and that God is there to look after us. But if we don't claim the Supreme as our Father, Mother and eternal Beloved, then we are helpless. As the child claims his mother or his father, we also have to claim Light, infinite Light, as our mother and father. Then there cannot be any fear. Only if we don't claim the right thing as our very own will we always have fear.

SCS 256. *Fate and free will*

Fate is the result of the past. Free will is the result of the present. Fate is sour; free will is sweet. Fate is the starving mouse in the church; free will is the blue bird flying in the vast sky. When we look backward, we feel the blow of fate. When we look forward, we see the dance of golden and energising free will.

The physical consciousness or the body consciousness is limited. When we live in the body, it is fate. The soul is ever free. When we live in the soul, it is all free will. It is up to us whether we live in the body consciousness or in the soul consciousness.

When the soul enters into the body and we see the light of day, at that moment ignorance tries to envelop us and fate starts its play. But light is not bound by fate. Light is the embodiment of free will. For our deplorable fate, we curse our forefathers, our friends, our neighbours, ourselves and finally God. But by cursing others, by cursing ourselves, we cannot solve our problems. We can solve our problems only if we know how to live the life of aspiration.

We are given ample opportunity to use our free will. It is we who have to utilise the opportunity in order to be fully, totally, unreservedly free. Most of you have read the *Mahabharata*, India's greatest epic. It tells of a great hero named Karna. His mother was Kunti, the mother of the Pandavas. Before she got married she brought this child into the world; and out of shame and embarrassment, she placed the child in a basket on the river. Finally somebody came to his rescue and he was saved. This child became a matchless hero. He said, "I am not responsible for my birth, but I am responsible for my life, for my life's activities." Each aspirant can also say this. Very often seekers tell me, "Oh, I have a very unsatisfactory background." I tell them, "Why do you care for the past? The past is dust. But if you aspire, nobody can steal away your present; nobody can steal away your future. Your future can easily be golden."

There are three kinds of karma: *sanchita* karma, *prarabdha* karma and *agami* karma. *Sanchita* karma is the accumulation of acts from a past life and this life whose results have not yet borne fruit. In *prarabdha* karma, the fruit of some of the accumulated karma we are starting to reap. If it is bad karma, then we suffer. If it is good karma, then we enjoy it. Finally comes *agami* karma. When one is totally free from all ignorance, suffering and imperfection, when one has realised God and is living only for the sake of God, at that time one is enjoying the Free Will of the Supreme. This is *agami* karma.

Most of us face *sanchita* karma, accumulated karma which starts functioning as *prarabdha* karma. There is no freedom, no free will, but only fate all around us. It is like a devouring lion, striking from the past. But when we have *agami* karma, this devouring lion becomes a roaring lion, roaring for the divine Victory, the divine fulfilment here on earth.

Fate can and must be changed. For that, what is required is God's Grace plus personal effort, self-effort. There are some seekers who feel, "If I care for God's Grace, what necessity is there to make personal effort?" But they are mistaken. Personal effort will never stand in the way of God's descending Grace. Personal effort expedites the descent of God's Grace. God's Grace does not negate personal effort. True, God can give us all that He wants without even an iota of personal effort on our part. But God says, "It is for your pride that I ask you to make this little personal effort."

If somebody asks us, "What have you done for God?" what will our answer be? We can be filled with pride when we say, "God has done this for me, God has done that for me, God has done everything for me." We can be spontaneously proud that God has accepted us as His very own. But if somebody asks us, "What have *you* done for God?" what will be our answer? Silence! So the little personal effort that we make is for our own good. When we make this personal effort, our whole life is surcharged with a divine pride. It is not our ego, but our conscious oneness with God that prompts us to do something for our Dearest. If we sincerely make personal effort, God is bound to be thrilled with us. Why? Because He can tell the world, "My child, My chosen instrument, has done this for Me and that for Me." Through personal effort we can make our existence on earth worthy and, at the same time, we can make God proud of us.

Ultimately, personal effort has to grow into a dynamic self-surrender. When we do something, we offer at the Feet of God the result of our action along with the aspiration that we have used to do that particular thing. When the results and the aspiration, the inner urge, we can offer to God, this is called true surrender. But just to lie at God's Feet like a corpse and let God work in us, through us and for us is wrong. God does not want to work in and through a dead body. He wants someone who is aspiring, someone who wants to be energised and who wants to do something for Him. He wants someone who is active and dynamic and who wants to manifest all the divine qualities here on earth.

At last I know my name.
My name is God's eternal Game.
At last I know my name.

At last I know my age.
My age is Infinity's page.
At last I know my age.

At last I know my home.
My home is where my flame-worlds roam.
At last I know my home.

When the play of fate is over, the play of free will begins. Right now we do not know our true name, we do not know our true age, we do not know our true home. But when we go beyond the play of fate, we come to realise that we are God's eternal Game and that we belong to Infinity. We come to realise that our home is where our flame-worlds roam. "Flame-worlds" means the world of aspiration, the world of our mounting inner cry where salvation, illumination and realisation grow.

Our free will is a child of God's infinite Will and at the same time it is part and parcel of God's infinite Will. This free will can let us know our true name, our true age, our true home. Free will is knocking at our heart's door. We have only to allow it to break through the wall of ignorance and make us one with the Cosmic Will. Fate is the gate which leads us to the failure of the past. Free will is our acceptance of the future that wants to transform us, mould us, guide us and liberate us from fear, doubt, ignorance and death.

scs 257. *Prison and prisoners*

People in prison are our brothers who have made mistakes. But before they can make inner progress, first they have to recognise that they have made mistakes and then they have to feel that there is another way of life which will prevent them from making further mistakes. This way of life is the way of aspiration, not the way of binding desire. When one wants to expand oneself inwardly, the light that is there is bound to guide and illumine him. Again, when one wants to bind himself, unconsciously or consciously, there are forces to misguide him.

Nobody wants to remain in prison. An individual feels that the judge was unjust or he feels that the judge was just, but the punishment he got was more than his due. So everybody who is in prison wants to get out. But we have to know whether a particular individual is coming out to lead a better life or to do something destructive. He has killed one person. Is he coming out with the idea that this time he will kill ten persons or is he coming out with the idea that he has done something wrong and now he wants to turn over a new leaf and only do the right thing? If he is determined to do the right thing, the divine thing, when he comes out of jail, then who is there to prevent him?

It was desire that prompted him to do something undivine, destructive. If he leaves the prison and aspiration does not come into his life, then again and again he will do the same thing. Temptation-world will again capture him. He has his own temptation; then there is the temptation of the world, which will try to capture his mind. He will again do something horrible and then he will be caught. What can save him? Obedience. Something inside him is bound to say, "Do this, don't do that," and this voice has to be obeyed.

A child's mother can say, "This is fire. Don't touch it; it will burn you," but if a child does not believe her, he will still touch it.

Just because of his innocence, do you think the fire will not burn his finger? No, it will burn him. He did not listen to his mother's warning. For a child there is his mother to warn him. For a grown-up there is something which is more powerful, and that is called conscience. You may say that someone's consciousness can be totally eclipsed by foul desire, but I will say no. Everybody's conscience is very powerful, but some people listen to it while others do not.

If somebody wants to come out of jail and lead a better life, he can pray to God, "O God, I did something wrong. Now inner illumination has dawned. Please forgive me. Now let me be Your real instrument and make You happy." If he prays like this, do you think that God will not listen to his prayer? God is bound to listen to everybody's prayer provided it is sincere.

A prisoner is he who has made a mistake, consciously or unconsciously. His mistake can be rectified provided there is an adamantine will. There is no mistake that cannot be rectified. But how many of the prisoners are trying to rectify their mistakes? When people do something wrong, very often a kind of inner arrogance comes forward against the authorities and against their own life of discipline. They become mad that they have done something wrong and then they try to destroy their own inner possibility. They say, "If I have done this, who asked me to do it, who allowed me?" There is no real answer. The vital may say, "If God was really compassionate, how did He allow me to become a thief, a hooligan?" This is how we blame God at every moment. First we become victim to our undivine desires and then, when we get the punishment, we blame God: "How is it that God allowed us to do this?" Poor God! What will He do? Right before us He kept two rooms. One room was full of light, illumination. The other was full of darkness. We didn't choose the illumined room, we chose the dark room. So naturally we shall have to meet with the consequences.

There is every hope for a prisoner. His case is not lost. As long as creation exists, God will supply him with hope and aspiration. It is up to him to accept inspiration from his inner life. A prisoner can start his spiritual journey, inner journey, right in the prison. If he is really sincere and wants to become spiritual and divine and work for mankind, then let him study a few spiritual books. There he may not have the guidance of a spiritual person, a spiritual Master, but I believe most prisons allow books. Let him start at the beginning and then, when he comes out of prison, let him go one step forward. First let him be satisfied with a few drops of water and when he comes out he can really try to quench his spiritual thirst. If he comes to a spiritual Master who has Light and Bliss, this spiritual Master will give him a glass full of water. He will say, "Drink as much as you want to. I have an inexhaustible source of Light." But the prisoner has to start like everyone else right from the beginning, with perhaps only one minute a day of spiritual life, of dedicated life. In prison he may not get the opportunity to lead a dedicated life, but he can study spiritual books, religious books, which will give him inspiration. The light from the spiritual books will enter into him and create a new field in his life.

SCS 258. *Imagination, inspiration, aspiration and realisation*[§]

Imagination is the creation's invisible beginning. Inspiration is the creation's visible beginning. Aspiration is the creation's illumining beginning. Realisation is the creation's fulfilling beginning.

The poet imagines. The singer inspires. The seeker aspires. The lover realises. The poet here is the seer-poet who envisions the realities of the world beyond. The singer here is the divine singer who has a free access to the world of celestial music. He is in tune with the music that elevates the consciousness of humanity. The seeker here is he who has freed himself from the desire-world, from the meshes of ignorance. He wants only the truth and nothing else. The lover here is a God-lover. Here on earth and there in Heaven he loves only God. Each creation of God he takes as the living manifestation of God. In each creation he sees and feels God's Silence-Vision and God's Sound-Reality.

Imagination says to inspiration, "I have discovered something great: God is great."

Inspiration says to imagination, "I fully agree with you. Your discovery and my discovery are the same. And you are speaking, I am sure, on the strength of your own personal experience, for I have had the same experience: God is great."

At this point, aspiration says to imagination and inspiration, "Friends, you two are right. I wish to add only one thing: God acts ceaselessly and compassionately."

Then realisation comes into the picture and says, "Friends, you three are perfectly right. Only allow me to add something more: God gives us everything unreservedly and unconditionally, but we receive according to our receptivity."

Imagination is not mental hallucination. Inspiration is not self-deception. Aspiration is not earth-negation. Realisation is not Heaven-glorification.

Imagination is not mental hallucination; it is the reality that grows and glows in our physical mind at God's choice Hour. Imagination has a world of its own. From there, the reality descends into our physical mind, our earth-bound mind.

Inspiration is not self-deception. Inside inspiration abides and looms large the reality of our own existence. Inspiration carries us to the farthest Beyond, to the highest Heights, to the universal Depths. It has the capacity to embody the transcendental Height and also to measure the universal Depth.

Aspiration is not earth-negation; aspiration is earth-acceptance. Earth is God's creation. If we accept God as our very own, we cannot separate earth from His Existence. God is everywhere in a greater or lesser degree. A true seeker is he who sees God not only in the highest plane of consciousness but also in the lowest, unlit plane of consciousness. The seeker enters into the lowest in order to bring down the Reality-light of the Highest so that he can transform the lowest into the Highest. The seeker accepts earth as a reality and in this reality, through this reality, the seeker knows that God-Vision manifests itself.

Realisation is not Heaven-glorification. Some people think that if someone realises God, he will all the time talk about Heaven-realities, for he alone knows what is happening in Heaven. Since he is an authority on Heaven, he will try to glorify the realities that exist in Heaven. But, on the contrary, a realised soul is he who feels that it is his bounden duty to spend most of his time starving with humanity's hunger, crying with humanity's pangs and smiling with humanity's joy. To serve God in humanity, to bring to the fore the divine Light that humanity embodies, is his soul's primary task. Here on earth he has to fulfil God's Dream. For him, not Heaven but earth is the reality supreme.

Imagination knows no obstruction. Inspiration knows no hesitation. Aspiration knows no test. Realisation knows no rest.

Imagination knows no obstruction. It runs, it flies, it dives. There is nothing here on earth that can remain a distant impossibility to imagination. Imagination has a free access to all of God's Reality.

Inspiration knows no hesitation. Once the divine in us is inspired, there is no delay, no hesitation whatsoever. It runs the fastest towards the destination.

Aspiration knows no test. Some people are of the opinion that God examines our aspiration, but this is absurd. God knows what we have and what we are. He never examines us. It is we who examine ourselves, for we are not sure of our own capacity, of our own reality or achievement. Also, we examine ourselves because we want to prove to God and to humanity our worth and value, and see whether we are fit to stand against teeming ignorance-night.

Realisation knows no rest. It would be a deplorable mistake to come to the conclusion that once we have achieved realisation, then for us it is the journey's close. No, realisation is preparatory to revelation, and revelation is preparatory to manifestation. Manifestation is preparatory to perfection, and perfection is the song of eternal transcendence. Perfection is not and cannot be a finished product. Perfection is continuously in the process of transcending its own height. Again, today's realisation has to be the beginning of tomorrow's new aspiration. As a matter of fact, inside realisation, revelation, manifestation and perfection there is always aspiration.

Imagination, inspiration, aspiration and realisation are all divine qualities, but aspiration preponderates. It has the strongest capacity to lift everything that it sees around or within, to lift it up to the ever-transcending Beyond. This is what our aspiration can do and always does.

The divine child in us is imagination. His very being is surcharged with imagination. The divine deer in us is inspiration. The deer symbolises speed, which inspiration has in abundant measure. The divine bird in us is aspiration. This bird flies and flies to the farthest Beyond. It embodies the inner flaming cry that has to reach the Highest, the Absolute, the farthest Beyond.

Imagination, inspiration and aspiration eventually grant us realisation. Realisation is the perfection of our inner nature and our conscious surrender to God's cosmic Will. At every moment a realised soul feels his conscious and constant oneness with the Will of the Absolute Supreme. Inside himself he sees a swan. This swan symbolises realisation. It is the swan of wisdom-light, the swan of victory-height and the swan of nectar-delight.

Usually, imagination is in the mind, inspiration is in the dynamic vital, aspiration is in the crying, loving heart and realisation is in the entire being. When we have imagination, we feel that we can do everything; it is only a matter of time. At God's choice Hour we shall be able to accomplish everything that we want to accomplish. When we have inspiration, we feel that everything can be done, for that is what our adamantine will wants to do for us. When we have aspiration, we feel that God is going to do everything for us, for we are helpless, we are hopeless, we are useless; yet we are still His loving children. Therefore, out of His infinite Bounty He will do everything for us. Finally, when we have realisation, we clearly see in unmistakable terms that God has already done everything for us. There is nothing that we have to accomplish; everything has been done for us by God Himself. Now we only have to share in His infinite Wisdom-Light.

scs 259. *I had an experience last year. I don't know where I was, but I felt quite within myself and I turned into currents of water. The source of the water was coming from behind me, and I realised that if the source of the water had stopped, I wouldn't have existed. I wanted to look in back of me because it was all light but I was frightened to turn around, partly because I thought I would break the connection and then I wouldn't exist any more, and partly because I thought it was a bit too bright. Was this all just imagination or did it have any spiritual significance?*

Sri Chinmoy: Yes, it had a tremendous spiritual significance. Water signifies consciousness. In the spiritual life, we are dealing with only one thing: consciousness. When consciousness is low, we are like animals; when consciousness is high, I tell you we are no longer inferior to the cosmic gods. And when our consciousness becomes part and parcel of the Supreme, at that time we become one, inseparably one, with the Universal Consciousness.

The current that you mentioned is the flow from the Supreme. Current means life. The life-movement will flow towards the ever-transcending Beyond. When you are aware of the Source and, at the same time, you feel that you belong to the Source, then you will not be afraid. But if you separate yourself and feel that you are not with the Source, then fear comes. If you are one with the finite consciousness, with the physical, you are frightened to death when you see the Source. You look behind you at the Source and you are frightened to death, because the Source is like the infinite ocean whereas you are like a tiny drop. Naturally, you will be frightened, because you are seeing something that can devour you at any moment. But if you can feel your oneness with the Source, you will have no fear. Your little finger is not afraid of the rest of your body, because it is part and parcel of the body. When you separate your little finger from your body-consciousness, you feel it is insignificant, it can do nothing. But when you bring your finger-consciousness into the whole body, then the finger feels that it is significant. Let somebody pinch your little finger and immediately your whole body starts screaming, because the body has established its oneness with the little finger.

The Infinite has already established its oneness with you. But the finite gets a kind of malicious pleasure in separating itself from the Source. It is like a mischievous, naughty child who gets satisfaction by staying out late so his parents will think of him and worry. He knows that he has a house, that his parents are waiting. He has a most comfortable bed and everything to eat, but he does not want that. If he can stay outside in the street or loiter somewhere, that is what gives him joy. The finite always wants to maintain its separativity; then, afterwards, the finite feels miserable because it has lost its connection with the Source. It feels helpless, hopeless, useless. When we accept the spiritual life, we have already discovered the limitations of the finite; we know the limitations of our body-consciousness, of our earth life. What do we do? We consciously try to enter into the Source and become the Infinite. When the finite is one with the Source, only then does the finite get a constant opportunity to manifest the Infinite.

So, in your case, in the beginning you came out of your Infinite Consciousness and became the finite consciousness. You were aware of the Infinite but unfortunately you did not establish your oneness with it. The connecting link was not strong enough. If you had had the connecting link well-established, then you would have heard the song of the Infinite in the finite and felt the total fulfilment of the finite in the Infinite. Water is consciousness and the current is the flow of life. This is how the finite and the Infinite can live together when the finite realises its incapacity and enters into the Infinite. The Source always knows that it has to manifest itself through the finite; only then will it get supreme satisfaction. And the finite gets its fulfilment by entering into the Infinite.

If the Vast plays its role in the tiniest drop, then this is a real miracle. Again, if the tiniest drop can become one with the Vast, this is also a miracle. The finite does not try; the finite feels it is impossible. In the case of the Infinite, the Infinite feels that nothing is impossible; only it is a matter of time.

SCS 260. *What is the meaning of maya?*

Sri Chinmoy: Maya is measurement. The outer meaning of maya is illusion. The inner meaning of maya is measurement. We try to measure the reality with our human eye. If we use the ordinary human eye, then our vision is very limited. But with our inner eye, our inner vision, if we try to measure the reality, then we see the reality in its totality. At that time we see that it has no separate existence from us. With the inner eye, we see that vision and reality are one. One moment you are the reality and I am the vision and the next moment I am the reality and you are the vision. Maya tells us that you as an individual are sitting in one place and that I as an individual am sitting at a different place. But when we use the inner vision, or third eye, then we see that both of us are one; we see that God's Vision and God's Reality are inseparable.

scs 261. *What is* sahaja *samadhi?*

Sri Chinmoy: The highest type of spiritual Masters first go to *savikalpa* samadhi. Thought-waves are there, but the Masters are not affected. Then they go to *nirvikalpa* samadhi, beyond the Cosmic Dance. Finally they go to *sahaja* samadhi: immutable silence within and the Cosmic Dance without. *Sahaja*, this rascal has been granted by the Supreme. I am fooling around, but inside me is the immutable Silence. *Sahaja* is the perfect synthesis. *Sahaja* embodies silence-power and sound-power together. In *sahaja* samadhi, silence will not stand in the way of sound or vice versa. On the contrary, they have free access to one another. Sound comes inside for perfection and silence goes outside for manifestation. Sound-life immediately enters into silence-life for greater and greater realisation and silence-life comes into sound-life for greater and greater manifestation.

scs 262. *What is the best way to bury the dead from the spiritual point of view?*

Sri Chinmoy: Once the soul has left the body, once the bird has flown away, it is up to you what to do with the cage. It is up to the individual. If you are a follower of Zoroaster, you will have to keep the dead body on top of the roof. Then the vultures and wild birds will come and the smell you will have to put up with. That is what they feel is the best way. Some say the body should be burned for purification. Others will say, "Why do you have to burn it? It is something Mother Earth gave to this individual. Let it remain with Mother Earth and then you won't see it." So they will bury the body. Somebody else will say, "Consciousness is the most important thing. Water is consciousness. Let water carry it to the unknown." Each one has his own explanation.

You have heard about the Indian custom of the past. When the husbands died, silly Indian tradition said the wives had to join the husbands. Always they had to enter into the burning pyre. Sometimes willingly they did it; most of the time it was unwillingly. They were forced. The wife was crying that she didn't want to die with her husband, but the relatives, even the parents of the husband, forced the wife into the burning fire because that was the tradition. "To show your oneness, you have to die with your husband," they said. That started right from the *Mahabharata*.

scs 263. *How can we increase our receptivity in our inner life?*

Sri Chinmoy: You can increase your receptivity to your inner life just by becoming more grateful to the Inner Pilot. The Inner Pilot will give you the inspiration and aspiration to become spiritual and He will be able to give you more receptivity if He sees that every day you are increasing your gratitude-capacity. The more you can offer your gratitude to the Supreme Pilot within you, the more and the sooner you will increase your receptivity. Gratitude means self-offering to one's highest self. This gratitude is not going to somebody else; it is going to your own highest self. Gratitude helps us identify and feel our oneness with our own highest reality.

Many of your near and dear ones are not following the spiritual life, but you have accepted the spiritual life. How is it possible? It is possible because the Supreme inside you has given you the aspiration, whereas there are many, many people who are still not aspiring. You should feel that He has selected you, accepted you to be spiritual; therefore, you should always be grateful to the Inner Pilot, the Supreme. And when you are grateful, your receptivity automatically increases.

scs 264. *I am a student of a Chinese Master, and my Master suggests that when we sleep we should recline on our right side, with one leg straight, and the other one tucked up, with the hand like this. I suppose it is like the images of Buddha. Do you feel that this is appropriate for sleep?*

Sri Chinmoy: I do not want to pronounce my judgement when it is a question of something your Master has said. If you follow a path, you have to have implicit faith in what your Master says. I am a Master, and I expect the same kind of implicit faith from my students. When a Master says something, it is absolutely correct according to his understanding for his own followers and disciples, just as what I say is absolutely correct for my followers and disciples. So I cannot pronounce any judgement. If you have a question which concerns your own aspiration, I will say what is best and what is not. But if you follow another Master's path, you should have implicit faith in what he says. I have no right to encourage you to doubt him. If you do not follow his path, naturally you have every right to suspect or doubt a Master. There are some teachers who indulge in judging other Master's teachings, but I am not one of those. If he is a Master, he has every right to offer his views, because God is expressing Himself through this particular Master in a unique way. God is expressing Himself not only through this Master, but through each of us in a unique way.

scs 258. *(p. 324)* Sir George Williams University, Montreal, 20 February 1976.

scs 259–264. *(p. 329)* Questions asked after *Imagination, inspiration, aspiration and realisation.*

SRI CHINMOY SPEAKS

BOOK 10

scs 265. *Prayer and meditation*[§]

Dear seekers, I wish to give a very short talk on prayer and meditation.

I pray. Why do I pray? I pray because I need God. I meditate. Why do I meditate? I meditate because God needs me.

When I pray, I think that God is high above me, above my head. When I meditate, I feel that God is deep inside me, inside my heart.

There are two types of prayer: right prayer and wrong prayer. Similarly, there are two types of meditation: right meditation and wrong meditation. The right prayer says, "I am helpless, I am innocent, I am weak. I need You, O Lord Supreme, to strengthen me, to purify me, to illumine me, to perfect me, to immortalise me. I need You, O Lord Supreme."

The wrong prayer says, "Although I need You, O Lord Supreme, I have some strength of my own, I have some capacity of my own. I need You because if I have Your Power and Capacity, then there shall come a time when I shall be able to lord it over the world and dominate the world. The whole world will be at my feet and I shall act according to my sweet will. But for that I need power in boundless measure. I have some power, but I need infinitely more. Therefore I invoke You, O Lord Supreme." This is wrong prayer. This prayer is for the fulfilment of the vital in us, the vital that wants to dominate the entire world.

The right meditation says, "Lord Supreme, out of Your infinite Bounty You have chosen me to be Your instrument. You could have chosen somebody else to play the role, but You have granted me the golden opportunity. To You I offer my constant gratitude, my gratitude-heart, for You have chosen me to become Your instrument to manifest You here on earth in Your own Way."

The wrong meditation says, "Lord Supreme, this world of ours is full of ignorance. We all are swimming in the sea of ignorance, wallowing in the pleasures of ignorance. You need me because in this world of ours, God-manifestation is extremely difficult. Your manifestation, Your full manifestation, is a far cry. Therefore You need considerable assistance from me here on earth. You need an ignorant human being like me to fight against ignorance in this strange world that You have entered into. You need my help for Your own manifestation; so I will be Your instrument."

Prayer is a flower. When we see the flower, we are inspired. Inspiration compels us to run the farthest, to climb the highest, to dive into the deepest depth. Meditation is a tree. The tree aspires. It aspires to reach the highest height, the highest plane of consciousness. When we see the flower, inspiration dawns in us. When we sit at the foot of the tree, our aspiration to reach the Highest, the absolute transcendental Consciousness, comes to the fore.

Prayer is purity. It purifies our mind. The mind is always subject to doubt, fear, worry and anxiety. It is always assailed by wrong thoughts, wrong movements. When we pray, purification takes place in our mind. Purity increases our God-receptivity. In fact, purity is nothing short of God-receptivity. Each time we pray, our inner receptacle becomes large, larger, largest. At that time, purity, beauty, light and delight can enter into our receptacle and they can sport together in the inmost recesses of our heart.

Meditation is luminosity. It illumines our heart. When il-lumination takes place in our heart, insecurity disappears, the sense of want disappears. At that time, we sing the song of inseparable oneness, our inseparable oneness with the universal

Consciousness, the transcendental Consciousness. When our heart is illumined, the finite in us enters into the Infinite and becomes the Infinite itself. The bondage of millenia leaves us and the freedom of infinite Truth and Light welcomes us.

Prayer is followed by meditation; not the other way around. First we must pray, then we meditate.

Asato ma sad gamaya
tamaso ma jyotir gamaya
mrityor ma amritam gamaya.

Lead me from the unreal to the Real.
Lead me from darkness to Light.
Lead me from death to Immortality.

This is the prayer that we have learned from the Vedic seers of the hoary past. This immortal prayer in the firmament of India knows no parallel.

Here in the West, the Saviour has taught us the supreme prayer: "Let Thy Will be done." Again, the same Saviour has taught us the supreme meditation: "I and my Father are one." *Tat twam asi:* "That Thou art." You are That, the ever-transcending Beyond, the Lord Supreme. This is the highest height of prayer. *Brahmasmi:* "I am the Brahman, I am the all-pervading Brahman, the Absolute Supreme." This is the supreme height and depth of meditation.

Prayer tells me, "O seeker, claim the Supreme Beloved as your own and say, 'O Beloved Supreme, You are mine. I claim You as my own, very own. Do grant me Your divine qualities in boundless measure so that I can be Your perfect instrument here on earth. You have infinite Peace, Light and Bliss. Do grant me infinite Peace, Light and Bliss so that I can be a most perfect instrument of Yours.'"

Meditation tells me, "O seeker, tell God, 'I am Yours.' Tell the Absolute Supreme, 'I am at Your command. Use me in Your own Way. At every moment You can manifest Yourself in and through me. You can utilise me at Your sweet Will at every moment, throughout Eternity. To fulfil You in Your own Way is to achieve immortal life. Through me fulfil Yourself here on earth, there in Heaven.'"

With a soulful prayer each seeker begins his day's journey; and with a soulful meditation the seeker ends his day's journey.

PART II

SCS 266. *What is the most important thing in the spiritual life?*

Sri Chinmoy: There is one most important thing in the spiritual life, and that most important thing is: God first and God last. God should come first in my life and God should come last in my life. I will start my journey with God, I will end my journey with God and, in between, God will be there, too. I don't need anybody save and except God. Whoever claims God as his own, I claim that person as my own. He who does not dare to claim God as his own is claiming ignorance as his own. I can't claim ignorance as my own. So whoever is in God, with God and for God is mine.

In the spiritual life there is no such thing as neutrality. In the ordinary life we say, "I don't want to be involved." But in the spiritual life that is impossible. Either you take God's side or the hostile forces will pull you, and you will be compelled to accept, consciously or unconsciously, world ignorance as your own. It will grab you and devour you. So please feel that those who are not aspiring have already taken the side of ignorance. And what is ignorance? Something that deliberately takes us away from the Real in us. Some people say that they are not practising spirituality, but they also say that they are not inside the prison of ignorance. But I will say, "You are already there, but you don't know it."

There are two magnets. If you allow the spiritual magnet to pull you, it will definitely pull you towards realisation. But if you don't allow it, then ignorance will pull you to itself. You can't stand in between; you can't remain neutral. You have to take one side.

scs 267. *How do we know that we are nearing our goal of liberation?*

Sri Chinmoy: When one is a student, one studies at the elementary school, high school, college and university. When one enters the university, one knows that he will soon be completing his course. In the spiritual life also, it is the same. When one starts the spiritual life, one knows how much peace he has. He grows into more peace, abundant peace, infinite peace. When one is a beginner in the spiritual life, one knows how much suffering he has, how difficult it is for him to meditate even for five minutes. Then gradually he gets the capacity to meditate for hours at a time. It happens in the same way that a student goes from first grade to a higher class and to the highest class. He knows when he goes to the highest class that his course is complete.

scs 268. *When people are gossiping about a negative quality in another person, can this gossip increase the strength of that quality?*

Sri Chinmoy: Certainly it does. Each time we open our mouth, we are bringing to the fore or we are using a power. It can be a good power or it can be a bad power. Even if we do not speak anything aloud, if we cherish an undivine thought about somebody else, then this undivine thought will enter into that person like an arrow. He will not be able to know who is the culprit, but the arrow will definitely enter into the person.

Gossip is very bad. It does not help anyone. Here we are all trying to be wise people. Anything that does not help us, we try to reject from our nature. We are all seekers. By becoming gossip-mongers, we will not be able to go to God. We need Peace, Light, Bliss and divine Love. If we care for these qualities, then we shall not speak ill of others. We are trying to love God. If we love God, then how can we hate God's children? To speak ill of someone is indirectly to hate him. If we really love the root, which is God, then we cannot speak ill of the branch or the leaf. If we really love the root, then the leaves, fruits and branches we also have to love.

scs 269. *What can we do about pride?*

Sri Chinmoy: Suppose I think that I am a good singer. Pride has entered into me. Then immediately I will compare myself with some great, well-known singers and my pride will be smashed. Or suppose I think that I am a good lecturer. Then immediately I will try to compare myself with some great orator. Then my pride will pale into insignificance. Each time pride enters, this is what we can do. This is the human way of dealing with pride. But the difficulty with this way is that it helps us conquer our pride only for the time being. Today pride has entered into me because I feel that I am a great singer. The moment I think of a really great singer, my pride goes away. But tomorrow it may come again. Tomorrow I will be proud of something else. But if I can bring down Peace and Light into my system, then what happens? I don't have the occasion to be proud of anything because I feel that every person who has really achieved something or accomplished something is my brother or sister. The right hand does not become jealous of the left hand. Both belong to the same body. So when there is oneness, pride goes away.

scs 270. *How can I fight comfort in the lower consciousness?*

Sri Chinmoy: What you call comfort, I wish to call pleasure. Comfort and pleasure go together. Pleasure is a form of passion, a form of destruction. Until the vital is completely purified, the human consciousness feels that pleasure is something very sweet.

Unconsciously a child takes poison. Just because unconsciously he is drinking poison, do you think that he will not be killed? Unconsciously a child places his finger in fire and he is burned. Just because he is not conscious of doing something, does it mean that he will not suffer the consequences? Since you have accepted the spiritual life, you do not consciously enter into the lower vital world. But unconsciously, in your mind, you do enter. On the physical plane you can remain thousands of miles away from the vital world. But mentally, if you cherish lower vital, emotional thoughts, destructive thoughts, naturally the mind will be destroyed.

If your aspiration is constant, then the burning flame inside you is climbing up, up, up. But if the flame is not burning, the pull of the vital becomes very strong, very strong. Again, if the flame is burning upward all the time, how can it go downward? When the flame is burning very brightly, the vital feels, "I have no place here." The lower vital has no chance to remain in that particular person. Then the lower vital gives the death blow, a most fatal blow. At that time the aspirant has to be very careful; he has to brave that blow. If he does brave that blow, then the lower vital feels, "Oh, he does not need me."

You want to have perfection in your nature and you want to have illumination. If you constantly feel that you want to become perfection and nothing else, then you are bound to remain at your own height. Gradually, from this height you will climb up to the highest height, which is your goal. Your own height right now is your upward aspiration and nothing else. Your ultimate goal is bound to come if you constantly strive to stay where you are right now, in your climbing aspiration.

Whoever wants to give up the spiritual life just because he is not making considerable progress or because he is falling down from time to time, is making a terrible mistake. And then something more I wish to say. After accepting the spiritual life, if you consciously leave it, then hostile forces torture you most ruthlessly and the divine forces show considerable indifference. If you don't accept the spiritual life, wonderful. Sleep, sleep; the time has not yet come for you to wake up. But if you already have started to run, and then you go again to sleep, at that time ignorance comes and covers you totally.

So, please run towards the sun. Then darkness has to leave you. Do not be afraid of your faults. Only be conscious of your height, conscious of your goal. If you are conscious of your height and you are conscious of your goal, then there can be no fall. But if there is no conscious awareness, then every moment is dismal darkness.

PART III

SCS 271. *Purity*

If I have to say what is most important in the spiritual life next to God-realisation, then immediately I will say "purity". Purity and God-realisation cannot be separated. Purity has to be in the physical, the vital, the mental and the psychic. In the ordinary life we use the term "cleanliness": he is clean, he is dirty. But purity is something which is infinitely higher and more fulfilling than mere outer cleanliness. A man may take a shower, and right after taking the shower he may cherish undivine thoughts and ugly evil forces. Now, what kind of purity has he got? He has cleansed his body, but his vital, his mind, his inner existence is all impurity. So outer cleanliness has very little to do with the heart's inner purity, the heart's reality. But again, outer cleanliness *can* be of great help and assistance to inner purity. If we take a shower and put on clean, fresh clothes, the things we are allowing to surround us are already pure and divine. Then it will be easier for us to prevent the undivine, hostile, lower vital forces from entering into us and keep our mind and vital pure and divine.

In the spiritual world, purity is the breath of our real inner existence. If we don't have purity, we can achieve only a little bit of reality by hook or by crook, by pulling and pushing. But that reality is very limited, and even that very limited achievement quickly goes away. Without purity we won't be able to achieve anything substantial in the spiritual life, and we won't be able to maintain the little that we do achieve. But if we have purity, then we can have all the divine qualities in boundless measure. If we have boundless purity, then our inner achievements can last forever. But unless and until we have established solid purity in boundless measure, God-realisation will remain a far cry.

How do we become pure? One way we acquire purity is by mixing with spiritual people, with pure people. From them we will get inspiration and guidance. The other way is to consciously think of ourselves as children, divine children. If we feel that we are divine children, we know that there is Somebody to take care of us. And who is that? It is our divine Parent. A child has no sense of impurity. He is always pure. Our outer mind may say that the child is very dirty, but that is only the physical. Inwardly, he is pure. If he has been playing outside, his body may be covered with dirt, mud, everything. An adult will say, "Look, he is so dirty!" But the child has no sense of guilt or wrongdoing. He just runs to his mother to be cleaned again. If we can always feel that we are divine children, then our sense of impurity will go away and our soul will spontaneously tell us what is the best thing for us. And inside that message purity will loom large.

In the spiritual life, each seeker must feel that he is a child. If we can feel that we are only four years old, we will be able to live in the heart. A child lives in the heart. When he is thirteen or fourteen his mind starts functioning. When the mind starts functioning, the heart is veiled; and when the heart is veiled, everything goes wrong and purity is nowhere to be found.

scs 272. *Temptation*

There are various kinds of temptation. One kind of temptation everybody knows, and that is physical temptation, the temptation to lead an ordinary life, a lower life. This temptation tempts us to enter into the pleasure world, the vital world, sex life and all kinds of undivine activities. If we listen to this temptation, it is the death of our spiritual life. If we give in to this temptation, it takes years and years and years to come out of this life.

Another temptation is aggressive vital temptation. This comes in the form of ego. Like Julius Caesar we want to say, "I came, I saw, I conquered." We are tempted to have everybody come and touch our feet. We want to be powerful and strong so that we can lord it over others. We feel that will give us real satisfaction. When ego comes forward and tempts us, we feel that we are the supreme lord and everybody else is useless.

In the mental world there is still another kind of temptation. We feel that we know everything, whereas the rest of the world is composed of fools. Everybody, everybody else, is an ignorant fool, and we are the only ones who know everything. In the mental world we are tempted to believe that we possess the sea of wisdom and everybody else possesses the sea of ignorance. We are tempted to believe that we are the only knowers, whereas the rest of the world is a mass of ignorance.

There is one other form of temptation. This is the temptation to feel that we alone are purity's flood, and that the rest of the world is all impurity. We are the only pure and divine persons around. This is a form of ego, but it is different from normal ego. It is very subtle and, at the same time, very damaging,

Now, how can we conquer these forms of temptation? We can conquer them only by surrendering — not to them, but to the divine Light, to the divine Will. How can we do this? We can do it by consciously trying during our meditation to feel that we are the instrument and somebody else is the player. And who is that somebody? It is the Inner Pilot. If we feel that we are the doer, the undivine forces will mock us. They will come and make us proud, haughty, undivine, impure and insecure. So we have to pray to the Supreme during our meditation: "O Lord, I am Your instrument. I am so grateful that You have accepted me as Your instrument, and I am so grateful that You have made me a conscious instrument. Please use me in Your own Way."

There are millions and millions of people on earth who are not conscious of the fact that they are the instruments of God. Just because we have accepted the spiritual life, we are fully conscious of the fact that we are the instruments and God is the Player. If we can maintain that kind of feeling, there will be no temptation. As long as we want to be the doers, wrong forces will come to attack us and devour us. But if we become absolutely helpless and feel, "I am the instrument, O God. You play, You utilise me," then all the temptation will come and attack our Inner Pilot, God, and He will not be affected at all.

When we become the lord, when we feel there is no other lord, then the temptation forces will come and attack us. But if we become clever and wise and say, "No, no, no, I am not the doer; I am the instrument. The doer is somebody else," then those forces will come and attack the Doer, the Omnipotent, the Supreme. And then we will be safe.

SCS 273. *The inner study*

Yoga is the only way to realise God and to get liberation. There is no other way. Yoga means union with God. If one wants to get a Master's degree, one goes to the university to study. If one says, "I will not study, but I will get my Master's degree anyway," it is impossible. Similarly, if one does not practise yoga, if one does not have discipline, if one does not meditate, if one does not aspire, then it is impossible to get liberation. Liberation is like the higher course. If I don't first go through high school and then go to college and university, how am I going to get my Master's degree? Similarly, in yoga also, step by step we go up, up, up, up. Then, at the end of our inner study, we get liberation.

If we offer our existence to God, to Truth, to Light, then we can expect Peace, Light and Bliss in boundless measure. If we study hard in school, naturally we will expect a high mark. As we sow, so we reap. If we sow divine seeds, seeds of aspiration, then sooner or later we are bound to see the bumper crop of God-realisation. If we can offer our inner cry, if we can cry for Peace, Light and Bliss, then God is bound to come. Our cry will be fulfilled by God, who is the possessor of infinite Peace, Light and Bliss.

Some spiritual Masters tell their disciples, even after they have meditated for ten years or twenty years, not to use the words "salvation", "liberation", "illumination". These are very big words. We start with the ABC's of spiritual life. Even while we are asleep if we think of reaching the goal, then we are just fooling ourselves. We will reach the goal, but at God's choice Hour. Salvation, liberation, realisation: these things come at the end of the road. Right now, all the seekers must think of the basic things in their spiritual life. Meditate for five minutes or ten minutes or half an hour: that is right now your study. A child does not think of his Master's degree when he has not yet learned the alphabet; it is impossible. So let him learn the preliminary things, the elementary things; then, when he is in the university, he can think of liberation and realisation.

Please don't think that I am discouraging you. Far from it. A child's ultimate goal is definitely to get his Master's degree. But just by all the time thinking of the highest course, he will never get his Master's degree. A seeker has to go step by step. If he always thinks of the goal, he will feel that the goal is very far. Here he has not yet started the journey, and the goal is millions of miles away. Then he will start thinking, "I am so weak, I am so insincere, I am so ignorant. How can I reach my goal?" These thoughts will come, and he will be disappointed and disheartened and he will give up spiritual life.

scs 274. *Seeing and feeling*

One thing is feeling; another thing is seeing. You don't have to see me twenty-four hours a day. If you can feel my inner presence, that is enough. When the mother is working in the kitchen and the child is playing in the living room, the child does not have to see the mother all the time. He knows that his mother is there. He is getting the vibration of his mother. The atmosphere in the room is surcharged with the mother's consciousness and the father's pride. So here also, when you meditate in the evening before you go to bed, if you can see me in your dreams, that is wonderful. But if you don't see me, you have to feel, "If he wants to come and be in my dream, well and good. But if he wants me only to feel his presence within me, that is more than enough."

Some of you want to see me. Yes, if you can see me, well and good. But more important than seeing is feeling. If the mother does not see the son, still she feels the presence of the son in her heart. When you use your vision, then you will see one thing in me and somebody else may see something different. Seeing is good, but it can be treacherous. But when you feel something in me, at that time you have already identified with it. Before you go to bed, if your heart identifies with my consciousness, then the following morning when you get up you are bound to feel my presence within you, without you, around you, everywhere. When you meditate in the evening, try to feel deep inside you my existence, or try to feel that there is a most beautiful child within you. This child is the soul that is coming forward.

So always try to pay more attention to feeling than seeing. When you are feeling, the mind should not be there at all. Act like a child, who knows only how to love. And do not expect anything in your own way. If you feel, "Oh, if the Master comes and stands in front of me, I will be so happy," then you are only indulging in fanciful dreams. Live only in Reality, divine Reality. This Reality will tell you, "Let God deal with my life. If He wants to come, let Him come. Mine is to dig the soil; mine is not to produce the bumper crop. He will do it. He will grow the bumper crop of realisation for me; I will only allow Him."

Then afterwards you can go one step forward and say, "I am not cultivating the soil. It is He who is cultivating in me."

Gradually, gradually give all responsibility to the Supreme in me. If you feel sincerely that I am responsible for your actions, then you won't be able to do anything wrong. Also, try to feel that whatever you cannot do right in front of me, that thing you won't do at all; whatever you cannot say in front of me, that thing you won't say. If you have that kind of inner feeling, then you will feel my presence at every moment of your life.

SCS 275. *Realising the Master's status*

When you leave the body, say, after forty or fifty years and become the soul, when you are totally in the soul-consciousness, then you will be able to know my real status. I am not asking you to leave the body, far from it, for at that time you will not be able to help me in my manifestation. But if you realise my inner status when you are in the body, in the physical, then your realisation is really something. Then you can participate and share in my game. Now you are participating with me while I am playing football and together we are playing against ignorance. This is the opportunity that you get on earth. But from the soul's world you will simply be an observer: I am playing football well and you are observing me. Sometimes you would like to participate, but in the soul's world you cannot participate directly in the game. You don't get the real satisfaction there, because the manifestation is taking place here on earth. There the joy that you get will come only from observing.

In rare cases, very close disciples, closest disciples, are very strong both on the physical plane and on the spiritual plane. On both the planes they are very powerful, dedicated, devoted and surrendered. When the Master plays his role on earth, even if the disciples are in the higher planes, their joy is solid and concrete; they get the same joy. But if one really wants to see me and manifest me here on earth, then one has to be with me here.

We get the greatest opportunity when a real spiritual Master comes into the world. At that time we make the fastest progress. Even those who would otherwise be absolutely useless in the spiritual life also make the fastest progress, according to their capacity. I have disciples who have had only one or two human incarnations. You can imagine how much of their existence is still in the animal world. But through the spiritual Master's direct intervention these people can still make fast progress in human life, although their progress may not be as great as that of a more advanced seeker. Although they may be in the animal consciousness, since they have accepted the Master, he will help them. At that time the Master's unconditional Compassion plays its role.

scs 276. *Expediting God's Hour*

If you feel that I am at least God's conscious representative, and if for twenty-four hours a day you can feel that I care for you, then you can easily expedite God's choice Hour. Most of you here have one common disease. We have to open up a hospital for all the patients suffering from this one disease. In our hospital, everybody is suffering from one disease: they feel that I don't care for them. But if you can feel that I *do* care for you as an individual, as a seeker and as a child of my soul, then immediately you can expedite God's Hour.

How I care for you, you will never know. Right now if I smile at you, then you feel that I care for you. But if you can feel my presence inside your heart, then always you will feel that I care for you. If you can consciously feel my presence, then gradually your joy will increase. When you cherish depression, doubt and all that, at that time you will give me a zero. Try to go deep within. If you can give me even one out of one hundred for my care for you, then I will be very grateful. When you can give me seventy, I tell you, at that time you are bound to feel that you are expediting God's Hour. When you can give me higher marks, then you are making the fastest progress. The easiest way to expedite God's Hour is to feel constantly that I care for you in my inner life and my outer life.

In the human way, you think that perhaps I need something from you, some favour, and that is why I care for you. But repeatedly I have told you that nobody is indispensable. Only feel that whoever is in a position to serve our mission in a divine way is getting the greatest opportunity. I am responsible to you, to your soul, to the Supreme. It is not your eagerness that will expedite God's Hour and make you run the fastest: It is *my* eagerness, *my* necessity. It is my constant inner necessity to take each individual the fastest towards the Goal. If you feel that it is your necessity and not my necessity, then you are mistaken. I have realised God; it is true. But until I make you realise God, I have not manifested Divinity in the earth-consciousness and my game is incomplete.

scs 277. *An April 13th message to disciples*[§]

We have one choice and one decision.
Our choice is to become one with God's Life.
Our decision is to be the ever-dedicated breath in
the fulfilment of God's universe.

— Sri Chinmoy

O Supreme, to Thee I offer what I am: my life's soulful
gratitude. O children of the Supreme, to you I give what I have:
my life of selfless dedication and oneness. My love is my weight.
My love is my height. My love is at once my weight and my
height. My love for the devoted disciples, on the strength of
my oneness with them, is my weight. My love for the Supreme,
on the strength of my oneness with Him, is my height.

For the past few years, the disciples have been entering into
my life and I have been entering into their lives. I am serving the
Supreme in them; they are serving the Supreme in me. Together
we are growing. Together we shall eternally grow. Gradually we
give and take. I expect from you absolute dedication and you
expect from me absolute realisation of the One Absolute.

According to grammar, "best" is the superlative degree. Everybody cannot be best in the ordinary life. Only one person can
be best; others can be good, better and so forth. But here we
are dealing with Infinity, Eternity and Immortality. Infinity has
no bounds. We are all spiritual seekers, seekers of the infinite
Truth. So each individual can have the aspiration to become
one with the Dearest, the Supreme. Each individual can be a
unique instrument of the Supreme on the strength of his absolute dedication and unconditional surrender to the Will of the
Supreme. Grammar is written by mortals, by ordinary human

beings. But our life is written by the Supreme, who can make each of us a unique instrument of His Will.

Each disciple can be like a petal of a divine lotus, a unique petal of the lotus. The whole lotus will be bloated with divine pride when it sees that each individual petal is helping and serving the whole to grow into the Supreme's perfect Perfection here on earth.

We know that slow and steady wins the race. The hare lost the race to the turtle. But again, I wish to say that when we live in the Divine, when we live in the Supreme, in the Supreme Consciousness, at that time we do not have to follow this principle. In our case, quick and dynamic can win the race. The Supreme is our Pilot, our Eternal Pilot. According to His Will, at His choice Hour we have started our journey. It is He who is inspiring us to run towards the Golden Shore of the Beyond. It is His race He is running in and through us, so we are bound to reach the destined Goal.

Some of you have the wrong impression that the Supreme is unknowable. But it is not true. Right now He is unknown to all human beings. But, at the same time, those who have realised Him are fully aware of the fact that He can be seen, He can be talked to, He can be felt. When I speak to Him, I see Him more clearly than I see you here with my eyes wide open. So you can say that God is unknown right now, because you have not realised Him. But if you say, "God is forever unknowable," then you are mistaken. God is our Father. How can our Father remain all the time unknowable? He can at most remain unknown for a short period of time, because now we are wallowing in the pleasures of ignorance. We are in a dark room that is wanting in light. But when our consciousness, our inner being, is flooded with the divine Light, then we are bound to see Him face to face.

So from now on, please change your opinion as regards God. God is unknown for the time being, but He can never be unknowable. He is our Father. He is our dearest, He is our closest. At His choice Hour He will open our third eye, the eye that actually sees the Truth. These two human eyes do not see the ultimate Truth. Only the third eye, which is the eye of our divine oneness with the Highest, with the Supreme, can make us see, feel and become one with the Supreme. The Supreme has inspired us to commence our journey. Our journey's Goal is destined. We shall never fail because the Supreme is our Pilot, the Supreme is our Way, He is our Guide, He is our eternal Goal.

SCS 278. *If I pray for my father, will this benefit his soul's evolution despite the fact that he does not lead a spiritual life?*

Sri Chinmoy: If one does not lead a spiritual life and another member of his family prays and meditates for him, naturally it will help. But if the person consciously rejects the love and the spiritual help that he is getting, then he won't get any benefit. Suppose a member of your family does not accept the spiritual life, but you have accepted it soulfully and you are praying for that person just because he is a member of your family. Your prayer will definitely work provided he does not reject it. He may say, "I am too lethargic. I don't want to do it, but if you do it for me, I will be grateful. I am hungry, true, but I don't want to go to the kitchen. Will you bring me some food?" Then you can go to your kitchen and open up your refrigerator and bring food. Just because he is lazy you are bringing him food. But if you bring him food and he just throws it aside and becomes annoyed, then what are you going to do? So it is up to him. When you bring him food, he should at least eat it. If he eats, then he will be nourished. At that time it doesn't matter whether he went to the kitchen himself. But if he rejects your food, then no matter how sincere you are, how well-meaning you are in bringing the food to him, you are wasting your time. It entirely depends on his acceptance or rejection. If he accepts, then naturally you will feel that the power of your prayer, the fruit of your prayer, will go to him. But if he rejects it, then it is impossible.

SCS 279. *What happens to geniuses like Bach or Shakespeare after they die?*

Sri Chinmoy: It depends on God's Will and also the eagerness of the soul. If Bach played his role as a great, supreme musician, and if he does not want to manifest any more music, and if it is the Will of the Supreme, then he will give up that life totally. In his next incarnation he may enter into the field of literary activity. If Shakespeare has finished his role as a great writer and if he wants to enter into music, he can do it. Again, if Shakespeare and Bach feel that they have not played their roles satisfactorily, that they could give more to the literary world or to the musical world, then they will continue in the same field in their next incarnation.

We feel that Bach composed such great music. Who could be a better musician than he or who could be a greater writer than Shakespeare? But only the souls of these two great figures know whether they contributed to the fullest extent what they embodied and what they came here to give us. If they have given everything, then they don't have to go through literary life or music life any more. But if they have not given everything and if they want to continue, and if the Will of the Supreme is for them to continue and give more of their soul-stirring music or soul-elevating literature, then they will give. Again, they may not want to continue this particular game. On the sports field, a game lasts for forty-five minutes or an hour. If one plays for forty-five minutes and then becomes tired, he may say, "I do not want to play this game anymore; I am ready to play some other game. I was playing football and it was very exhausting; now I want to play something else, some indoor game." And then God may say, "All right, you don't have to play that game. You can play some other game. I am offering you My Compassion."

Usually great geniuses like Shakespeare and Bach have completed their roles. Then, God may take them into science or spirituality. In the case of Bach, he had already accepted spirituality, whereas Shakespeare had not consciously accepted spirituality. So Bach's music is full of spirituality. But Shakespeare's higher ideals are not spiritual; they are something else. Spirituality is everywhere, true, but you have to know what spirituality you are aiming at. The one has already touched spirituality; the other has not properly touched the real spirituality. It is entirely up to God's Will what they will do next.

SCS 280. *Is there any question you cannot answer?*

Sri Chinmoy: If I use my mind, there will be millions of questions that I cannot answer. But if I use my oneness-heart with the Absolute Supreme, there will be no question that I will not be able to answer, if it has to do with spirituality. Thousands of times I have answered questions, believe me, and when I heard it on the tape or read it in the book, I could not believe that it was I who had said it. Or after I have answered a question, when everything is all done and my physical mind gets the message of the answer that I have given, I cannot believe that I have answered that question. When I try to understand the question afterwards, I cannot understand it. It has happened to me once or twice that I have answered a question one hundred per cent correctly; but if I use my mind in order to know what the question is, I do not even understand the question. So how many times I have answered questions most correctly on the strength of my heart's oneness with God's Will. My heart immediately becomes one with God's Will. Many times it has happened that before the question is even formulated, just when the person opens his mouth, the question has already come to me. You are standing with the question and you have completed two or three words, but your question has already come to me and the answer has already come to me. Then you go on, go on, using so many words; but it is all unnecessary. When you open your mouth, the question and the answer both have come together, and I am just waiting for you to complete your question.

SCS 281. *Why is it that some religions do not mention reincarnation?*

Sri Chinmoy: Some religions say, "Our Father is in Heaven. He is there and we are here, in hell." So naturally they try to go to Heaven, where He is. And then, once they are there, they say, "Oh, He is our Beloved. Are we such fools that we will come back to earth? Who needs reincarnation?"

But if we know that He is in Heaven and also here on earth, then naturally we will come back. Wherever we are, God, poor fellow, is also there; He is bound to be with us. If we are on the ground floor, in the basement, He is also there. And also when we are on the top floor, in the attic, He is with us. So if you accept God's Universality, then you know that reincarnation is absolutely real. But if you accept only God the Transcendental Height, then you will only stay with Him upstairs. You shall not come back. When people say that God is only in Heaven, it creates a problem. But if we say He is both in Heaven and on earth, then this problem doesn't arise.

SCS 282. *Does the vibration of the city reflect the aspiration of its inhabitants?*

Sri Chinmoy: At times the vibration of a city is like the aspiration of its inhabitants. And also, the inhabitants may have a vibration of their own. It is like a house. A house has a vibration of its own and the inhabitants also have a vibration of their own. The inhabitants have a vibration and they are giving it to the house; and the house has some vibration, which it is giving to the inhabitants.

scs 283. *Are there delicate and beautiful worlds of the psychic imagination that the artist should try to seek access to for inspiration?*

Sri Chinmoy: Yes, there are many, many beautiful, delicate psychic worlds. You are using the term "imagination", but this is absolutely wrong. These are not imagination; they are psychic realities. What you call imagination is not imagination as such; it is a reality in another world. Here on earth we call it imagination. But when we go to a higher plane, where we get the message of creativity, the light of creativity, it is not imagination at all. It is real. Only we don't see its reality in the physical form here. We are on the first floor and a flower is on the second floor. We don't see the flower because we are on the first floor. But when the fragrance comes down, we know there is a flower, a source, and the source is on the second floor.

So imagination is a world of its own, a reality-world. But here we don't see it because it is stationed a little higher. The good artist must always seek access to the higher worlds for inspiration, for if one wants to create something, one has to get something from a higher plane. Then only will the world be illumined and fulfilled. Anything that comes from above has more beauty in it, more purity in it, more reality in it. Our goal is to bring down from above divinity, reality, beauty — everything that is divine.

The imagination-world is not a mental hallucination; it is reality-world far above this physical world. Let us try to have an access to this world so we can get inspiration and create something new, something unprecedented.

scs 284. *When I do my daily activities, I do not feel concerned about them. Is this the right attitude?*

Sri Chinmoy: While you are doing your daily activities you should pray to the Supreme, to the Inner Pilot, who is operating in and through you. God has infinite Concern for human beings in each of their activities. If you are not concerned, that is a mistake. You will have concern, but you will not feel that this concern is coming from you. Feel that it is coming from somewhere else and that an Inner Hand is guiding you. This is the right approach.

scs 285. *When you perform meditation and concentration, if you can't break through the electromagnetic field around you, it will cause a certain amount of frustration, since you are not able to express what is inside you.*

Sri Chinmoy: When you concentrate or meditate, you have to surrender to God's Will. The will that is inside your concentration, the will that is in your meditation, you have to surrender to God's Will. If you really love God, then you have to surrender the capacity that you have and also the results that you get from your capacity. When you concentrate dynamically and powerfully, then you have to feel that your capacity has come from God. When you soulfully meditate, you have to feel that this capacity has also come from God. Now, if the result that you want you are not getting, then you should not be disturbed. A child knows how to crawl, but he wants to walk. He will definitely be able to walk one day, but today he can only crawl. Just because he can't reach his goal today, he will not give up his desire to walk. He will crawl today and one day he will be able to walk. While you are concentrating, you meet with some obstruction, some frustration-barrier. If you are not achieving the thing that you want, naturally you will meet with frustration. But you have to take this frustration as a barrier that can be easily overcome. It is only a matter of time.

It is like walking through a tunnel. You know that on the other side there will be light. Right now it is night, but light is bound to come. If you can take frustration as night, then you will know that a few hours later there will be day. But if you feel that only night exists, that there is a barrier and there is nothing beyond that barrier, then you are making a mistake.

When we concentrate, we pierce like a bullet through the thing that is standing in our way. But when we meditate, we don't reject the thing. Because of our oneness with God, we try to accept the obstruction and illumine it. Anything that is discouraging or destructive in us, we don't discard. If we leave aside frustration or other negative things, then they remain on earth and bother somebody else. So when it is a matter of concentration, we will cast aside all obstructions; but when it is a matter of meditation, when our mind has achieved vastness, we will accept obstructions and transform them. In the beginning, when we want to run towards our goal, we don't keep anything negative. But when we reach our goal, then we have to feel that the things we have left aside may create problems for our brothers and sisters. So after reaching our goal, we will come back to illumine them so that they won't stand in the way of others.

scs 286. *How do we know who is our real teacher?*

Sri Chinmoy: When you see four or five persons in front of you, automatically one person attracts most of your attention, or gives you much more joy. Four persons are walking along the street, but when you look at one of them, you will get tremendous joy. That means that you have already become aware in the inner world of your affinity with that particular person. Your mind cannot account for it, but your soul has already recognised its oneness.

A teacher is supposed to be your most intimate, eternal friend. If I give you more joy than other teachers, then I am your teacher. If somebody else gives you much more joy, then that person is your teacher. It is like choosing a school. There are quite a few schools; so you go to a school that you like. You are under no compulsion to go to a particular school. Just because you like a particular school, just because you like the teachers of that school, you will go there. In the spiritual life also, when a seeker sincerely wants help from a spiritual Master, he makes a choice. The one that gives him utmost joy, the one for whom he feels utmost love, is the right one for him.

scs 287. *Is there such a thing as false light?*

Sri Chinmoy: Yes, there is false light. There are many destructive forces which attack light and use it to deceive seekers. We can tell whether it is true or false light by seeing if it is all purity. If it is false light, there will be a certain amount of impurity.

These false, destructive forces often take the form of the cosmic gods. Once a hostile force came to me in the form of Vishnu. I was meditating at about half-past two or three o'clock in the morning and this force came and stood in front of me. I was about fifteen or sixteen years of age and I had seen Vishnu three or four times before. He is a most beautiful god. When I concentrated on this being, I noticed impurity within him, so I did not bow down to him. Then a tremendous fight took place and after three or four minutes the figure of Vishnu exploded. There was a tremendous noise and my brother came running to my room. They even heard it in the house right down the street. They all wondered what had happened at that time of the morning. They thought the stove had exploded. But my brother was the only one I told. On another occasion I was attacked by a hostile force during my meditation; then, afterwards, I discovered that my mosquito net had been torn to shreds.

Very often a hostile force takes the form of a seeker's own Guru. The seeker has to be absolutely certain it is his Guru. Otherwise, if he bows down to it, it can cause real harm on the physical plane. It can harm our limbs, even give us a heart attack or stroke. Once a hostile force appeared before the dearest disciple of a spiritual Master. When she saw her Master in front of her she was overjoyed, and she immediately bowed down. Then she was at the mercy of this hostile force and immediately suffered a heart attack. Afterwards, it went upstairs to see who else it could find. But it found only one of the ordinary disciples. When this disciple bowed down to it, the demon could not be bothered with him. It felt it was beneath its dignity in that particular case, and it went away.

So you have to be very careful that the light you see is real light. Never bow to any form which appears before you unless you feel peace and purity in it.

SCS 288. *Is God wholly good, or is He both good and evil?*

Sri Chinmoy: God is both good and evil and, again, He is above them both. It is like a tree. Let us say the roots are evil and the branches are good. But they are one; they are part of the same tree. Evil is a lower manifestation of Truth and good is a higher manifestation of Truth. There is no night without light; even in the blackest night there is always at least an iota of light. But God is in both of these and above them both, as the sky is above the tree. If you say God is not in evil, then you are saying that God is not omnipresent. And that is like saying that God is not God. God is in both, but He is not bound by them. He is like a boat which is in the water and also above the water.

From the strictly spiritual point of view, there is no such thing as good or evil. Evil only exists in the mental world. What we think of as being evil is actually lesser truth or imperfection growing into greater truth or more perfect reality.

SCS 289. *Can you please explain what* shakti *is and its role in Creation?*

Sri Chinmoy: Shakti is the source of infinite Energy. This infinite Energy can be transmitted as infinite Light, infinite Peace, infinite Bliss. With this Power, we can climb up the tree, we can climb back down, we can walk, we can run, we can fly, we can dive, we can do anything that we want to do. Power is necessary capacity. Naturally we need the necessary capacity for flying, for running, for each activity we do. So this capacity is power here.

On the spiritual plane, God is infinite Light. This infinite Light is also infinite Energy and infinite Peace. Peace is Power and Power is Peace. Light is Power and Power is Light. It is the movement that is Shakti. God has two aspects: one is His static aspect and the other is His dynamic aspect. When He wants to manifest, He employs His dynamic capacity, while His other aspect remains silent. Here Shakti becomes the universal manifesting Force.

How is it that we say that the Power aspect of the Supreme created the Universe? If we say that the Power aspect can only create something vast, then we are mistaken. If God has infinite Power, then with His infinite Power He can create something vast and also something very tiny. Infinite Power does not mean that He can create only something big. If the infinite Power can create the vast, then it can also create a grain of sand.

Infinite Power is experienced in various forms inside the heart of each seeker. One seeker will experience Power as Bliss, another will experience it as Peace, a third as Light; and a fourth will experience it as Consciousness.

The seeker feels and experiences Shakti, the Power, inside him, according to his own evolution. Shakti is the manifestation of God's Vision. When this manifestation takes form, each individual has the right to issue a name to it. The Form remains the same, but the seeker recognises the Form, accepts the Form, in various ways. Then, when this Power operates inside the seeker, if the seeker needs Peace, he will call it Peace. If the seeker needs Light, then he will call that Power Light. If somebody needs Delight, then he will take that Power as Delight.

SCS 290. *Does each soul have a task and, if so, how is it known?*

Sri Chinmoy: Each soul has a task and you can know it only through your sincere aspiration. Let us take each soul as a limb of God's own Existence. With His Hand He does one thing, with His Nose He does something else, with His Eye and Ear something else. It is like a football game. Somebody has to play at the goalpost, somebody has to play on the left and somebody has to be on the right. If all the players stay at the goal, there will be no game. No, the players have to be well distributed. So like that, each soul has its respective job to do. And you will know which position you are going to play only when you deal with the captain. God will tell you where your post is.

SCS 291. *What is the difference between intelligence and consciousness?*

Sri Chinmoy: Intelligence is limited. Someone may have a bigger thumb than someone else, but at most it is only half an inch or so bigger, and this is not very important. Intelligence also can be a little bigger or smaller, but it is finite and will always remain so.

With consciousness it is quite different. Consciousness is vast, very vast. The finite consciousness is itself finite, but it is capable of expanding into infinite consciousness, into the Infinite itself.

SCS 292. *When you come into the dream of somebody who is not yet your disciple, what does it mean?*

Sri Chinmoy: If a Master comes to someone in a dream, it means that the soul of that particular person has already recognised the Master. Like a magnet, the soul is pulling the Master's love, concern, blessings and affection. The soul is pulling the presence of that Master. Then, a few days or a few months later, the physical mind, the earthly, physical eyes will be able to see the Master. The soul has recognised the Master on the soul's plane, the inner plane; then it has transmitted this truth, this reality, to the dream-plane, to the dream-consciousness. From the dream-consciousness, in the course of time, the reality will come to the physical consciousness, to the physical plane. It is a very good sign, a very good indication, that sooner or later the student will be able to meet with his Master.

scs 265. *(p. 339)* University of Massachusetts, 29 September 1975.

scs 266–270. *(p. 343)* Questions and answers following the lecture *Prayer and meditation*.

scs 277. *(p. 357)* Sri Chinmoy delivered this message on 13 April 1969, the fifth anniversary of his arrival in the West.

scs 278–283. *(p. 360)* Questions asked by seekers attending a lecture that Sri Chinmoy gave at Oxford University on 19 June 1976.

APPENDIX

PREFACE TO ORIGINAL EDITION

Editor's prefaces to the original edition of Sri Chinmoy speaks*:*

Sri Chinmoy speaks, part 1
This volume consists of several lectures delivered by Sri Chinmoy in recent years, plus a wide-ranging interview with two Boston journalists.

Sri Chinmoy speaks, part 2
This volume consists of a series of lectures Sri Chinmoy gave at various universities and public places, as well as miscellaneous talks he delivered at his Centres.

Sri Chinmoy speaks, part 3
This volume consists of a series of lectures Sri Chinmoy gave at various universities and public places, as well as miscellaneous talks he delivered at his Centres, with selected questions and answers.

Sri Chinmoy speaks, part 4
This volume contains informal talks, lectures, a radio interview and selected questions and answers by Sri Chinmoy.

Sri Chinmoy speaks, part 5
This volume consists of a series of essays by Sri Chinmoy dealing with a spiritual seeker's inner life, plus a selection of questions and answers.

Sri Chinmoy speaks, part 6
In this volume Sri Chinmoy discusses a number of subjects about a Master's relationship with his disciples, including inner receptivity and the experience of meditation.

Sri Chinmoy speaks, part 7
In this volume Sri Chinmoy tells how to overcome some of the problems seekers encounter after they have entered the spiritual life. Also included is a series of significant questions that seekers and disciples have asked the Master about his path, as well as a group of general spiritual questions.

Sri Chinmoy speaks, part 8
In this volume Sri Chinmoy answers a series of questions on purity, compassion and justice.

BIBLIOGRAPHY

SRI CHINMOY SPEAKS (10 VOLUMES)

SRI CHINMOY:

  −*Sri Chinmoy speaks, part 1*, New York, Agni Press, 1976.
  −*Sri Chinmoy speaks, part 2*, New York, Agni Press, 1976.
  −*Sri Chinmoy speaks, part 3*, New York, Agni Press, 1976.
  −*Sri Chinmoy speaks, part 4*, New York, Agni Press, 1976.
  −*Sri Chinmoy speaks, part 5*, New York, Agni Press, 1976.
  −*Sri Chinmoy speaks, part 6*, New York, Agni Press, 1976.
  −*Sri Chinmoy speaks, part 7*, New York, Agni Press, 1976.
  −*Sri Chinmoy speaks, part 8*, New York, Agni Press, 1976.
  −*Sri Chinmoy speaks, part 9*, New York, Agni Press, 1976.
  −*Sri Chinmoy speaks, part 10*, New York, Agni Press, 1977.

Suggested citation key is SCS.

POSTFACE

Publishing principles

This edition of *The works of Sri Chinmoy* aims to obey the Author's wish: scrupulous fidelity to his original words, use of typographical style by him selected, specific spelling choices, end placement of any editorial content (i.e. not written by Sri Chinmoy himself), particular treatment of some personal nouns in special cases, etc.

Textual accuracy

This edition has been checked to ensure faithful accuracy to the originals. Although much effort has been put in proofreading and comparing different versions of the text, this print may still present lingering errors. The Publisher would be grateful to be apprised of any mistypes via postal mail or facsimile, possibly with scan of the original page where the text is different. Please use original books only, specifying the year of publication, as no online version can be considered authoritative.

Ongoing reprints will include any revised text from these errata.

Acknowledgements

The Publisher is very grateful to the late Professor Lambert and his équipe for his invaluable advice. For many decades Prof. Lambert conducted a small publishing house specialising in hand-made prints of philological edition of the classics. The standard of this edition would not have been the same without his scholarly advice.

The Publisher is also grateful to the international team of collaborators that spent countless hours proofreading and checking the current text against the originals.

Our deepest gratitude to Sri Chinmoy. His living presence can be felt breathing throughout his writings. It is a privilege to be involved with his works, in any form.

Citation keys

Citation keys are used throughout *The works of Sri Chinmoy* to allow accurate cross-reference of texts across titles and editions. Examples: EA 13, ST 50000, UPA 7.

Sri Chinmoy Canon

We could not use better words than Professor Lambert's, who kindly offered the name *Sri Chinmoy Canon*:

> «By defining Sri Chinmoy's first editions as *editio princeps* we chose to follow classical scholarship criteria, not because we consider Sri Chinmoy's work antique, but because we believe it is among the few post ‹classical antiquity› works to rightly deserve to be considered a *classicus*, designating by that term *superiority, authority* and *perfection*.
> «The monumental work Sri Chinmoy is offering to mankind is awe-inspiring and supremely pre-eminent in proportions and quality. It is manifest that Sri Chinmoy's work — which we feel right to call *The Sri Chinmoy Canon* — will be of profound help and source of enlightenment to anyone seeking a higher wisdom, truth and reality supreme.»

[Translated from French by M. G.S.]

TABLE OF CONTENTS

Composition typographique par imprimerie
Ab Academia Aoidon, Paris & Lyon.

Un grand merci à Prof Knuth pour
l'utilisation avancée de TEX.

A LYON, LE 27 DÉCEMBRE LXXXVII Æ.G.